Out of Alabama, Into Mississippi

**Out of Alabama, Into Mississippi:**
**A Tale of Love and Sacrifice**
A strong family that lives together shares lc
By Terry Winfred Williamson
© 2024 by Terry W. Williamson
All rights reserved. This book or any portion thereof may not
be reproduced or used in any manner whatsoever without the
express written permission of the publisher except for the use
of brief quotations in a book review.
ISBN: 979-8-35098-218-3

## Contents

Introduction......................................................................3

Boy Meets Girl and Gets Hitched ...............................3

Sooie! Sooie! How Many Pigs Do You Own?...........12

Don't be Afraid of the Choo-Choo ...........................26

Giddy Up! Whoa! ......................................................29

The Williamsons ......................................................38

Toys We Never Had ...................................................43

My Big Brother Alvin ...............................................47

The Pastor, Jack .......................................................59

The Transition to the North .....................................65

School #1...................................................................74

The Angel of Death ..................................................82

The Four P's .............................................................88

Schools and Education............................................110

The St. John's Nazarites .........................................121

A Trip to Michigan .................................................142

Music Carries Words...............................................150

What's the West Coast Like?...................................166

The Assault on South Pearl Street—February 22, 2022 ..........175

A Strong Family That Lives Together Shares Love Together .186

Conclusion ..............................................................207

Acknowledgments........................................................208

Special Thanks to the Five Females in My Life.......................208

About the Author........................................................209

Gratitude to the Following People and Organizations.............209

Formal Recognition/Citation ......................................210

## Introduction

My name is Terry Winfred Williamson. I'm a twin, and we are Libras, sons of a sharecropper from the Deep South. I love adventure and excitement; taking long journeys is something my twin and I loved as we grew up. My family had to endure many sacrifices during our stay in the South. We all had our hard times dealing with the struggles, the bigotry, prejudice, and jealousy from the white man, which made our lives a living nightmare in the early 1960s. The words "boy" and "nigger" were unpleasant words for us as little boys. My older brother Alvin hated those words with a passion. You will soon see, how *his feelings became a great part of what we had to endure.* The white man gave my older brother a hard time, and even their children called us those names with smiles on their faces as they laughed at us with pointing fingers—it was so degrading. Treating us like unwanted trash. We never played with white kids in our town, not even out in the country. It got to the point that something had to change before real trouble commenced. My parents had to get Alvin out of this one-stoplight town, with no time to spare. Making a transition to the North was my parents' only option. The North changed our lives. We settled in the city of Albany, New York. The school system there gave me a great education; I earned my associate degree in the culinary arts. Get ready as I take you on a magnificent adventure of my life's experience, in the form of words. My greatest hope is that my story touches you: the joy, sadness, drama, comedy, murder and suspense, and some lifesaving situations. Finally,… on to a wonderful love story. Remember, "Life is short, but death is sure." Stay safe, and may God continue to bless us all.

T.T.F.N.

## ONE

### Boy Meets Girl and Gets Hitched

I was born and raised in a small one-stoplight town called Waynesboro, a town where I was certain to make the expression, "Boys will be Boys" (repeated often by my mom) live up to its very description. It is a key factor in all that I am expressing and sharing with you and will keep you on the edge of your seat. So much so, that you may have problems putting this book down. There will be some twist and turns, mysteries and revelations; however, no matter which direction you're taken, it will not let you down.

In looking back, I now realize that my twin and I were a gift, a blessing given to our parents from God. Remember my mantra—*"A strong family that lives together shares love together"*—this simple message: this story is for everyone near and far, especially for my own family. My family's history starts in the state of Alabama, ending in the state of Mississippi. My grandparents were born here during the midst of slavery, during the sharecropping period, working for the white man, sometimes as field hands and sometimes as a stable boy. Although it's very painful to know my grandparents were born and raised during slavery, the most delightful aspect of their story that I'd like to share with you is about my wonderful mother, Velma Davis, *"a tall, slim, beautiful black woman"* with self-discipline and a determined mind: characteristic of that Choctaw Indian blood, just like her mom. My brother Alvin told us as little boys, our mom would not hesitate to reach for the shot-gun when needed, and she wouldn't be hesitant to use it as well. My father was aware of that; he made sure he didn't make our mom upset in and around the house. Her focus: the ten siblings and their education and well-being, striving for a better life in the Deep South. Making a brighter future for the whole family; demonstrating that *"A strong family that lives together shares love together."* She took charge of our family back in the early sixties; she's number one in my book. Way to go, Mom! She was born and bred in the northern part of the good old state of Alabama in a small county town called Choctaw County. She was the middle child of several brothers and sisters. My mom's parents had a large house, with several large rooms for everyone to share. One thing is for sure, they weren't farmers. I'm not sure of the means of their income, but they didn't struggle. I wonder if they had a car or maybe just a horse and wagon. The Davis family during this time considered themselves middle class, and they carried themselves in the same manner. They all went to school at some point or another. I know my mom attended school, but what grade she completed, that, I'm not sure. I do know she was smart just like the rest of her family.

I don't know when or how my grandparents managed the hard times during that period. One thing is for sure—they all were Alabamians. It was before the period of the 1920s, and during this time my parents were born. My mom was born on September 28, 1919, and my dad on August 27, 1917. They both lived and grew up in the state of Alabama until young adulthood. Later, my mom would devise a plan that would change the lives of those two young people forever.

That change would involve eloping and crossing that mysterious Choctaw County line. This would turn out to be one of the best love stories ever lived. My mom is very smart and had a strong will and determination to boot. Here's two young people making plans to one day cross over the state lines from the state

Figure 1 Choctaw County Line

of Alabama into the state of Mississippi (making me part Mississippian, and part Alabamian) just to make a better life for themselves. Looking back, I now have a clearer understanding of the hard times they had to endure. But look at the Williamson's and Davis's today, they are all doing well! I'm glad I had the opportunity to share this phenomenal history with my four sons.

At an early age, I do remember some of my mom's brothers and sisters. I remember Uncle Jack—I'm not sure if he was one of the oldest ones or not, there's Uncle Herman the contractor and builder of homes, and Uncle J.C. He was the quietest one in the family. My mother's sisters, as far as I can remember some of their names . . . there was Aunt Betsy and Aunt Irma Dee. They were all still living at home at the time with their parents, Vaden and Mary, during this time. We all know how parents are when it comes to their children, and they were very strict and protective, especially of their young girls.

My dad's name is Andrew, he was also born and bred in the small country town called Deer Park in the southern part of the state of Alabama, and he was also a son of sharecroppers. Some folks had the tendency to look down on people who worked in the fields, but my dad had no care in the world. He was just a hard worker; he worked very hard every day.

My dad comes from a large family as well, there were ten brothers and sisters. On the boys' side, not in any order—though I do believe my father was the second oldest—were Dan, Michael, Andrew, Stan, Jim boy, and Uncle James. Later, you will see why Uncle James was my favorite. They lived in this old, rusty house of a shack with no more than three rooms; the size of the rooms, I'm not sure. But there was room for everyone; my dad's father, Augusta Williamson, and his wife, Mary Williamson, were strict. My grandfather was a very stingy and demanding man who controlled the house and all the finances. My father told me a story of how one day, my grandfather and his wife got into an argument. At one point my grandfather hit his wife on the head with a piece of firewood for not doing what he told her.

Figure 2 My grandfather Augusta Williamson, on my father side

Figure 3 My grandmother Mary Williamson, on my father side

In my grandfather's house, all the cooking and heating was done with firewood. They had to cook with a potbelly cast iron stove. During this time every house had a fireplace; it was common all through their neighborhood in the South. They did all they could to make ends meet. One of the most important things is that they were all healthy, making life a little better for themselves. Even though my grandfather was a demanding and controlling man, he helped with the chores. Everyone did their share of chores around the house, and that's the only way things could ever be. My mom had several girlfriends in her hometown; they would walk and talk about schoolwork and, of course, boys.

One of her friends came up to her, saying, "Velma! Have you heard?"

My mom said, "Heard what?"

She said, "There's a fish fry this weekend next to the county fairground hosted by Choctaw County. There's posters and flyers all over the area, I think we should make plans to attend. There will be lots of food and fun and it will last all day."

My mom said, "You don't know my parents."

Her girlfriend replied, "Yes, I know, I know! Are you okay with the plan?"

My mom said, "Girl, I'll be ready."

During this time my dad wasn't attending school because everyone had to work the white man's fields - this was common for Black families in the Deep South of Alabama at the time. The fish fry at the fair is the event that would bring two young people face-to-face for the first time, and change their lives more than they could have ever imagined. Well, that day came sooner than they expected. Everyone was there from all over the different counties, and my mom and dad met for the first time. My mom didn't tell my dad about her parents, Mary and Vaden, and how strict they were - she was too focused on having a good time. After all the food and fun at the fish fry, they went back to their own counties. Soon after, they began seeing each other. The courtship went on for a while; they had no problems and nothing to worry about at the time... not until my mom's parents found out what was going on with their daughter—because she started slacking on her share of the work around the house, and often daydreaming. They didn't realize their daughter's life was beginning to change.

*Figure 4 This is my Grandmother Mary Davis*

They began to see this strange boy around the house a lot, and her parents asked her, "Velma, who is this boy? He doesn't look like he's from our neighborhood; we've never seen him before."

She answered, "His name is Andrew, and he's from the other side of town."

Insisting on finding out more about him, they asked, "What township is he from?"

7

She said, "Deer Park County."

They said, "No, you can't see him; besides, you don't know anything about him. What school does he attend?"

She said, "He don't go to school; he has to work all the time."

My dad had to be careful if he came anywhere near my mom's parents' house, because her father was on the watch for this country boy from another county who didn't attend school at all. My dad really wanted to see her; he wasn't giving up, and he was willing to take that chance. My mom was willing to take a chance too; that's the only way the two of them could make this courtship work.

They started seeing each other on a regular basis, and the distance they both had to travel was more than two hours away from each town with Choctaw being in the northern part of the state, and Deer Park in the southern part of the state. Everything was fine for a while, but then it began to change for the two of them; as a matter of fact, things took a change for the worse. The constant arguing with her mother and father about this boy reached high tension; something had to change real soon in this family! It continued to the point that things really got out of hand; her parents still insisted that she stay away from this boy who lived in a different county. My mom tried talking to her parents to see if they would change their minds, but to no avail; they were very strict. I'm not sure if that was for the best or not. So, my mom and dad started seeing each other secretly. I can only imagine what they were going through, a country boy from one county seeing this girl from another county. I bet that it was both a scary, yet exciting time for the young couple, and they had yet to realize the outcome of it all.

My dad couldn't drive, and neither could my mom. And I don't believe the white man, the owner and sharecropper, would let my dad use his horse, mules, and wagon; he made sure his animals were for farming only. He barely paid my dad any wages; he would pay in the form of produce from the fields. Since it wasn't easy to get things past my mom, she took charge of their relationship. Being fully ready to execute on the plans she had for her and my dad, she told him there would be a hayride next month in Waynesboro, Mississippi, and she planned on attending that hayride. . She knew they had to cross over that Choctaw County line that would take them out of Alabama and into Mississippi. My mom assured my dad everything would work out fine." I can see them now sneaking out of their houses and finalizing her scheme. My dad still had to be very careful when he came around; he knew her parents were on the watch for him.

My grandparents on my mother's side, Mary and Vaden, were set in their ways. We all know that was the truth in a large family, especially in the Deep

*Figure 5 Photo of my grand mother and grand father Mary and Vaden Davis*

South. Unfortunately, every time there's a good situation, something or someone would throw a wrench into the mix of it. My mother's parents were still upset over their daughter being with this boy. They thought their daughter was too good for him. However, those two lovebirds didn't let that stop them. Although my mom would get caught sneaking out of the house by her dad sometimes, that still didn't stop her from meeting up with my dad. My grandfather was the quiet one in their house, but my grandmother she was the total opposite. She took charge and she also made all the decisions as well. Again, that's that good ole Choctaw Indian blood!

I do remember when we were little boys, we would ask our mom Madea if we could go down the train track to grandmother's house to visit our great-grandmother, and she would say, "Okay, but boys—be careful on the track and look out for that dangerous train." At the time, she was old, and we used to be afraid of her. She had a room at the side of the house. She would say, "Come on in, boys," and offer us some of her freshly made biscuits—to us they didn't look very fresh. We'd sneak them in our pockets; they were hard as rocks. We only stayed for a short time because she looked scary to us; she wore this dingy white scarf on her head all the time. My older brother Alvin told me that we called our great-grandmother Aunt Mag, Margaret. She, too, had the blood of the Choctaw Indians, just as her daughter-in-law, Mary. Aunt Mag lived to the great age of 108 years old. Talk about good genes—here's hoping those genes are passed down to the rest of the family.

Now, back to the two lovebirds. Some very good news: we all know she was smart. Remember that plan my mom devised? Now she's putting that plan into action. She had had the conversation with her girlfriends about the hayride in the town of Waynesboro. But there was one slight problem—remember, they had to cross over the state line out of Alabama into the state of Mississippi, which was another two hours from both towns, from Deer Park and Choctaw County, but she didn't care. She told my dad they were attending this hayride. There wasn't anything to lose. And it was free to the public; everyone was invited. The hayride was in the Black folks in the neighborhood. This wouldn't cause any problem with the white man. They didn't like it when Black people were having a good time. They thought all Blacks should stay home or remain working in the fields or go eat watermelon under a shade of a tree, even though I know white people are the ones who love watermelon; I've witnessed this my whole life, and it's a fact. Now that the word was out—everyone in the area knew about the hayride going to Waynesboro. So, they were ready to get things rolling; they would make the best of this great opportunity.

Figure 6A photo of my Great-grandmother Aunt

They kept it a secret until that day of the hayride. My mom snuck out to meet with my dad somewhere between the two counties. The day had arrived when they would make the trip to the big hayride in Waynesboro. The farmer that had the most horses and enough wagons was the one in charge of the hayride. The owner of the wagon put hay all over the bed of the wagon, then he placed bales of hay all around, which gave all the people a place to sit down. I wonder if it will be a country parade for Black folks? One thing was for sure—you could smell the fresh hay as it blows in the wind and fell to the ground, as well as the droppings from the horses as they passed by. The smells are all part of a good hayride out in the country.

When it came time for the actual hayride, in Alabama, they made their way to the wagon, found a good place to sit down, and got comfortable, looking each other in the eye with big smiles. I wonder if they were all hugged up. I often wondered how bumpy the hayride was, and how long they had stayed on that old, dusty dirt road. The hayride started at the farmer's property, located close to Highway 45 North, so they would have come from the South, heading toward Waynesboro. I guess it wasn't a hard ride after all.

*Figure 7 This is the building, the City Hall in Waynesboro M.I.*

Once in the city of Waynesboro, they stayed on Highway 45 North for about four miles, then made a right-hand turn into Highway 84 East and travelled for another three miles. Then they took a right turn into the parking lot. This was the place where the townsfolk did their shopping, next to the farmer's market. Once there, everyone climbed off the wagon. They'd made it to their destination. "We are here, we did it!" The best news of all is that they had a ton of fun on the hayride, fun they could cherish for the rest of their lives, sharing it with their sibling as well. Way to go, Mom and Dad!

Now, I'm wondering, what will their parents think? They were the first in our whole family to elope. The plan wasn't finished yet. She told my dad, "This is our secret, we will go straight to City Hall. There, we will get married." Of course, my dad was ecstatic about my mother's perfect plan to get married. I'm so happy my parents were at the right age—eighteen in the state of Mississippi. If not, there would have been a big problem at the City Hall.

*"Boy Meets Girl and Gets Hitched."* I like the sound of that! This is one love story I will never forget. I will carry those special moments with me all my days, and I know my brothers and sisters will agree with me as well. It didn't take long before my mom's parents accepted the outcome of it all. My mom didn't care about what kind of work my dad did for a living. As I said before, she was a smart young lady, and it would carry over later in life. We would all benefit from it. "Hmm . . . What's next for the newlyweds? They have to start looking for

a place to settle down, a place they can call their own." She devised the perfect plan, and I know for a fact they were the first in our whole family to elope. I'm so proud of my mom. This should make all my brothers and sisters feel the same about our parents. Now that the two lovebirds were married, it wouldn't be long before they heard the sound of small footsteps running across the living room floor.

# TWO

### Sooie! Sooie! How Many Pigs Do You Own?

My mother and father wanted to be able to say one day, "This is our house." But first, they had to find a place to live in a good location as well. One of my father's brothers, Uncle James, who lived in Waynesboro on Highway North 63—yes, that part of town everyone that lived in Waynesboro knew had a very bad reputation, in around that neighborhood—I'm not sure Uncle James was the older brother or not, but he lived in that part of town. He was a pig farmer; He's been living there for many years. My dad, Neshia, asked his brother if he could put them up for a while, until they could find a place of their own. My uncle was more than happy to put them up, saying, "We're family." So, my father, and his brother, a pig farmer, were living together. Remember our family mantra? *"A strong family that lives together shares love together."*

Figure 8 This photo of my Father Andrew Neshia.

Figure 9 My favor Uncle James my dad's brother.

During this time, my mom didn't have any working skills, so as a new housewife, it was just fine with her. My dad had been working hard all his life and he was going to make sure his family was taken care of financially, and that was the bottom line.. Now all my dad needed to do was find extra work. Since there were sharecroppers' jobs all around the Waynesboro area; he knew he wouldn't have any problems. He'd been working with his hands all his life. For now, he would work with his brother James, and for a while they would be slopping hogs. "Sooie, sooie!" *At least it would bring home the bacon!* I'm overjoyed at the love and happiness my mom and dad shared with each other over the years. It was a struggle sometimes, and they persevered. Working hard together, it didn't take long at all before they became that perfect couple. They made a solid promise to each other; it would be a lifetime relationship and commitment between the two. That was a beautiful thing here. I was hoping for a life just like that. Now everything had panned out the way my mom wanted it. Maybe it was time to move on to other things. Who knows? It could be the sound of little footsteps running across the dining room floor; that would make the two lovebirds a very happy married family.

Uncle James's place was the first place for my mom and dad to live as a couple, because they left the border of Alabama. And Madea's mother and father were still upset about the elopement. Things were getting tight for the newlyweds; there wasn't much room for them all at Uncle James's house. Uncle James wife, Aunt Bee, and his daughter, May Jewel occupants of the home. Aunt Bee— was special! Why? She was the first person I saw with gold in her mouth; it was mostly in her front teeth—all four on the top. My parents were happy there, and they didn't want to go back to their hometowns either. That's where they started, but not where they would finish. They needed a place of their own. The new residence had to be somewhere in Wayne County.

They didn't have very much—basically the clothes on their backs. How much money did the two have between themselves? It will always be a mystery to me. I guess my mom could do some housework for the white people who lived close to town; at this point they needed extra money coming in, and they would like to help my dad's brother as well for letting them stay there for the time being. For a long time, my grandparents would never come to Waynesboro. maybe it was because of the elopement years earlier.

They hadn't seen each other in some time. Besides, the distance from Waynesboro to her mother was very long, and adding to the difficulty, all the roads were old, dusty dirt roads. Only Highways 63, 84, and 45 were paved in blacktop and stone. Years later, my mom's mother and father finally moved out of the state of Alabama, and of all places they moved to Waynesboro on Highway North 45, just about three to four miles from Uncle James's house. Maybe that was good news, because at this time, just about all of my mother's brothers and sisters had moved out of the house in Choctaw, and now it's just an old empty big house.

That old house was just too large for my grandparents; that's why they moved to Waynesboro. That was a good move—now mother and daughter were back together again, with no hard feelings. In fact, my mother and father had buried the hatchet, between her and her parents and that boy from another county. Now it was time to go house-hunting for the two lovebirds. Uncle James told my dad there was one place they could look at; it was very cheap to rent, and it was really close to town. My Uncle, Madea, "Neshia," headed out to look at this place. Uncle James said we are here! They all got out of his truck, and as they all stood there looking at this old house, they began to look at each other with amazement!

My mom took a very long look and she said, "I don't know, Neshia." That's the name she called him. Then she went on to say it looks kind of funny. "Besides, it doesn't look like a regular house at all." She said, "Okay, if you like it, I'm fine with your decision." Well, this will be our mom and dad's first home. My mom also said, "Neshia, it would need a lot of work." What did this house really look like? It was originally a train station, a depot, and it was used for the United States Postal Service as a drop-off station for all the mail in the Wayne County area. This old train station was just sitting there for so many years. From what Uncle James said, the county was about to tear it down, so the railroad department gave them the okay to purchase the building. Uncle James and my father would prepare to do some major renovations on this old train station. He also said, "If you all don't have enough money, don't worry; I'm here for you." My mom was so happy for the financial support from her brother-in-law.

So they began, and with all the supplies they needed, they started the renovation. After some hard work and some major changes, in no time at all, it was finished—their own home. Pretty soon, hopefully there would be an addition to those lovebirds' family. My parents' siblings all called my mom "Madea," at an early age. My mother knew what kind of work my dad did for a living? She knew he was a sharecropper just like his parents were in the past, and she was okay with that as his new wife. During the time that my mom was living with her parents, there were a few health problems in the household. There wasn't anything very serious, I guess, just an everyday bug I suppose. First, my mom's dad, Vaden Davis, wasn't in the best of health.

My twin and I saw this in him, the first time we were introduced. There's something about his face—that's why we looked at him the way we did. Well, he's our grandpa, and we love him. I was told our grandpa was a little sickly, so that's why he always sat on the porch of their house with a glass of water in his hand all the time—I mean, just about every day. Well, I didn't realize it wasn't water—it was hard moonshine whiskey. My older brother Alvin told me that Waynesboro was a dry county. Somehow my grandfather found a way to buy his bootleg whisky. Maybe it gave him some relief at the time. It was clear, and that's why it looked like water, but we thought nothing about it as little boys. It got worse later, but no one knew what the problem was. All he did was sit out on the porch with that glass in his hands.

Later in life, my twin and I used to look at my grandfather sitting on the porch. We thought he was just our quiet grandpa. We didn't know he was sick at all, and he stayed to himself. He never called to me and my twin to see if we needed something. He didn't even yell at us as little boys. Like, "Stop," "What are you boys doing," "Stay out of the road," or "Go play somewhere else, you are making too much noise." We were expecting some kind of discipline from him. I guess he knew our grandma would take care of all the discipline around the house, and that was something she continually did every day. For us twins, it was either the belt or go find a switch. Another thing is that we never saw our grandmother under the weather.

When my parents moved to Waynesboro, in their first home my mom began to experience strange symptoms. She was still young and strong—it was more like a bug or something, she thought. My dad noticed the change in our mom, so my mom had my dad take her to the hospital for a check-up. What the doctor told my mom and dad gave them both an unbelievable shock. The diagnosis was an acute touch of asthma. "Don't worry; in most cases, it will dissipate over time, especially in young people." His orders for her were to eat the right food, drink plenty of water, and not to forget to exercise. So she began to walk to our grandmother's house. She didn't want to walk on Highway North 45 because it was too dangerous, so she chose to walk on the train tracks. That was the way to keep healthy. Our grandmother didn't want my mom walking on the train tracks at all; she said it wasn't safe. They came to an agreement that it was much safer than Highway North 45. By the time she was blessed with two little boys, the asthma had gotten much worse. So she had to deal with this acute asthma for many years. To add insult to injury, she developed high blood pressure to boot. I'm not sure what she did for her blood pressure at the time, but the asthma she couldn't hide; everyone in the family knew our mom was very sick. My mom used to sit around the house breathing heavily, and it was sad to see this. My twin and I would sit and look at her trying to catch her breath and start crying. She would say to us, "Boys, don't cry. *Everything will be all right.*" These words stuck with me; I had no idea many years later, my mom would use these same words again. My mom was still strong, we could see it in her every day. When she got sick, she would tell me and my twin, "Boys, go out and gather those leaves from that plant." She showed us once; she said, "If I ever need this plant, this is what it looks like." So we would go into the fields and find this same plant; with some research I found out its name it was called the Mullein plant. The above photo is what it looks like. We would take as much as we could and head back to the house. We'd give it to our mother, and she would take the plant, rub it together, and place the leaves in a pot with a fire under it. When it started to burn, she would take a towel, put it over her head, lean forward over the thick, blueish smoke and begin to breathe the smoke and fumes. Within no time at all, she was breathing well. What a sign of relief for those two little boys. This special plant was a gift from God, and it grows on Earth freely. My older sister Gloria Jean stayed home most of the time because of my mom's asthma. It didn't bother her; she

Figure 10 This wonderful mullein plant, Verbascum Thapsus. My mom depended on it when her Asthma flared up

had a male friend that would visit from time to time, but it was understood that it was not a committed relationship. I remember the boy she was keeping company with his name was Benny and he was living over by the front. Jerry and I used to talk with him as little boys; I still remember his face as a fair-skinned, tall boy. The last time I saw him, he came to visit Gloria Jean in Schenectady, New York. I stopped by my sister's house, and he was there. He greeted me and said, "What's going on—which one are you?" I said, "I'm Terry." He came from Chicago one weekend, and my sister was happy to see him again; they reminisced about school and life in our hometown. My sister enjoyed cooking great meals like Madea, those delicious meals and set a nice table; it was something she enjoyed very much. Memories of Each time my mom would say grace to God, thinking of him for a good healthy family was special. When a family is poor, there's always better things.

What about my mom and dad's house down by the train tracks? Years earlier, it had only two large rooms. There was a large porch that ran the length of the house, five steps in the front of the house, and four posts that held the roof over the porch. There was one door, which was the entrance into the house. There were no windows in the front of the house. There was a total of two doors and two windows in the large two-room house. Once inside, the first room to the right was for my mom and dad. There you would find some of my mom and dad's personal items. First, there was the large fireplace. To the left side of this room was my mom's ironing board and the table and chairs, and my mom and dad's bed was in the back of the room. The fireplace kept the room heated, and it was very warm where my mom and dad slept. We never ran out of wood for the fireplace; there was a wood box that held all the wood for the fireplace. There was a wood box for the kitchen stove as well. It was me and my twin's job to keep plenty of wood in both wood boxes. There was a wall between both large rooms. The fireplace was on one side, and the kitchen stove was on the other side of the wall and the other small window by the back

Figure 11 My mom and oldest child that lived, Gloria Jean Koonce Williamson

door. That back door was the way to get outside. My mother's cast-iron stove kept the other room warm as well; my twin and I also had to keep the wood box filled. There, our mother did all the cooking for the family. It was also the sleeping quarters for my two older sisters and six brothers. My little sister Vonda and little brother Billy slept with our mom and dad. There were no problems; we all were a big, happy family.

One day, my mom was making supper for the night and my older sister Gloria Jean was helping her in the kitchen. I was in the next room where the fireplace was. Gloria Jean was still helping my mom with the cooking. I went to be close to the fire; it was cool out. The fire in the fireplace was very hot; I could hear the popping and cracking coming from the hot wood in the fireplace. Some of the wood chips kept falling out of the fire and landing on the floor, so I just kicked some of the wood chips back into the fire. My big sister Gloria Jean came into the room and told me to stop before I got burned.

I continued to kick the wood chips back into the fireplace, and before long, I gave off this loud scream. "Why is my pants on fire?!" My big sister Gloria Jean grabbed me and threw me down on the floor and began to put out the fire on my right leg. Our mom came running into the room screaming, "Gloria! What's going on?" Well, Gloria told our mom, "I told Terry to stop kicking the wood chips back into the fire, and this is the result."

I knew what was next, either the belt or the switch, but first, she had to take me to the hospital. So Jerry ran next door to get Uncle John. We got into his truck and were off to the hospital. My leg was very burned; it felt as it would fall off. The doctors said it was a second-degree burn. He also told my mom it could have been worse if we hadn't gotten to the hospital early. So after all that, I knew the switch was next. Now I had a lifetime scarring on my right leg and a sore behind to boot. My mom came and told me, "Please, Terry, be careful in and around the house." My response was, "Yes, Madea." I knew us twins were her favorite.

My mom's special sewing machine was my mom's favorite item. That sewing machine was always busy, making dresses and shirts, blouses, and, of course, our blankets and such. There was a window on the right side of the room. There wasn't a door in the room they slept in. There was the first door, which was the entrance into the house, and the other door was out back. My mom had four wooden posts she used to make quilts and blankets for the people in the neighborhood and around town. I used to watch her when she was making them. She used to sing her favorite song when she was working; it goes like this: "I want to die easy when I die." At the time, I didn't understand the meaning of that song. Now it's hard for me to even think about the song, and hearing it again makes me feel sad. People all around loved her work; she had different patterns.

To the left of the stove was an icebox, which kept all the food cold. Let's not forget the iceman—he would bring ice over to the house all the time, at least two or three times a week. I clearly remember him. He wore this strange leather strap on his left shoulder, the side he carried the ice on, and a crooked-looking hook in his hands. Our mom always kept a large pot on the stove so that if anyone needed to take a quick wash-up, there would

*Figure 12 Singer sewing machine: Courtesy of A Yee via Flickr*

be plenty of hot water ready. My dad didn't like to shave with cold water, so she made sure he had very hot water for shaving. My big sister Gloria Jean did a lot of work with our mother—doing the dishes, cleaning around the house. Not to mention, my mom was still bothered with asthma; it flared up once in a while, but she was a very strong woman, and she was doing fine. My mom always wanted a water pump inside the house but that wasn't possible because of the train station, so the pump was always on the outside. My mom hung a rope on two nails, from wall to wall, with a blanket over the rope. This was for privacy when taking a bath. My mom and dad couldn't afford a traditional folding screen. I'd seen them in town—just another thing my mom wanted, but the blanket on a rope from wall to wall was good enough. That's why things were so special in and around our house.

My mom, the homemaker, her husband, and their sibling—not only did she take care of all of us, but she also found a job other than homemaking. She landed a job at the blanket factory down the tracks from the left of our house. She didn't work there for very long, because there was an incident at the factory one afternoon. One of the other workers had stolen a blanket and placed it outside of the building between the train tracks. That day when my mom was on her way home, she walked down the tracks and noticed a box in the wooded area. She picked it up and it was a brand-new blanket, so she thought someone threw it away or it fell off the train when unloading. One of the bosses saw my mom pick up the box, and he asked her to stop, telling her she was fired for taking the blanket. She said, "I thought someone threw it away." The boss said to my mom, "Don't worry, just go home and don't come back tomorrow," and he went on to say, "Don't say anything to anyone; it's between you and me." My mom thought she was in deep trouble and might go to jail. He told her he would take care of everything; he said he thought she was an honest woman. That was my mom's last outside job, and it was a scary one at that. She came home and told my dad. He said, "Velma, don't worry about it; you have a large family to take care of, and we'll be just fine with what we got, and there's some good coming out of what happened."

Here's an unforgettable moment in us twins life. My dad worked very hard every day in the fields for the white man. My twin and I could see him coming home from work. He would walk over to the porch and grab his favorite porcelain basin with a red ring all around it. He'd pour some water in it and begin to wash his face and hands, then reach back for that dingy old towel he used every day. Then he would hang it on that rusty nail. My mom always told him, "Neshia, did I tell you to put that dirty towel in the hamper?" That was his daily ritual. Besides, he was always so tired from all that hard work. Afterward he would mosey over to his favorite chair, and most of the time he would fall asleep. I know now he had to be very tired from work. She kept a bucket of very cold drinking water for the family, especially during the night. Here's the fun part: there was one dipper in that family, and there was no problem with the family drinking from the same dipper. We'd just drink, and when finished, we'd hang the dipper on a nail in the wall. That's real family love. Remember, "A strong family shares love together." That's because our house was so special; we were a special family, and it was a blessing from God. Nowadays it's hard for people to drink from the same cup or glass with other folks.

Since I'm on the topic of the water bucket, there was also one on the outside of the house, which sat next to the water pump where our mom did the washing. The fresh, cold water made the difference when the clothes were washed and hanging on the clothesline, when the wind blows through the clothes, what freshness it brings. It was the freshest smell one could ever wish for.

At this time, my twin and I used to play around the icehouse in town until we got into some trouble with the white men. Our mom said, "Boys, don't let me catch you around the icehouse." It was one of the places the white men would hang around. The other place they hung around was on the back streets of Waynesboro; there was a red Coca-Cola machine. If you wanted to find a group of white men, they would all be standing smoking cigarettes and sitting around this Coca-Cola machine, looking and staring at people that walked by— especially little Black boys, which I thought was weird—as they didn't have anything to do.

Our mom didn't have to worry; you couldn't catch my twin brother and I in that part of town. We tried it once, and it wasn't pleasant at all. This I'll never forget. They would yell, "Hey there, you two double twins. We don't want to see any little niggers around here." Do you want to see two little boys run? Remember the old saying, "Eat my dust"? It was fitting. Off we went running home. My twin and I used to run and call the white man names. By teasing them, calling them "White soda cracker"—you know the Saltine crackers that come in a box—we didn't let our mom catch us doing this. Not just us twins, all my brothers and sisters used that term. I don't know where it came from; for us it was fitting. It was the only way to get back at the white man; they tried to make us feel sad and it hurt. When the white man called us "nigger," it hurt a lot and they were very serious, so "even Steven." We had to keep it to ourselves; otherwise he'd come over with the switch or the belt. So, it was better if we just minded our own business and just go home and play or sit on the porch for a while. By doing so, we wouldn't get into any more trouble in town.

My twin and I sat there next to the steps. We weren't allowed to go to town for a while, so sitting there, we could smell the sweet aroma from the pine trees, coming from the direction of town, and we could hear that very loud, noisy whistle that goes off every day. It's been a while, so we tried it again. We asked Madea if we could go to town later that day just for fun and a game. She said, "Yes boys—remember what I said and be careful around the white man," and we would say, "Yes, Madea."

Meanwhile, our next older brother Ervin stopped us, and he asked us twins if we wanted to go for a ride in Dad's old car. It was parked to the left of the house. No one had a driver's license at the time, so it sat there parked, because no one could drive it . . . So, us twins got into the car with Ervin and off we went—no more just two twin boys, now it's the three of us. Ervin could barely see over the steering wheel and the dashboard to drive, and here we go, down that old dusty road we went. He was doing good for a while until he got close to this giant log truck that carry tons of logs on the back of it. We were fine until the truck made a quick, sharp turn. Some of the logs were too long so Ervin could see them. Without any warning, Ervin lost control of the car, and we ran into the back of the log truck, knocking out the windshield. We all were lucky, if there such a word; I call it a blessing. Although we all got into trouble that day, we didn't get the belt or the switch. We never went down that path again. Ervin never drove that car again; he learned his lesson that day.

What's that loud noise coming from the train tracks? It's an everyday event. Our house would shake violently, as if it were an earthquake.

Our house was close to that old dusty dirt road, and that very noisy train—it would put you to sleep or keep you awake during the night, that noise from the wheels coming into contact with the rails. In our house there was no electricity, so we were used to the noisy train during the night. We had to use kerosene lamps to light the whole house. All the cooking and the kids' homework was done under the lamp lighting. Both rooms were mostly in some darkness. Having the kerosene lamp was so important to the family, for cooking and reading or just sitting around thinking.

These kerosene lamps were for indoor use only. There were several of them throughout the house. There wasn't a strong smell from the kerosene because the burning of the wood in the fireplace masked the smell in the house—again, my dad used fresh pine wood from the sawmill. The only thing that was a concern with kerosene was that when we had to put the flame out, it left this thick smoke, and it gave off this unpleasant smell. All in all, things inside the house were good. From the house there was a path that led to the outhouse. What did my dad use for lighting during the middle of the night on the way to the outhouse? That's when the kerosene lantern came into play on a cold, dark night with the snakes and frogs about. That outhouse was smelly sometimes, according to how the wind was blowing. It was close to Aunt Lelee's house as well. They didn't complain at all; they were good neighbors. There were a few of our neighbors who complained about the outhouse. Sometimes they used to drive or walk by with their hand over their mouth and nose; well, it's something they had to do to experience all parts of living in the Deep South. My dad did all he could to keep it clean and fresh. My dad would go over to the sawmill and collect pine wood chips that gave off a sweet smell of fresh pine, and he

*Figure 13 This is what our outhouse looks back int the day.*

would place the wood chips in and around the structure of the outhouse to combat at least some of the odors. Our parents weren't ashamed of owning an outhouse because there was no other choice. My dad knew he had to build another one because the old one was used out. He found a new spot and decided to build it there.

My dad had my twin and I help him dig the big hole for the new outhouse. There was a problem. Uncle John came running out screaming, "Neshia, you can't build the outhouse there, because it would be too close to my house, also it would be in plain view of my house!" He didn't say anything about the smell. My dad agreed with him and looked for a better place to build it. Jerry and I, we started digging the hole in another spot. After digging for a while, we came up on some bones, which gave us a scare at the time. We stopped and told dad what we found. He called Uncle John then looked and decided it was the bones of an animal. Us twins looked at each other with different thoughts, so we continued to dig until it was finished. Then our dad started building the new outhouse.

Figure 14 chamber pot we owned several of them

Again, if you had to go in the middle of the night, and if it was dark outside, you had to use what we called the chamber pot. It, too, was the sanitation facility for the house during the night. It was well-known in most Southern homes. There was one in each room of our house. They were mostly white, made from sheet metal, and they were glazed with porcelain with a wire handle to carry it. There was a red ring around it, with a white lid that covered the top.

Moving to the outside of the house, I mentioned the large porch with the five steps. If you looked straight ahead, you'd be looking at a large, wooded area. If you looked to your right, there was a very tall tree called a Chinaberry tree. It had poisonous berries on it. As little children, we could not eat the berries; this order came from our mom. But my twin and I would pick them up and use them in our slingshot; we remembered what our mom told us about those Chinaberries.

Back to the porch at our house: if you stood on the porch and looked to your left, you'd see this very large oak tree, and it gave lots of shade, especially on a hot summer day. My father also had a medium-sized garden to the left of the oak tree. There was a dirt road behind the house. Our house was the only house on the left-hand side of this dusty dirt road. All the other families' homes were on the right side. In fact, there were seven families, and I knew them all. We always played on that road, my twin and I, and we used to get into all kinds of trouble playing around the neighborhood. In fact, the Bells, Aunt Lelee, and Uncle John's mother (her name was Mrs. Gracey); she was mean to us. She used to yell at us a lot of the time.

"What are you boys doing? Go away; get back to your house!" And she didn't hesitate in using the switch on us. We used to run and cry to our mom, and she would tell us boys to just try to play safely, and we wouldn't get in trouble with Mrs. Gracey down the road, especially in front of her house. Many times, she used to chase us up the road to our house. "You boys stay out of the middle of the road; go play somewhere else. Play in front of your house, you little bad boys, and if I see you boys down here in front of my house, I will put the belt to your bottom. Velma wouldn't mind if I gave you boys a lashing, so git!" So, we would head back to our house; there's always something for us to do. Jerry said, "Hey Terry, what is it?" I said, "I don't know." He replied, "How can you forget to think hard?" I said, "I can't remember; maybe it's because of Mrs. Gracey."

Jerry said to me, "It's tadpole season!" My twin and I do this every year. This season came early this summer. We are on the hunt for young tadpoles; they are bottom feeders. Like always, the best place to look is in front of our house. By now you should know all about our house and its surroundings. In front of our house are three major landmarks: the small front yard, the old noisy railroad tracks, and the main one is the small stream that runs out in front of our house all the time. It even runs all the way in front of our small town. Out front— that's where we will find all the tadpoles we need for the year, and we only need one. Jerry and I both had a small bucket, and in those buckets we put small holes in the bottom; this way we could catch them with ease. I would start at one end and Jerry at the other end. We would make noise in the water, and out of nowhere, the tadpoles would come swimming up to the surface. We would catch all the large ones, keeping them in the bucket with no holes in them. Then we would separate the ones we need to keep.

Then we would put them in a large jar until it was time for the transformation. It would take about three to five weeks before it commenced and reached its final stage. It seems like it happened overnight; before long we had our baby frogs. That made us happy—and what was the first thing we did? Run inside the house to show our mom our brand-new frogs. She would give off this loud scream, "Boys, get those frogs out of this house!"

With a quiet voice we would say, "Yes, Madea," and out of the house we would run. We would keep our frogs in the jar in a box as long as we could before they either hopped away or just succumb to the heat and weather or just die. That's okay; we will repeat the same next year, us little twins. "We have to stop putting our mom on edge for sure," but "Boys will be boys." See you next year!

## **THREE**

### Don't be Afraid of the Choo-Choo

To the left of the house is the direction that will take you to my grandmother's house, about two and a half to three miles

*Figure 15 locomotive in front of our house*

down those noisy and dangerous train tracks. Since I'm talking about train tracks, and that same old noisy train, there was a terrible train derailment. This accident sounded and felt like an earthquake. The ground was shaking violently. I'm sure everyone in the neighborhood heard and felt this very loud sound coming from the accident. It was a terrible thing to see." My whole family experienced the train derailment. It happened just in front of our house. There was a lot of noise. This loud sound was the result of large freight boxcars—it was a squeaking, crushing sound of those steel rails. I never thought a train rail could bend so easily, just like a large rubber band— the sounds of heavy metal that stretched all the way to town. This was very scary and amazing. Many of the boxcars were carrying fruits and vegetables. Some were filled with dry goods. Our mom said to us, "Don't go near the wreck." But all those fruits and vegetables sure looked good to my twin and I. Well, it didn't take very long for the engineers to clean up that even larger mess. Then things were back to the norm, but now the smell of hot tar was coming from the cross tires. It's amazing how much goes on in and around our house and town.

In the front of the house, in the direction of that big oak tree, my dad had a cast-iron water pump that was installed before they moved into the house. There was no running water inside the house.

At this point, if one needed water, the pump had to be primed with water first to get the water to flow out of the spout. After priming the pump, the water would come cascading out, and it was very cold. Next to the pump was a large, silver, soft, metal tub. This tub's purpose was soaking clothes and washing and rinsing the clothes. We took one of my mom's wash tubs and filled it with water.

The game was to see who could dunk their head under the water and hold their breath the longest. Jerry went first, so I kept track of the time. When he submerged his head into the water, we noticed there was too much water in the tub. Now it was my turn to dunk my head in the water. I didn't notice Jerry had taken a broken glass to bail some of the water out of the tub, so I dunked my head into the water, but when I came up I could see the water was red. I wiped my face, and I felt this burning, stinging sensation. Jerry screamed for our mother, "Madea, Madea, come quick, Terry got a bad cut on his face!"

I was screaming "Madea!" with blood all over the place. I didn't know what to do. So our mom ran to the place where the washtub was, screaming, "What have you boys done now?!" My face seemed like it was on fire, and the blood didn't want to stop. Off to the hospital. I got several stitches and a lifetime scar. That scar would come into play later on in my life. That was not the end of this story—what came next was a switch and a sore behind. The two of us never played that game again.

What could two little bad boys do now? Well, our mom always told us not to touch the iron because she did all the ironing. One day, she was at home, so Jerry decided to iron his own clothes. At first, you have to get the iron hot by placing it on the stove in the kitchen. After getting the iron hot, he took it into the other room, our mother and father's room. He started ironing his clothes. He sat down in the chair and proceeded to iron his pants, but the iron slipped out of his hand and landed on his lap, his right thigh in fact. He let out a loud scream.

After he screamed, our mom came running and said, "What are you boys doing now?" And I said, "Madea! Madea! Jerry dropped the iron on his lap!" So, I ran next door to get Uncle John, who owned a pickup truck. "Okay, off to the hospital."

There, he was diagnosed with a second-degree burn on his right thigh, and we all know what's next: the belt or the switch. Madea said to us, "Didn't I tell you to be careful in and around the house?" "Yes, Madea." Well, boys will be boys. He will carry the imprint of a cast iron on his thigh forever. I used to tease him, saying, "Jerry, you are carrying an iron on your leg," just for laughs.

There were more scary moments and trouble to come for us, and we certainly got into it as little boys. I must share one more event with you! The house was empty, just Jerry and I there. We got hungry, so I decided to cook us some hotdogs. The stove was always very hot, so I put the frying pan on the stove. It had grease in it, and by the time I got the hotdogs, the pan was too hot, but I didn't notice that. I put the hotdogs in the pan and from out of nowhere, the water mixed with the grease and exploded. The grease splashed all over my left arm, and I gave off a loud scream. I had three very bad burns on my left arm that left three lifetime scars. One is the size of a quarter, the other is the size of a nickel, and one is the size of a dime, and those scars are still there today. Now I have forty cents on my left arm. Yes, I knew what was next—the belt or the switch! I got the belt, this time from our dad, another lesson well-learned. Madea said, "Terry, what did I tell you boys? Stay away from the that hot stove."

Well, the next morning our dad said, "Everyone, it's time to head to the fields; it's time to start working for the white man." That meant everyone except me and mom; she always stayed home but it was a day off for me, but Jerry was on his own this day. Now one can see—boys will be boys. Those good memories will be part of our lives forever. For number of scars, I got Jerry beat, three to one.

She made sure everyone went to bed real early. We had to be up by six-thirty in the morning and get ready to go to the white man's fields. She woke everyone up and made breakfast. Eventually everyone could hear the sound from the white man's truck horn. It was time to go. They all climbed on the back of the truck, and it was off to the fields. My twin had to be at the field by himself and work all by himself this day. One thing is for sure—he would give it his best. We will be careful around the bugs and spiders when they come out. It's nice if our dad leaves work early today; this will give us some time to play when Jerry gets home. I do have my scars. I'm okay; the burns won't stop me from having fun with my twin.

What's next for those twins? It's June bug season! But first, what does one look like? It has a very hard shell, blueish and greenish mixed with some silver, all in one color. It has six legs to tunnel through the dirt and grass. It has two bulging eyes on top. What are those twin boys going to do this part of the summer? Look for the biggest June bug we can find. The first things we would do is sneak into our mom's room and go over next to the sewing machine. We would find the sewing box and get the strongest thread our mom has.

Then we would sneak out and run down by that big oak tree in our front yard. It was very hot out that day, and we could see June bugs flying in the air—that's the first good sign. As soon as we see the biggest June bug, we both would attack. The best way to find the first big one is by crawling on the ground; it makes our job much easier. First Jerry would sneak behind the one we wanted, and I would approach from the front in case it started to crawl and fly away.

Jerry would catch it, holding it in his hands real gentle-like, not to squeeze it too tight or he would kill it by crushing it to death. I would have the string from our mom's sewing box, then I would tie the string on one of the June bug's hind legs. A June bug flies by its own power, and it could fly with ease, but when it has some string tied on its hind leg, which altered his flight. As soon as Jerry let the June bug go, it would take off and start flying, but at a very slow speed, and that way we could keep up with it as it flies. Those twins running down that old dusty road chasing their June bug . . . now that's how little boys would have fun in our one-stoplight town. Everyone, you are welcome to join us in our next hunt for June bugs next year. Boys will be boys! See you next year!


## **FOUR**

### Giddy Up! Whoa!

As little boys, my twin and I knew there was a big fire in Waynesboro. It was a bad one. Everyone knew about the fire—it lit up the sky and burned until the next day. It took place in this huge brick building on the main street in town. Back then I didn't know what it meant about a three-alarm fire. The Wayne County put up posters; they were looking for people to help clean bricks from the ruins. They wanted Black and white folks, but they didn't let the white folks work with the Black folks. We all knew the white man was tricky. They called us "boy" or even worse, "nigger." The only time they didn't call us those names is when they were in the company of parents. They wanted my parents to say "yes, sir" or "yes, ma'am, and they weren't happy with the word "no." Then they would call us "*COLORED*." For example, they would say, "All colored folks could work over to that side of the building. And the white folks work on another." When it came time to clean the bricks, my twin and I asked our mom, "Madea, can we go to town to help clean bricks?" She'd say, "Okay, but be very careful around those white folks." When we got there, they told everyone what to do and how much money everyone would receive for pay at the end of the day.

They gave the white folks twelve cents a brick, they gave all the Black folks five cents a brick. Now what am I saying—the white man will never change to the end of time, that's how I feel and what I believe. But that didn't stop us; we still cleaned bricks and made a small amount of money until it was time to go back home. We couldn't wait to tell our mom what kind of day it was cleaning bricks—again, another lesson we learned by living in the Deep South. And we had to be very careful in their presence; the only dishonest thing we did as little boys was playing a game called "pitching pennies" for keeps or playing the game of marbles. We would play the game with other kids in the neighborhood, and they were both fun games most of the time—just don't lose. Our mom gave us a call when it was time for supper, we ate and then off to bed we went. We had to work with our dad in the white man's fields the next day.

Up and at'em! Our mom got us up early for breakfast, then she packed a lunch. We all could hear the white man's truck outside. We all climbed on the back of the pickup truck like always, and it was off to the fields. When working that early in the morning, everything was still wet. Today we all would be picking sweet potatoes. My twin brother and I watched our dad plowing the fields as he tried to keep the

*Figure 16 plowing for sweet potatoes.*

horse in a straight line, wearing his old, wrinkled coveralls, his dingy handkerchief hanging out of his left pocket, and that rumpled hat, the one you could see the sweat stains on.

He would yell to the horse, "Giddy up!" which meant, "let's go, horse," and he'd say "Whoa!" which meant "let's stop, horse." He stopped, looked at us, and said, "Boys! Bring me some water!" So, we got him his water and he continued to plow. When our dad finished plowing, it seemed there were sweet potatoes on the ground for miles. And then it was time to pick the sweet potatoes. Everyone had their separate bucket to put the potatoes in. When all the buckets were filled, we put them in croker sacks. As we filled the croker sacks with the sweet potatoes, my twin and I started eating them, and my dad said, "Stop boys, before you get sick!" And those twins of course didn't listen, and we got very sick. We learned a painful lesson that day: don't eat sweet potatoes in the middle of the day on a very hot, sunny day.

Now it was time for the cotton season. Did we pick cotton? The answer is yes. We were young and didn't understand the importance of picking cotton. The leaves were very sharp most of the time, we had more cuts than anyone else, clean cuts like razor blade cuts. Ultimately, it didn't pan out because we got in the way more than anything else. At least, we tried.

We were there mostly for show, and we couldn't stay at home with our mom; she would never get her work done because we would keep her on edge, so we had to go to the cotton fields. What did my twin and I find out about the white man? That he was cheating our dad, we seen it with our own eyes, and that's a fact. How did we know? At the end of the day, all the cotton had to be weighed - my dad and the rest of the family brought their share of cotton to the scales to be weighed.

We knew the scale had to be straight in order to get an accurate account of the cotton. But when the white man was weighing our father's share, the scales were always off-center. The scale and pea were placed on the scale incorrectly; the scale and the pea work together in order to get the correct weight to be counted. When we told our dad, he confronted the white man. The weighing of the cotton never changed. He said the pea was set correctly on the scale bar. We knew that was not true; he was lying to our father, and adding insult to injury, he had a straight face. The white man knew my dad didn't go to school, so to swindle him was no problem. Yet somehow, God was looking down on my dad that day for sure. He placed an equalizer in the mix: a nuisance, a bothersome, destructive boll weevil. This bothersome bug was a hard-shelled, scratchy insect. My twin and I feared it, along with the spiders, snakes, and the large green worms with a horn on their head. The boll weevil was the scariest of them all. This same boll weevil destroyed the white man's cotton crops. That was a very bad year for the white man and his cotton. God was protecting my dad and his family, which made me and my brother very happy. I know that if you believe and trust in God, he will take care of you. It's a good thing our mother and father believed in going to church. We are thankful for that pesty boll weevil.

Figure 17 bull weevil that bothersome bug.

We hated all of those fields because there was always some kind of insect about, especially those large spiders. They drove us crazy. It was so horrible; we both had really bad dreams about spiders. And it was worse as we got older; we never watched a spider movie; it was too much to bear. We developed arachnophobia. After a long day at the white man's fields, it was time to go home, and time for the good cooking our mom had waiting for us all.

Here's was the best part of the day, which my twin and I loved the most. It was lunchtime, the best part of the day because the food Madea prepared made the difference. It seemed like time stopped. I can still smell those soft brown biscuits our mom made. They were so "mmm, good!" My dad would take us to the nearest oak tree, which would have plenty of shade to sit down and eat.

The food was outstandingly good, and so delicious to boot. Our mom put so much into her cooking. Everyone was fat and happy.

Then it was time to get back to work, which we couldn't do because we'd both gotten very sick. This was the day we had eaten raw sweet potatoes. Thank goodness for that large oak tree with lots of shade. There we were, laying on the ground trying to recover. Another good part of the day was when it was time to go home. This was music to our ears, and we couldn't wait.

The white man will continue to cheat any Black man that works for him. And it was getting worse as time went on, now that the mechanization of farming became widespread, and it ended the time of the sharecropper. That included Mr. White Man as well, who would no longer be needed. Now it would be much harder for the Black man to make a living, especially in the Deep South like in this small one-stoplight town called Waynesboro.

The end of the day had arrived, and it was time to head home. We jumped on the back of the white man's pickup truck. It was a fun ride in, the warm wind blowing on our faces, and the anticipation of reaching our destination shortly. We knew our dad would tell our mom what happened in the fields that day with those sweet potatoes. At least we didn't have to go and get a switch or the belt that time. This would give us a short time to play in the front yard, and soon it would be time for supper. What would Mom be cooking for us tonight? Our dad said to us, "First, the wood has to be chopped and stacked and taken into the house, then you boys can go and play for a while."

For supper, it was time for the boys to go and wash up. One thing was for sure: we all couldn't wait for suppertime. Our mom cooked just like our grandmother. Their food had that special aroma and taste, and those unforgettable soft brown biscuits seemed to melt in our mouths. We didn't have a TV or radio, so we just sat around the house eating roasted peanuts. You could always tell we did this often, sitting by the fireplace and just looking at the leftover peanut shells on the floor. My dad would sit on the porch sometimes in his old chair, and there you could see peanut shells all over the porch and on the ground in front of the house.

Well, it was the same ritual the next day: back to the fields. There, my twin and I would not look forward to fighting those spiders and boll weevils, and there'd be no eating raw sweet potatoes. But my dad gave us some good news. A friend of his got him a job at the sawmill. Wow, that was the best news ever; the whole family was happy for him. Jerry, my twin brother, and I would always watch to see when our dad came home. He always came the same way. He would come from the right of our house with his coveralls on and his dusty boots, and we knew he was tired.

There were two reasons we always looked to the right of the house: one, knowing our father was on his way home, and two, because the smell of fresh-cut pine from the sawmill once it'd hit the air it travels through the whole town. That and the sound of the evening whistle ending the workday, which was always part of living so close to town. Sometimes our dad would be so tired, he'd forget to tend the garden, which he usually did, with a straw from the broom dangling in his mouth. He would tell us, "Boys, take care of the garden for me," so we did our best to keep it up for him, and we too would put a straw in our mouths.

The other day my dad was talking with our mom. He wanted to start a singing group, and he knew several guys in the neighborhood who could sing. My mom told him okay—it could be a good thing for the neighborhood. The church was just down the railroad tracks or that old dusty dirt road. So, my dad formed his singing group. He called it the "Blue Jays." They sang only gospel songs. My father was the lead singer, and they could really sing. Everyone in town knew about the Blue Jays. They sang all over the Wayne County area— Bucatini, Quitman, Shubuta, and Altaire—every town they could sing in, they were there. I loved to hear them sing.

There was one guy that sang with my dad in the Blue Jays, and there is a situation I would like to share with you. As you know, my twin and I always waited for my dad to come home from work at the sawmill, but this day was different. One day, he came home with a very sad face, and my mom came to him, saying, "Neshia, what's going on, what's wrong?" As our mom was talking with him, he told her there was a big accident at the sawmill. He said the guy's name, but I didn't recognize his name.

My dad told my mom one of his best friends had just gotten killed. He was carrying a load of logs that was too heavy for the tractor, and it tipped over and he tried to jump. In doing so, he slipped and fell to the ground, and the tractor fell on him, crushing him to death. It was so sad, and I felt so bad for my dad losing one of his best friends and one of the members of the singing group.

The owner of the sawmill offered his condolences to our family. My father was hurt so badly that the owner gave him the day off. I had no idea it would affect me as a little boy, but it hurt me. I cried, and I was very sad as well. There was so much happening in this small one-stoplight town. My father not only lost one of his best friends, but he lost a member of the quartet group, and now he had to go find another singer. He found a new guy from a little town called Shubuta to join the group so he could continue to sing with the Blue Jays.

Here's something my twin and I did just about every day as little boys. Many times, we waited and watched for our dad. He would come walking across the dry, grassy field from work at the sawmill. We waited with anticipation for his arrival because he always had something for us.

I remember his work attire like it was yesterday, with those dusty blue-jean overalls on and those dusty, old high-top boots. There was an unforgettable wrinkled old gray hat he wore all the time, and you could see the sweat stains around the brim. And let's not forget the Camel cigarette hanging out of his mouth. It seemed like he smoked all the time. Our mom tried often to get him to quit smoking, but to no avail. I still remember the brand: Camel nonfiltered cigarettes. He smoked every single day, but he never left cigarette butts in front of the house. Why? My mom insisted, "Neshia, don't throw your cigarettes on the ground in front of the house," so he didn't throw cigarettes or peanuts in the front yard.

It was time for our dad to get out of work from the sawmill. My twin and I could see him far in the distance, and we waited for a surprise as he got closer to the house. Most of the time, it was those sugar cookies filled with coconut. When our father got to the house, this is something he would do every day: grab his favorite washbasin—it, too, was made of porcelain—and he would fill the basin with water and give himself a good washing, both his head and his face. Then he'd reach for that dull white towel and begin to dry himself. Our mom told him time after time, "Neshia, put that dirty towel in the dirty clothes hamper." Well, that was his ritual, and afterward he would hang that old towel on that rusty nail on the porch post. Just before suppertime (here comes the fun part!), he would climb those five steps onto the porch with his favorite old chair. We were watching him all the time as he leaned back with the back of the chair pressing against the wall.

He had that long straw from the house broom stuck in his mouth. In the back of our minds, we were also waiting for the call from our mom: "It's suppertime!" As we waited, like any other time, we could smell the aroma from our mom's cooking. That day, it happened to be our dad's favorite: pork chops smothered in onions and gravy, with those soft, fluffy brown biscuits and real mashed potatoes. Our dad would be so tired from his work, he would fall asleep in his favorite chair. And before long, *WHAM!* Down to the floor he went. We would run over to him saying, "Dad, are you okay?" He would look at us, saying, "Boys, go and play." To us it was really funny.

I was so happy my dad had landed a new job at the sawmill. The smell of the fresh pine from the lumberyard was sweeter now. It became even sweeter when the wind was blowing in the direction of our house from the sawmill. When we all got the call that it was time for supper, we all gathered around the large table. My mom gave thanks to God for his blessing on our family and all the good food placed on the table. I don't remember my dad ever saying the blessing at the dinner table. That was fine, for we were thankful for what we had: a healthy family.

One thing is for sure: like I said before, if you stood on our front porch and looked to your right, you'd be facing the direction of that tall, dry grass field. The outhouse and the sawmill were all close to town, so the smell of pine would always come from that direction. One day, I went into the house, and my oldest sister Gloria Jean was helping my mom after supper with the leftovers and cleaning all the dishes. After supper, everyone went their own way to relax. So, I decided to go into the other room, where my mom and dad slept. Remember, there were only two rooms in the big house. It was in the evening time when there was some coolness in the house. We didn't have electric power for the house, so when the sun went down, so we had to use kerosene lanterns or lamps.

What's that whistling sound coming from outside? My twin and I ran to the door, and what did we see? A real dust devil. Out the door we went with no shoes on, chasing and trying to catch the dust devil. Around and around, it goes. It started in the front of the house, and we chased it over by the road. Our mom called to us, "Boys, here are some forks. If you can catch the dust devil with a fork in your hand, you can catch the devil."

We tried and tried without any success at all. I believe our mom was kidding just to keep us busy. She always told us to play it safe in and around the house. She was watchful for those twins of hers; we were her heart. Jerry said to me, "Let's go to town," so we yelled out to Madea, "Can we go to town?" She said, "Okay, but be careful, and stay out of the way of the white man!" We replied, "Yes, Madea." Then our mom said, "Boys, how about some ice cream?" Well, that trip to town will have to wait. Our mom got her old ice cream–making machine out, with that crank shaft that goes around and around to make ice cream. We took turns turning the handle until the ice made heavy cream became ice cream. Well, that stopped us twins from going to town that day. Our mom outsmarted us this time! After the ice cream it was too late to go to town, but we didn't care—that ice cream made us very happy. That's what our mom wanted all along.

*Figure 18 My Twin and I chased the Dust Devil in our front yard and on the road.*

Speaking about our mom, here is something I would like to share with you as well. All my childhood, I never forgot our mom's polka-dot dress. I can't remember all her other clothing, but this dress was my mom's special dress, and she looked good as she wore it. She always kept her dress inside a long, plastic bag. My mom would wear it to church services and on special occasions around the neighborhood. This polka-dot dress had long sleeves and didn't have a really low collar.

It wasn't a tight dress but was very loose as she wore it. The dress wasn't too long, but just below her knees. It had a navy-blue background with medium white spots or dots that covered all over it. This dress will be in the back of my mind forever. Sometimes she would wear different shoes and different purses to match the dress. I remember looking for a dress just like hers with no success at all, until my baby sister Vonda called, telling me, "Terry, I found just what you were looking for." Now that was a magical turn of events for me. I suggested she wear the dress instead of taking photos of the dress, so now I could put the dress in my memoir. She said, "Yes, I will wear the dress." Now that would make it more memorable. Now that the search is over, I can hang on much longer to that dream of my mother's favorite dress. Take a good look: Vonda looks just like our mom in that polka-dot dress. They look so alike. In fact, they have the same bone structure, and that pretty smile as well.

Figure 19 Everyone should know my little sister Vonda Joyce the

But don't let that smile fool you; our mom could be very intimidating, and she wouldn't take no for an answer if things weren't the way she wanted. She was in control of our family.

## FIVE

### The Williamsons

In our house, down by the railroad tracks, we always had a cozy, close-knit environment, and we were all happy. Here are some important notes about our home, that old shack down by the tracks. We were the only family on that side of the old dirt road, which was dusty and became very muddy after a heavy rainstorm. Even after all that, it was our happy home.

The property was owned by the railroad company back in the day. That's why it didn't have many windows and doors. As I mentioned earlier, there were two doors and two windows. One door was much larger than a normal house door; there was another small door in the rear of the building and a special path at the beginning of that small door.

Because of the United States Postal Service, there was lots of traffic here. It was a building for working people.

There was a chimney that led to the left a bit, in the middle of the building that served the fireplace and the kitchen stove, where my mom did all the cooking for the family. The building was a real ugly building before the work was done on it, and my mom and dad were proud to have a place of their own. They owed Uncle James a great deal of thanks for what he did for them, the newlyweds and the first in our family to elope. That's my mom and dad! With some renovation work done on the inside and the outside, it became our home. And the amazing thing about this house was that it was very close to those noisy train tracks. One could see, it was unbelievable to the naked eye. It sat next to this old, dusty dirt road. This you had to see as well. There were two big rooms in this old house, and we made it our home. My mom didn't think twice; the house was good enough for her and my dad as a young married couple. It's a big part of my memories.

Figure 20 I so happy to find an old house close to our two-room house down by the train tracks

We all love her so very much. That's my mom. All my childhood life, I never saw my mom and dad argue about anything at all. Once in a while, she'd ask him to stop smoking. She was a very special mom and wife.

One day, my mom came with some good news for us all: she got a job close to town. It was in the same area as the hospital and the sawmill, close enough that she could walk. This lady named Mrs. Mamie Russell had a friend of hers who was looking for someone to help with cleaning and taking care of her house. No one in the family ever knew the lady's name. My mom took the job, and we could see the house from the streets. In other words, if one could stand in Mrs. Mamie's front yard and look to the right, they could see her lady friend's house.

They both lived on the same street in that neighborhood. Many times, we used to walk by to see if we could see our mom working, but she was always working inside this big house. Both houses looked like those plantation houses in New Orleans, Louisiana, with those large pillars about the front and two floors or more, and what had to be several bedrooms. To see one of these houses was a sight, and there were many in our town. For some reason, most of the houses were white in color, but there was also brown, beige, and yellow. She wanted my mom to work five days a week.

Figure 21 This is a replica of Mrs. Mammie House

The lady that got my mom the job, Mrs. Mamie Russell, wanted us to work for her as well, picking up pecans in her backyard. So, we went over to see what she wanted; we'd passed by her house many times before. To be on her property was kind of scary to us. She had this very big plantation-looking house. We already knew not to go to the front door of this huge house. Here we went, heading across the backyard to the back door, where she had a Confederate flag hanging. I always wondered if she was a part of the KKK.

She came out of the back door, saying, "How you boys doing?" When she talked, it seemed as if she were singing her words—that's a Southern thing. We said, "All right, ma'am." She told us what to do, saying, "Pick all you can then come to the back door and knock for me."

There were four big pecan trees, and they were filled with pecans. This had to be the best year for pecans, and they were the very large ones. So, us twins, we got busy. We were too small to climb those huge trees, so we would take some large sticks and throw them up to the branches, which would jar or shake the limbs. Then here came all the pecans falling to the ground. We would gather them in large metal buckets. There were tons of pecans all over the place.

Afterward, we went to the back door and knocked, and she came out and sat down and began to give us our share of the pecans. She had this small quart can, and she began to divide the pecans. She gave us one can full of pecans and gave herself three cans full of pecans. We were just two little boys in the South who didn't know any better.

All the same, we knew it wasn't right, and we didn't understand why she was doing this to us. So, the next time we picked pecans for her, we devised a plan which would be in our favor and would give us a better share of the pecans. Jerry and I launched our plan; we hid some large paper bags in the hedges, so in the process of picking them off the ground, we would take a large portion of the pecans and put them in the large bag hidden in the hedges.

Now, we approached the back door, and she came out with the same procedure, giving herself three and us one. We were happy with the results of our plan. We told our mom what we'd done, and she was okay with that. She knew how Mrs. Mamie Russell was. Her husband and all the white men around town called us "boy," and we didn't like it. We thought it was part of life in the South. When any Black person came to a white man's house, they had to enter at the back door, even if it was in town at the stores. My older brother Alvin really hated the word "boy." I will elaborate on it later.

Figure 22 My big brother Alvin in our hometown in the South

Back to the job at our house, my dad had a good job at the sawmill, and my mom was working cleaning houses for the white lady. The rest of the family did odd jobs to help.

My twin and I asked our mom if we could go to town just to look around; this was one of our secret adventures. We would go out to find something to get into, no trouble this time we'd hope, because we didn't want our mom telling us, "Boys, go outside and get a switch."

By now, everyone knew what that meant, the switch— we might not have been able to sit down for a while. We just wanted a short walk around town. Maybe the white store owners would have some work for us to do. We'd got work from them before; this would give us some money to go to the stores on the front. Then we could buy our favorite cookies, filled with coconut and vanilla filling. Remember, if you stood on our porch and looked to the right, that was the direction of our small town. We'd walk on the train tracks for a short time, then there was a path to walk on parallel to the train racks, which led to the first street in town.

   Mrs. Mamie Russell lived on that same street; I mentioned it earlier. That same street also crossed the train tracks, one of many in this small one-stoplight country town. When Jerry and I saw this white car stalled on the train tracks, we didn't know what to think at the time. The white man tried to get the car started, but it wouldn't start, and we both saw the train coming from our right.

   But the man didn't get out of his car. The train was blowing its whistle very loud and the lights on the train were flashing side to side. The sound from the train's wheels also made a scary sound; imagine the metal-to-metal contact and it trying to stop but couldn't. That whistle from the train made this officially weird sound. I'll never forget the combination of the two high-pitched sounds. The man couldn't get his car started; he tried time after time with no success. One of the puzzling things is that he didn't try to get out of his car, not once—just sat there trying to start it over and over, and it wouldn't start. The train got closer and closer, and we couldn't believe our eyes as the tears run down our faces. Then suddenly the one-hundred-ton locomotive T-boned the car, carrying it down the tracks and almost to our house. It made such a loud crashing sound, with pieces of glass and metal from the car flying all over the place. The train just couldn't stop. We also saw the conductor of the train just sitting there; it had to have given him a big shock as well. All we could do was stand and watch with fear and disbelief; I'm not sure if we had tears in our eyes or not. What goes on in the minds of two little boys who would witness this kind of tragedy?

Figure 23 My twin and I witnessed the train T-bone the white man car

One thing is for sure: I'll never forget this crazy, scary train-to-car accident. That really shook us up. The trip to town was made short. We turned and ran back home. We could see part of the car on our way home, and it was so hard to believe. Even today when I hear or see the train, it brings tears to my eyes. In fact, where I live today in Albany, New York, at Madison Avenue and South Pearl Street, I still can hear the sound of a train, just a few blocks away off Broadway, the same high pitch from the train whistle and that very loud sound from the train's steel wheels making contact with the steel track. Another déjà-vu of that terrible shocking sound we experienced at the railroad crossing. Here in the city of Albany there are train tracks all over. I can see them from my window at South Pearl Street, and the sound of the wheels and the loud sound of the whistle are scary to me. It seems as if I am in a teleportation machine that takes me back to the same place where my twin and I witnessed that terrible train wreck in our town.

I used to like trains before the accident, because one ran just in front of our house all the time. They fascinated me. During the night, it would either keep me awake or put me to sleep. The sound of the railroad tires crashing against the steel rails and that heavy, loud sound of the whistle that appeared to have three different sounds all in one were all part of putting one to sleep—but not anymore. It's scary, at least for me and my twin. My feelings were different now at this stage of my life; it's a very significant part of our lives, and it brings back those dreams and nightmares. It will be in the back if my mind and in my heart forever.

## SIX

### Toys We Never Had

One day, my twin and I got some good news from our mom. Boy, were we excited! We couldn't wait for the good news. Every Christmas, my twin and I would always look for our father coming through the fields from the sawmill with a crate of oranges on his shoulders. This happened every year. This was a big part of our Christmas holiday season. Our parents also gave us some money so we could go to the front to buy things from the stores.

My father would always take the axe and head to the woods for the best tree he could find. He always came back with the most plump and full tree. There's something special about fireplaces and Christmas trees—the smoke from the fireplace, the smell from the pine tree! My mother took care of the decorations. There weren't a lot of toys, so underneath the tree, it looked a little bare. My twin and I always wanted a red wagon to play with, or a little tricycle, or best of all, our own cowboy hats and a two-gun holster. Let's not forget the boots.

What about the game of marbles? Yes, we played the game at home and all through the neighborhood and across town. We both had our own marble bags. Inside each marble bag was fifteen to twenty marbles total, with one very large marble made of solid steel in each bag. It was called the breaker. Its purpose was to disperse, or break up, the marbles. Within the circle there could be as many as twelve to fourteen marbles.

Carting marbles with you was just like carrying a wallet. It's the pride of all little kids. The bag was made of canvas, with a string to tie off the top. Just about every kid in the neighborhood played marbles at some time or another and owned a marble bag, filled with all sizes and colors. Some of the marbles were made of hard glass, and others were made of porcelain. The porcelain marbles were twice the price.

Well, I guess you know—we couldn't afford the porcelain marbles. Everyone on our block played marbles. For the game itself, everyone who was playing had to shoot one marble into the circle, and the marble that came closest to the edge of the circle would win and its owner would start first.

Next came the big breaks. Leaving a small number of marbles inside the circle, you have to shoot and hit the marble, and it must go outside the circle to count. You shoot until you miss. This game was called a "one-one" competition. We were all shooting for keeps, and it was a challenging game. It was like shooting pool on a smaller scale. It was a game for all little boys only. Little girls couldn't play, because they wore dresses and couldn't get down on all fours like little boys because they would get their knees scraped on the rough gravel and sand. It's not that they couldn't play with boys. They spent a lot of time playing "ball-jacks." Now, my two sisters Gloria Jean and Geraldine could play for hours. No one could beat Geraldine;

she was master at the game of ball-jacks. In fact, she taught me and my twin. I still can play a good game today.

My twin and I would never play this game of marbles over on Highway 63. Like I mentioned before, that was one part of town our parents told us to stay away from. Could you imagine two little boys playing marbles over there? It would worry our mom to pieces, seeing we were her favorite and all. Well, you know what I mean!

This is one game I must teach my four boys; they are not too old to learn. It will take some good skills; they might have to practice a lot, and it might take them some time. In fact, do you have time to play? I will spot you three marbles to start the game. It's fascinating; you have nothing to lose but your bag of marbles.

One day, my twin and I went with our big brother Alvin across the train tracks into the woody area. As I said many times before, if you stood on our porch and looked straight ahead, you would see the small yard, the small stream, the train tracks, stick weeds, and a woody area with tall trees and the train tracks and Highway 63. When we went into the woods, our big brother spotted this very humongous snapping turtle. It was very scary looking. Our big brother always told me and my twin that if we saw a snapping turtle at any time, we should not go near it. They could grab a hold of your hand or finger and never let go, no matter what you did, so the three of us surrounded the turtle and my big brother grabbed a large stick and put it close to the turtle's mouth. Without any warning, the turtle snapped and grabbed the stick, and he wouldn't let go. Alvin gave off this big yell, "We got you!" because Jerry and I knew the turtle wouldn't let go.

Alvin picked the turtle up with the stick still in his mouth. It was so scary-looking, with its very hard scales just like an alligator, those rough-looking feet, those piercing eyes—like he was watching and waiting for his next victim—and that pointed nose. Snapping turtles are strong and swift. Everyone thinks turtles are very slow, but these were slow only when they were walking alone across the road. Any other time they were very dangerous and quick. They could move in any direction as quick as lightning.

Our big brother told us, "Don't underestimate the speed and quickness of those snapping turtles." And its protection was unreal, a perfect camouflage. It could make its whole body submerge inside its hard shell so that no other animal could get to it. My twin and I saw a different animal trying to get it to come out of its shell, with no success at all—a perfectly dangerous machine. Now we had one in our sight, and it was unbelievable that we caught one.

Just looking at our big brother, he was more excited than we were. And it had a golden-brown color. Alvin had me and Jerry hold the stick and headed back across the train tracks to the house. Once we arrived, we put on a pot of hot water to prep for some turtle soup.

Figure 24 this Armadillo was all over our little town

Our big brother told us, "Let this be a lesson, boys." To capture a snapping turtle, take carefulness. And we always listened to him, as our protector. This showed how much he was willing to do to protect his twin brothers and everyone else in the whole family.

But I'm not done yet. After scaling the turtle with hot water, he began to clean and take it apart. He told us, "Now it's time to make turtle soup." This was from the horse's mouth. Along with the turtle meat, he needed some vegetables—of various kinds—cut small. He mixed everything up well, cooked it slowly, and before you knew it, the stew was ready to go. When it was all finished, Alvin placed it on the table for everyone. It was the *soup du jour*." It was very tasty soup, and it lasted for some time. Now one could see why my twin and I needed our big brother around the house, not only us, my mom and dad, and the rest of the siblings. Alvin also told me he not only cooks turtle soup, but we would also cook squirrel and rabbit as well. He said it tasted just like chicken; we didn't know the difference. I guess he was watching our mom as she did her cooking.

What's next after the turtle for those twins? Let's take a walk over to Uncle James's house. To get there, we needed to cross Highway 63 and walk for about half a block. We would walk straight to his house, and it wasn't too far from the highway. As we approached his house, we could see him and his wife Aunt Bee sitting there on their swing on the front porch. We gave them a yell, and he said, "Come on over, boys." The strangest thing—as they sat there, we could see his big double-barreled shotgun in his lap. And before we could reach the front porch of his house, Uncle James jumped to his feet, and *bang, bang*—with both barrels, he shot this big armadillo that came from beneath his front porch of the house.

It too had a very hard shell that covered 95 percent of its body. However, one shot with a double-barreled shotgun would stop anything in its path. He only had to fire it once, hitting the armadillo and tearing it apart. Well, this was an extra experience for us twins and some extra excitement for us as well. Afterward, Aunt Bee would take us to her kitchen, and she would make us something good to eat. She was special, with the gold on her two front teeth; I think that's where Gloria Jean got the idea from, because she also has gold in her mouth, not both front teeth, but she has it between both front teeth. It looked good to me. Looking back, it was something people did in the South.

## SEVEN

### My Big Brother Alvin

At the time, our parents didn't have extra money; the main thing was we were all happy for what we had. Sometimes our dad had extra money, so he would let us go to the picture show. There was a twenty-five-cent special at the picture show in town. He would say, "Okay, boys, you can go; be careful and stay to yourselves." He said there wouldn't be enough money for popcorn, but that was all right with us. So off we went for some fun at the picture show. Again, we had to deal with the white man's ways. We paid our fare, and our hearts were filled with excitement because we didn't get to do this that often.

There were signs posted that all Black folks had to sit in the balconies, and the white people were sitting on the lower level. That was better for us—sitting on top gave us a better view of the movie, and it was good to be on top for a change. We also talked about how if we were sitting on the lower level, we knew the white people would throw things down on us. So the sitting arrangement panned out well for us. One thing for sure, I'll never forget the movie was in black and white. And it was a scary movie at that. It was *Frankenstein and Dracula*, and no, we didn't tell our mom what kind of movie we saw at the picture show. It probably would be our last time going to the picture show for a while.

What about my big brother Alvin? He's the second oldest of all the boys and girls. Gloria Jean was the firstborn. All through town, the white man continued to call all Black men "boy." You could be a young child or a fully grown man, and they made sure they called you "boy." My big brother was independent; he didn't take any nonsense from the white man or anyone else. Everyone knew Al. He didn't take no for an answer, especially when he was right. I looked up to my big brother; I thought he could do anything. He did a lot of hunting all around the wooded areas. He always took me and my twin brother with him as he hunted.

We carried all the things he needed for hunting. He had two shotguns and one single-shot rifle, and he had this special hat with a canister on top. It burned with this very bad odor coming from it: the smell of sulfur. Our big brother told us it's carbide that really gave him the light he needed at night. Jerry and I carried the extra guns, and Alvin would have us take the rifle and shoot up into the squirrel nest. This was called "stirring the nest." As soon as the squirrel jumped out of the nest, he would shoot his shotgun at the squirrel, and then Jerry and I would go and find the squirrel.

We did the same when hunting for any other small animals. We did all kinds of things with our big brother; he always looked out for his younger brothers and sisters. That's because we loved and respected him.

There was a contest at the Cooley's Chevrolet car dealership that was posted in the newspaper. Any family could attend. They were looking for the largest family in the Wayne County area, and the largest family would win first prize—a gift certificate from the dealership. Of course, In my opinion I felt we were the biggest family there. But when it came down to who was the overall winner, a white couple won the contest. And I felt their family wasn't as large as ours, so they took pictures of all three families. Over the years we lost that newspaper clipping. But they won anyway.

The Cooley family also owned the backstreet Hamburger Shop, which had some of the best-tasting hamburgers in Wayne County. My big brother Alvin always told us the white man would never treat us fair. That's one of the main reasons he had so many problems with the white man. That's why one day he would have to leave Waynesboro.

One of the items in our front yard was our mom's black cast-iron pot. As I said before, if you stood on our front porch and looked straight ahead, you would see those long, noisy railroad tracks and the heavily wooded area. Beyond those trees lived some white people. You could hear them all the time, especially during the weekends. They reminded me of the Hatfields and the McCoy's back in West Virginia and Kentucky in the late 1800s with their screaming and yelling and that old rusty truck that didn't start most of the time; it seemed as if it would fall to the ground. All that noise was on a day-to-day basis, shooting off their guns—it was scary both night and day. Yes, it took some getting used to, just like that very noisy freight train that shook our house all the time. So, one day, Jerry and I were playing in the front yard, and we noticed our mom's black pot wasn't there. Off we ran, telling our mom the pot wasn't there anymore. And we told our big brother someone had stolen our black cast-iron washpot. He said, "Madea, the black washing pot is missing. Who took it?" We told him we didn't know. My big brother put his thoughts together. "Hmm . . . I have an idea. It was those crazy white people across the tracks! And I'm going over and getting it back." My mom and dad told him, "No, don't go over to those white peoples' houses." Well, this was our big brother. He always took care of things around the house.

Figure 25 Our mom cast iron black wash pot, the one the white man stole from Our mom.

He said, "I'm going to get it back." He took off across the train tracks, went through the wooded area, and within no time at all, he came back with the pot. My dad was glad he got it back. You can only imagine how our mom felt. That was her source of heating the water for washing the clothes. That pot wasn't cheap, especially for a poor family. We had no more problems with the people across the tracks. Again, my big brother was a protector.

There was this guy called Alan who lived over by Highway 63. If you stood on our porch and looked straight ahead through the woods, on the other side of Highway 63 was Alan, who always picked on my twin brother and I. He was much older than we were. Well, one day, our big brother came to us and said, "This is what I want out of both you guys. The next time this guy called Alan comes over here, don't let this guy beat on you." Within a few days, he did come over again.

When Jerry and I finished beating him up, we had no problems with him again. In fact, the three of us became friends. Later on, during the summer, we concluded that all he wanted were some friends to play with. At this time, my older sister Gloria didn't have a boyfriend, but our next older sister Geraldine did.

She was seeing this guy named Tommy Joe Huntley. He lived over on Highway 63. Everyone knew the Huntley's, and they had a bad reputation on that side of town. Well, everyone called him Tommy Joe, and they knew he was a really bad individual in his neck of town. He and his brothers all thought they were Black cowboys, and they carried guns, guns with holsters on their sides, and they even drew against each other. Making it a family duel seemed a little strange to me.

I'd never heard of civilians around town who carried real guns on their sides, not even the white men—they carried it tucked into their pants and shirts. The only other person I'd seen with guns and gun holsters was the sheriff in town; they would always flash their power around town.

Tommy Joe had two other brothers, Ulysses and Calmus. Tom and Ulysses actually drew against each other. Tommy Joe shot Ulysses in his right hip, and the bullet is still there.

My sister Geraldine began to go out with Tommy Joe, and my big brother did not like that at all. He kept quiet for a while. He wanted to see what would happen between them,

so, Tommy Joe started to come over to our house to see my sister on regular basis. Our big brother Alvin didn't like

Tommy Joe all that well; he had a very bad feeling, and that's not good. My twin and I began to like him a whole lot because of the way he carried himself. We thought he was a real Black cowboy. He took us just about every place he went alone with my sister Geraldine.

Well, she too went everywhere with Tommy Joe, so I guessed they were girlfriend and boyfriend then. He even took us to that dangerous river, the Chickasawhay River, for a swim, but we were too little to get into the water. We thought we could do the doggie-paddle; it was mostly splashing water. That river was a death trap. It took the lives of so many people, both young and old. Everyone in Waynesboro knew that the river was very dangerous. But that didn't stop people from going swimming there. Our mom told us many times, "Boys, don't you let me find out you been to that river. If I find out you have, you know what's next. It's your choice, the switch or the belt. And if I do hear you been there, your father will also give you the same treatment." Our mom told us to be careful around those hustle boys! So please don't go down to the river alone. We told our mom, "We will be with Tommy Joe," and we felt safe around him. He didn't let us swim alone; he was always close. Besides, we didn't know how to swim all that well. We would just put our feet in the water and play in the sand or try some fishing; there's always good fishing in this river. Tommy Joe didn't take us there very often because he knew how our mom felt about that river. But all the other things we enjoyed, and being with him, we felt safe—hunting and fishing, using the bow and arrow, and the biggest thing: he taught us how to use the bullwhip.

He could kill anything with that whip, and he was good. It was unreal. Jerry and I saw him kill all kinds of snakes. He would pop soda cans, leaves from trees—that bullwhip was so loud when he snapped it over his head. The best news was that he taught us how to use it. Not long after, Jerry and I could use the bullwhip. He could ride horses with no problem at all, and he could fight with his fist man to man. Here was the most beautiful thing of all: he could swim so fast for a long time with ease; we couldn't believe it.

Even though Jerry and I swam, he taught us how to swim much stronger. We really thought he was a Black cowboy and a Black Tarzan, like Johnny Weissmuller, the TV actor. He used to dive off the bridge into the Chickasawhay River, and we thought that was far out. We really trusted Tommy Joe Huntley. He came second only to our big brother—no one could take his place. My sister and Tommy Joe were always together. To me, they looked happy, but my brother didn't see it that way. He felt something wasn't right. Then my sister told my mother and father that she was pregnant. That didn't sit well with my big brother at all. My mom and dad were upset when my sister got pregnant; the family was still struggling. Remember, we were a poor family. This was a setback for my mom and dad. So, my big brother confronted Tommy Joe; some words were exchanged, and the argument escalated. Before long, a fight broke out. This was one event I'll never forget. It went on for hours. It seemed like they went back and forth, and we were there to witness the whole fight—my big brother and my sister's boyfriend, the big tussle on our front porch.

It went on for a long time. They both fell off the porch, landing on the ground in the dirt and grass. They rolled and twisted in the front yard. They almost went under the front porch. It seemed like it took forever as my twin and I just stood there looking at them fight, wondering when they would stop fighting each other. Before long, it was all over. My brother got the better of the two.

Tommy Joe made his way to his brown-and-white 1956 Chevrolet car and drove off down that old, dusty dirt road. We didn't see him for a short time. Then, for my sister's sake, my big brother talked with her, saying, "I knew Tommy Joe would wind up doing something like this." He said he would have to bear some of the responsibility and take care of the baby when it was born.

Things got better later after they cooled down. He was my sister's boyfriend. Meanwhile my big brother got in an argument with this white man in town. He was treating him very badly, calling him "boy." My big brother couldn't stand it at all. He would talk back to any white man that called him "boy." In fact, we all felt the same. I thought it was part of life living in the Deep South. Those words— "boy," "yes, sir"— were all we knew. My parents knew they had to do something before my big brother got into real trouble.

Back in the '60s in our one-stoplight hometown called Waynesboro, Mississippi, my mom and dad had a problem with my big brother, Alvin. Every now and then, something would get out of hand. The word got out, and my mom and dad learned that someone saw my big brother arguing with another white man in town.

We all knew the reason behind the arguments. It started to escalate with the white men. They would not stop calling him names. They knew my brother by sight. They would say, "Hey, nigger boy, what are you doing here?" and they knew that would bother my big brother. All my brother was doing was trying to find some work in town.

And one thing was for sure: the white men were the owners, and they operated all the businesses thereabouts. This was a big problem for us as a poor Black family trying to make ends meet. My big brother wouldn't say "yes, sir" to the white men. They didn't like that, and it made them angry. It was known that all Black men and boys had to say "yes, sir" to all the white people here in this small one-stoplight town.

But I'm not finished yet. My twin and I, we were just little boys, but they would call us "those two little nigger twins." Our mom dressed us alike the majority of the time, so it was much easier to recognize us. We were very scared and didn't go to town that much. But our brother Alvin, he was much bigger than we were, and he was so brave—to look at him made my heart flutter; that's why us twins loved him so much. The white man knew they could not get under his skin. Instead, my big brother would stand his ground. That wasn't kosher, and they couldn't stand my big brother. It seems like they were waiting for him to come to town, just to start more trouble with him. My mom knew what was going on, and that gave her more concern about her first-born son. Let me tell you, in this small town, it was bad.

It happened all the time. Well, this time, it escalated to the point that something had to be done right away. Alvin was a good-hearted, warm person. He kept to himself most of the time, and he never went out of his way to bother other people. It didn't make a difference if one was Black or not. That also included the bothersome white men, a group that constantly harassed all Blacks, especially boys and men, in our small town. However, this was my brother Alvin. He just wouldn't say "yes, sir" to the white men. My twin and I were much smaller and were too afraid to say no to the white men, so we always said "yes, sir." They loved that.

We were told by our mom what happened to little Black boys in this part of Mississippi. They'd find them hanged in trees out in the woods or buried in a shallow grave, and their parents wouldn't know where they were. My mother didn't want this to happen to her sons. She wanted Alvin to be able to live his life. That's why she had to get him out of Waynesboro, Mississippi. Besides, he was my parents' firstborn boy, and she didn't want him dead in some godforsaken wooded area here in the deep part of Mississippi.

My twin and I thought the world of our big brother. To us, he was something special. Could you imagine what he meant to our mom? My parents told him he had to start being "nicer" to the white men. My big brother said, "If anything, the white men are the problem." My brother told my parents he wasn't the problem at all, because back then, and even today, the white men thought they were much better than all Black folks here in this small country town.

They could do some crazy things at any time, with no warning. Alvin told dad he wasn't afraid of the white man; those were the kinds of words my parents were afraid of. This kind of talk could get him in serious trouble with the white people. My big brother said, "Don't forget! Yes, it's our hometown as well." All my parents wanted was for him to stay out of their way, not to go to town so much, and to keep a low profile until they could figure out what to do in case something bad happened.

Figure 26 Here's the Black Sambo there's one just about every white man yard.

My mother and father and the rest of my family knew there was a problem here and about. There were so many young boys and men missing, or worse—they would be found weeks or months later somewhere in the deep woods. Now that's a scary feeling, especially for me and my twin brother. We all know what happened to little Black boys and young men back then. It was so sad. The other day it was very hot, and we were walking down Highway 45. Jerry said, "Let's go swimming," and I said, "What spot?" He said either the bunny-hole or Mrs. Billy William Pond on the other side of Highway 45. Jerry said, "I tell you what we'll do! Let's go to both places." So, we went to Mrs. Billy William Pond first. We had no idea it was cow pond; we tried it anyway and it was dirty and nasty. We walked in the water to learn how to swim. We could feel mud gushing between our toes, and to make matters worse, the pond had several cows bathing in it. Swim or not, we left that pond quickly and made our way to the bunny-hole. It was down this dirt road parallel to Highway 45. Once there, we couldn't believe how clear and cold the water was. "This is the place to learn how to swim!" we said, knowing our mom would give us a licking if we got caught. Yes, she told us not to go too far from the house, unless one of our big brothers went with us. We wouldn't stay long—just enough to cool off, then we would run as fast as we could to get back to the house.

We saw something strange as we were walking past Mr. Billy Williams's hotel. It too was on Highway 45, and his house was next door. On the front porch of his house, he had his big Confederate flag flying in the wind, letting the Black folks know that the white folks were better than they were. So, we stayed to ourselves and headed back to the house. Besides, it was scary to see that.

And we saw another strange thing. Every Black person that lived in Waynesboro knew about the Black Sambo. It was made of porcelain, almost like plaster of Paris. The white man made sure the face was black and the clothes were in different colors. Next to the hotel, I didn't understand why when the white man entered his house, he would rub the head of the Black Sambo. I guess it was supposed to bring good luck. That was something I didn't understand at all.

If so, why did they treat the Black men and young boys so badly? That was something very strange, and it would continue in my hometown. It was very dangerous in the state of Mississippi at that time, and there was nothing anyone could do about it. All Black folks that wanted or needed anything came at the mercy of the white man. My parents told Alvin, "Please try to keep out of their way. Don't even look in their direction, if possible," at least until we could find a foolproof solution to all the problems heading my brother's way. Our family and friends didn't want a tragic ending for Alvin; this would break my mother's heart.

Everyone in the neighborhood was trying to find a solution for Alvin. It was also important to keep my twin and I safe as well, and the rest of my brothers here and about. One thing was for sure, my big brother Alvin wasn't wrong for what he believed in. All he wanted was to be left alone. There was danger all around, especially when walking on the main highway, as we know. In fact, again we were walking to our grandmothers on Highway 45; this time, our mom knew we were going to see Grandma. There was talk all around town about how little boys and men were murdered by hanging them out in the wooded area, or worse, buried in a shallow grave, and no one could do anything about. My parents didn't want this to happen to their boys. My mom was very frightened when it came to all her boys, especially her oldest son Alvin.

Again, she told us to be careful. This time, we were walking, minding our business. All of a sudden, here came the white men driving by in their old beat-up pickup truck with that large Confederate flag waving in the wind on the back of the truck. They always seemed to be angry. They would be screaming and yelling all kinds of words. "Where are you going, little nigger boys?" They would drive by and throw things at us as we were walking on the side of the road. Let's not forget this was the main highway. There were four major highways in this town, as I mentioned before.

On Highway 45, Highway 63, and Highway 84, they would throw old fruit, beer cans, and, of course, pieces of watermelon. They were trying to make a statement, throwing the watermelon pieces. It was their way of telling us they were superior, and we were only good for laying around in the shade of a tree eating watermelon. Like we were nothing compared to them.

Let's look back. I remember what it felt like, as if your life was in their hands. To avoid trouble, our mom always told us we had to walk on the train tracks most of the time.

By the late '60s, we thought our big brother Alvin was too old for a lashing. My big brother had had a big argument before concerning the trouble with the white men. My dad didn't want this to get to that point again. My father was tired of the crazy things the white men were doing altogether, because he had the same problem with the white men as a sharecropper or working as a field hand. This problem will never cease for Black folks. My dad was aware of the same problem, and my brother couldn't take it anymore. Neither could my twin and I, and in fact, we all knew what our brother was going through.

No matter what happened around here, things would not change in the South, here in our one-stoplight hometown of Waynesboro, Mississippi. Alvin didn't want to hear this anymore; he was sick and tired of it all. So, this led to another argument between my dad and my big brother. They were outside on the porch. My dad grabbed his old favorite chair, sat down, and leaned back against the wall.

This was his daily ritual and his place to wind down and relax. There, he and my big brother began to talk about what was going on in town with the white men. Well, at first, it was just small talk. Before long, it led to some unpleasant words.

We could hear some loud talking and screaming, and my mom came running out the door onto the porch, screaming, "Neshia, what's going on?" My big brother was screaming at my dad.

My mom said, "Alvin, stop that!"

Then my big brother began to scream very loudly, "I'm going to run away!"

My dad said, "What did you say?"

Again, my big brother screamed, "I'm going to run away!"

My dad, as he leaned back against the wall in his favorite chair, slipped to the floor, and the chair went crashing onto the floor of the porch. My dad pushed his favorite chair to the side, got to his feet, and screamed back at my big brother, saying, "No, you are not!"

They struggled on the porch. This was the same porch that dad and Alvin, my big brother, fought on that hot summer day. My dad tried to stop him. They both struggled as they wrestled, and they too both fell off the porch and landed on the ground. My dad did all he could to hold him down.

This I'll never forget; my twin and I just stood there watching as they continued to struggle, rolling in the grass and dirt. Alvin somehow got loose from my dad's grip and started running from the house toward Mrs. Barnes's house. The direction he started running was to the left of our house. My dad got to his feet and ran after him. Alvin kept running as my dad screamed, "Stop! You can't do this! I will see to that!" as he chased after him.

But my big brother tripped on some barbed wire fence, and this was all my dad needed. My dad ran after him, reached up and grabbed a branch from the nearest tree, and started giving him many lashes on his backside and anywhere else the switch would land. And it had to sting; my twin brother and I will attest to that. It leaves some nice welts on your backside. We couldn't believe our big brother got a whipping from our dad.

It was probably the last whipping he would ever get. I guess he didn't know how strong and fast my father was. Afterward, things settled down quickly. Everyone was surprised and shocked throughout the whole ordeal. My dad said, "Enough of this nonsense. Get back to the house now. I mean, right now!" They headed back to the house, and I guess Alvin learned his lesson that day. Never say to your parents, "I'm going to run away from home." They love you too much.

Besides, Alvin was the oldest boy of six other brothers. We were relieved and excited throughout the whole struggle. My mom was so sad. Like always, she couldn't hold back the tears streaming down her face. She told him, "What was you thinking?" (This makes me feel so sad and emotional, sitting here writing my memoir.)

It was so real, just like it happened yesterday. My mom and dad went over to our neighbors' house, the Bells, to see if they had any suggestions for what to do about our big brother. Aunt Lelee and Uncle John Henry Bell . . . Remember how they wanted us to call them Aunt Lelee and Uncle John, the names they wanted us to call them when we first met them, when our mom and dad first moved there a long time ago?

They were not related to the Williamson family. Aunt Lelee said they would talk to her brother; his name was John, aka "Pastor Jack". He moved away many years ago from this area to a place called Albany, New York. He was one of her older brothers. She said she would talk with him and see if he could help my mom and dad. Aunt Lelee made the call and talked with her brother.

He said he would be glad to help my family and any family that needed help in the Deep South, because he himself was born and bred in the Deep South. He said to just let him know what he could do in the very near future, and he would make some arrangements. This made my mom and dad feel so happy, knowing something would be done very soon to get our brother out of this small one-stoplight town, Waynesboro.

All my brothers and sisters were born and raised here. This was our home; it was all we knew all our lives. Our mother and father would never have to worry about our welfare, because we were their pride and joy, especially when there were seven boys and three girls around. And the white men wouldn't stop all the nonsense and unnecessary prejudice against all Black people, especially the Black men and young boys, here in this town. I personally believe it will continue throughout the South forever.

## EIGHT

### The Pastor, Jack

Mrs. Vera, my mom's friend, we called her "Aunt Lelee"—came over to our house and told our mom and dad some good news. Her big brother, Jack from Albany, New York, would make a special trip back to Waynesboro to help with supporting my mom and dad with any problems that occurred between the white men and my big brother.

He also mentioned that he would be coming real soon, because our parents were really in desperate need of support. My parents were blessed and very happy for Aunt Lelee's suggestion. Now help was on the way. My parents had met Pastor Jack only once some years earlier. My parents didn't know too much about Pastor Jack back then, only what his sister Aunt Lelee had told them.

They were all from a small town called Shubuta, Mississippi. Pastor Jack was born in Shubuta on August 17, 1909. There, his parents had several brothers and sisters. They lived on a very large piece of land. I'm not sure of the acreage they owned. I was told it was "hundreds of acres." I saw it with my own eyes; it was a lot of land. Their parents owned cows, pigs, sheep, horses . . . I could go on, they had so much. They also owned land on the other side of the road as well. I didn't think Black people owned that much land.

I still to this day remember the pastor's mother as she stood there on the front porch of this big brown-whitish house with large trees all about. They had this large pecan tree, and my twin and I asked her if we could pick some pecans. She said to us, "Go ahead boys, pick all you want," because they would fall to the ground and rot anyways. And they were the large pecans. I won't forget her name; it was a biblical name, Mary. She had a pretty face and long, black hair. One of the pastor's other sisters lived next door—Mrs. Janney.

I talked about how we used to play with his four nephews, Junior, Leroy, George, and Don, our next-door playmates. Pastor Jack left Shubuta, Mississippi, on December 14, 1931. He told me about his brothers and sisters. There were fifteen children in all, and one died at birth. So, his mother and father had fourteen children. Pastor Jack said he would be there by the weekend. This would make my mother and father really happy. It was time for a change in our family. My dad could concentrate on his job and my mom would be busy with all the things around the house and trying to keep watch on us twins. The rest of my siblings would also stay busy because there was plenty of work around there.

So, we were all happy for our big brother. Not long after we got the call from Aunt Lelee, her brother had arrived at our house from Albany, and it was about time. My brother was hesitant for a while, as if he didn't want to leave this one-stoplight town, but he after giving it some deep thought, he was ready for this change. He stood there with tears running down his face.

Of course, this made Mom do the same as they both looked at each other. She told him, "Alvin, this is for the good of our family. Besides, you won't be gone forever. You will come for a visit one day soon." He looked at our mom, saying, "Madea, I will write every week to let you know how I'm getting along in this new place." It was so sad for everyone in our family; everyone was fighting the tears. Now it was time for lots of hugs and good-byes and "I will miss you, big brother."

Even Aunt Lelee was fighting back the tears. As I looked, I could see Uncle John fighting tears as well. It was a big gathering around the house, and Uncle John and Aunt Lelee's kids were there as well. They knew what was going on and that it was for a good cause. Now that all the good-byes had come to an end, it was time for my big brother to make the big trip.

My brother was finally leaving this small town. It's amazing what a good cry can do to change a person's mind. Pastor Jack and his son, Samuel, were ready to make the trip back to Albany. My mom and dad were so happy for what the Beals had done for the family. They always said that if we needed anything we shouldn't hesitate to ask.

My mom got some of my brother's things and put them in this big white car called a Cadillac. I was told it was a Fleetwood Cadillac. It was the biggest car I'd ever seen, with four doors to boot. It was sad for me and my twin brother. Now what were we to do without him? Alvin saw the sadness on our faces. He began to tell us, "I'll be back," and that was a promise to all of us. As our mom wiped the tears from her face—they were happy tears as well—I could see the relief from the ordeal in her face, Pastor Jack looked at our mom, then at my big brother.

He told my big brother, "This is what I want you to do for me and your family, especially your mom. I want you to work very hard."

He said, "Okay,"

We all just stood there as this white Cadillac car drove off into the distance down this old, dusty dirt road. It was as if we would never see our big brother again. There was tears all over the place, but at the same time we were filled with love and joy.

After he left, the house was quiet for some time; everyone had to get along without our big brother until he returned back home for the whole family, and I hoped it would be soon.

In continuing to keep busy, my mom would make more quilts and blankets. Our dad was still working as a field hand for the white men and doing some sharecroppers' work as well. Talking about our town, the sawmill was just across that field through those trees and bushes. As I mentioned before, my twin and I waited for our dad to come home from the sawmill. That sawmill was a big part of our lives. Every single day we could smell the aroma coming from the sawmill, the smell of fresh pine traveling through the air. It was even better when the wind would blow in our direction. That's why my father brought some of the woodchip's home for the outhouse. I must give it to him; that was a smart move on his part. He even put some of the chips around the house. Now I guess you can see why we were a happy family.

Now we all had enough to keep us busy, and time would pass by quickly.

I mentioned earlier that I would explain and talk about the path that led from the back door of our house. That path led to what we call the outhouse. It was our bathroom and sanitation facility. It was the way of the South for minority families, if you were poor like we were, and we were very poor. The outhouse was approximately seventy-five feet from our house. To the right. It was the only one on this side of this old, dusty dirt road; in fact, it was the only one in the neighborhood,

What made our family a success in our lives, is the love our parents surrounded us with. Joy and peace. Our family — Happiness is what love is all about. Meanwhile, the family that lived next door, the Beals, had a nice house with a driveway and a truck. They had running water and electricity in their house. Since we didn't, Aunt Lelee and Uncle John had us come over and watch TV with their kids many times. That was the best invite ever. We watched the old black-and-white movies, like *Gunsmoke, Wagon Train*, and *Have Gun – Will Travel* to name a few.

Now in the rest of their house, there were three bedrooms and two bathrooms. I'd never seen a bathroom inside a house before. I'll talk about the bathroom later on. They had a nice front yard and backyard. They were considered middle class. There were six other families living on this dusty dirt road. Our house was the only one located on the left side of the road. All the other families lived on the right side of the road. Everybody on the other side of the road wore shoes. Running on the train tracks, through the fields, we never wore our shoes. We didn't start wearing our shoes until we got to the City of Albany. Remember us twins? Well, we couldn't wait for that day to come. We missed those days carrying those guns for our big brother. Jerry and I would carry his two rifless, and he would tell us to shoot the rifle into the squirrel nest, and the squirrel would jump out. Then Alvin would shoot the squirrel, and down to the ground he would fall. He took us hunting and fishing, but not down at the Chickasawhay's River area. He told us twins many funny stories when we were little boys.

There was good news: a letter from our big brother. Pastor Jack would be helping him to find a good job there in Albany. It was in a restaurant called Joe's Bar and Tavern, located on Western Avenue and Ontario Avenue. And he didn't have to worry about a place to stay for the first three months of rent. Pastor Jack owned plenty of houses, and he did all he could for Alvin in anything. My mom and dad were overjoyed with the good news, and my big brother Alvin said, "I will not forget the promise I made to the family."

when we were little boys. We all were waiting for our big brother to return back to our hometown, and take us back with him to Albany, New York.

This would be a long time waiting, and we couldn't wait to get the answer from Aunt Lelee. She said she would let my mom know when she got news. It would be coming from her brother (Jack) the pastor, all the way from Albany, a little more than 1,800 miles away.

He would not do the driving all by himself; he would have his son, Samuel, help him drive to Waynesboro. When my twin and I saw that big, long Fleetwood Cadillac come driving down this old, dusty dirt road, then and only then would we jump for joy, saying, "Madea, they are here!" I knew this would warm my mom's heart when she saw her oldest son in person. I would be looking to see my mom's face shine with joyfulness and thankfulness to boot. We all would share the joy of seeing him again. I wondered how much he had changed in the last year. Would he bring his twin brothers something, a gift from the North?

And our whole family would be making that same trip to the North for the first time. There was so much excitement in the air. The time is finally here for him to leave, so what could two little boys get into now, knowing their big brother wasn't there to help our mother stop those twins from getting into trouble? Well, we weren't that bad, if you know what I mean!

We thought of it as twins on an adventure. Just as long as we didn't play on the train tracks when the train was nearby, she told us to just sit on the steps or on the porch until the train had passed. Out of all the things we as twins did, playing near the train scared our mom the most. She always told us to just play safe in and around the house, and it was always, "Yes, Madea."

My mom had gotten a call from my big brother, and she said to us, "Everyone, Alvin is coming back for us in two weeks." Now it was time to start packing, but just the important things. There were a lot of things in the house that had some value, like my mom's sewing machine. Imagine my mom and dad and six boys and two girls, plus Pastor Jack and his son, all had to fit in this Cadillac, making that very long trip back to Albany, New York. His sister Aunt Lelee packed a large box of food for us on the way. This was in the late '60s. We all were greatly thankful and gave all praise to the Almighty. We were leaving this one-stoplight town in about one or two hours. It was a long time coming. For now, I was hung up on two possibilities: leaving my hometown and looking for a brand-new place we all could call home. There wasn't any room in my brain or subconscious for trying to imagine what a big city like Albany would look like, and nobody around could tell me or give me any idea. I'd just have to wait and see.

The younger siblings all leaving for the North didn't even have shoes on our feet, but we were still so happy to be leaving that one-stoplight town. That day was not too far away. I was very anxious, filled with anticipation—what would I do when we got there? I wished I could imagine how it would look.

So far, I've talked about some wonderful things and adventures. Most of the adventures were about my twin and me. There were bad times in our lives; it seemed sometimes as if we would never make it in this town. We had to endure the good and the bad, but with God's help, we made life as a family in a beautiful place to live. This was home, and this was our town.

I think it's so beautiful, and I wish all families could practice making this work for their family in some kind of way. My mom and the rest of my siblings were making that transition from the South to the North, 1,800 miles—a long drive. Living in the Deep South was a living nightmare for all Blacks. We are miracles of creation; we can capture and replicate the present, past, and future.

He that can't remember the past is most certainly condemned to repeat it, at least some part of that memory. We as Black folks must focus on the future. One must not forget their past; it's so important in making and completing one's life. Remember, life has so much to offer to anyone looking for a change or a miracle. Our whole family was ready for that 1,800-mile drive to the North, and it was so exciting to say we were finally out of that small town and the state of Mississippi.

Like God said to Lot and his wife, "Whatever happens, don't look back." That would not be a problem for my family. Now that everything was set, we were on that same old, dusty dirt road that led from our house, heading north. I hoped Pastor Jack had air conditioning in his big Fleetwood Cadillac car, because it was going to be a long ride for him and his son, Samuel, my mom and dad and two sisters, Vonda and my oldest sister Gloria Jean, and six boys. This big car was really packed to the max. My whole family could say we were finally on our way.

## NINE

### The Transition to the North

This was another exciting time in our lives as little boys in a family from the Deep South. It was a struggle for us all in this small, one-stoplight town as my parents were trying to make ends meet. One thing was for sure: we owed a great deal of gratitude to our big brother, Alvin E. Williamson, and the promise he made early before the big trip to the North that he would work very hard and save $300 so Pastor Jack could return for the whole family.

Now that we were on our way to the big city, everyone was so happy, especially those twins. We were making that transition to the North, that big city called Albany, New York. I had heard of this place from the pastor's sister Aunt Lelee, but

I never thought I'd be living there. My mom was happy that Aunt Lelee prepared some things for the trip. We would be there soon, and it would be unreal. Everyone was excited for our family—we were all making this move, and we couldn't wait.

The pastor's car had lots of room for us all, but it was still a little crowded. I had no idea what the different state was about. As we traveled, all we did was sit and ride as long as we could stand it. Pastor Jack made several stops along the way.

My twin and I were very excited traveling to an unknown place. Soon we would have a brand-new place to live. Pastor Jackson said, "Well, everyone, we are in New York State. We should be in Albany in three hours." It was still a long way, so we all just sat back and tried to relax. The next time Pastor Jack talked, he said, "Everyone, look around; we are in Albany." Now this threw me for a big shock. I couldn't believe what I was seeing. This was a very large place; look at all those very tall buildings! It seemed as if they were touching the sky.

I'd never seen so many cars, trucks, and buses. With all that noise they produced, I think our mom and dad were shocked as well. It was unreal hearing those high-pitched sounds coming from the police cars, fire trucks, and ambulances. And to see so many people walking the streets in all directions . . . the streets looked to be miles long, crossing each other. Everyone in the car was looking out the windows, trying to see all they could. My mom and dad looked a little lost and surprised.

Everywhere we looked, the houses were either two floors or higher. The pastor two daughters Cherise and Pattie were living there at the time. So Pastor Jack had them stay upstate with their aunts, just until our family got settled. At our new place, we had plenty of room to sleep and some privacy for my mom and dad. No more two-bedroom houses for us.

Everyone was very happy in Albany. My mother and father and the rest of their siblings were all comfortable, and there was no shame at all when neighbors passed by like it was back home, in the house we lived in next to the train tracks, close to that very dusty dirt road. Remember, we were in God's hands. Pastor Jack told my mom and dad about the house we would be living in before we left for the North. Now that we were there, it was unreal.

Now that we had settled down, my twin and I were out looking for some adventure—you know those twins. We said, "Madea, could we go outside?" Our mom said yes, "Don't go too far, boys. You may get lost." Pastor Jack said, "I told you, it's a large place. I'll drive you around for a few minutes so you can see this big city." I guess people on the sidewalk were looking at us funny. We were all staring out the windows, looking at the people as we passed by. Then Pastor Jack went on to say, "I will show you where you will be living. Here we are at your new home."

It was a two-story building, and it was tall. I will never forget the address—189 Green Street in Albany, New York, near the corner of Rensselaer Street. We all got out and went into the house. It was upstairs. We'd never been in or stayed in a house with two floors. But there were lots of buildings much taller. There were some people living downstairs. Later on, we were introduced. They were the Jackson family, and they were very nice to us all. Once inside, the place was unbelievable— there was so much room. There was a front dining room, and it had a large living room. It had three large bedrooms as well.

What a relief—no more two large rooms for our family house anymore. I would miss our old house; it was all my mom and dad could afford, and it was our home. I'll keep those memories in the back of my mind forever. My twin and I got into so much trouble in and around that old house. Maybe they would turn it back into a train station again; who knows? Out of all of us, our mom was the happiest. She could hardly breathe. No, it wasn't her asthma; it was the excitement for our new home. The whole family was out of that one-stoplight town called Waynesboro.

We all made it a memorable moment. Our big brother wasn't at the house yet. He was still working at Joe's Restaurant out on Western Avenue and Ontario Street. But not for long; here he came with hugs and kisses and arms waving in the air. "How is everyone doing?" That really brought tears to my mom's eyes. Again, her plan worked out very well. Our whole family was together again. We would all miss our other sister Geraldine, who was still in Waynesboro with her boyfriend Tommy Joe Huntley.

Tommy Joe made a promise to our mom and dad that he would bring our sister to Albany as soon as the baby came. Well, my mom and dad would have to take his word. Now it was time for our mom to get busy with all the little ones. It was summer, and soon it would be time for school, after we all got settled, walked around, and got more comfortable in our new environment. It would make things much easier for us all. Afterward, we would have our place in this new house. I had no idea our house would be like this. It was just a big dream. Everyone seemed to be happy in these strange surroundings, and it felt so good to be around brand-new things. It seemed like I'd dreamed about it.

This day, my twin and I asked our mom, "Madea, can we go down the street?" Again, she said, "Boys, be very careful on the streets. They are dangerous, and don't try crossing them at all." And the same reply, "Yes, Madea," and off we went on some brand-new adventures in a brand-new city—no more little country town. So my twin and I discussed which way we would go, down the street or the opposite way on Green Street.

Jerry said, "Let's go that way, down Green Street and around the corner on Rensselaer Street." We decided to go down the street, and we were happy and excited. For the first time in our lives, we saw this boy riding his bike on its rear wheel. Now that threw us for a real loop. Something like that wouldn't happen in our hometown. Up and down the street he went, and he was very good. Maybe one day we could do that as well. We had no toys to play with, and no bikes, so we decided to continue our walk down Rensselaer for a while, then we came back to the house. We asked Madea, "Can we go a little further this time?" She said, "Sit on this step for now." We sat on the steps. There were three steps that connected to the flat solid surface that led to the hallway and the steps upstairs. We just sat there in front of the house. We asked our mom a second time, "Madea, could we go down the street?" She said, "Yes, but be careful on the streets."

We went around the corner from our house on Green Street to Rensselaer Street again. Here we go, down Rensselaer Street. We heard some very loud noises coming from down the street. There were these boys playing basketball. They were much older than my twin and me. The strangest thing was that the basketball hoop was an old bicycle rim; they'd made it to look like a basketball hoop. It was nailed to the telephone pole. Now that was strange to see, but it was working, and they were having a ton of fun to boot. Another very strange thing occurred to us. The white boys and the Black boys were all playing basketball together. I thought to myself, something like this would never happen back in our hometown. It was impossible.

One of the white boys came up to us, saying, "Hi, my name is Frankie Travis." Imagine, the first person we met was white. Frankie Travis: his skin wasn't white like the people in our hometown, and his hair was jet black. That was strange to us. "What's you guys' names?" We told him our names: "We are Terry and Jerry Williamson."

He said, "You guys are twins."

We replied, "Yes."

He said, "Hang around, I want you to meet my family." So he went back to the basketball game. Then, this big, tall Black guy with all these muscles came over to us. "Who are you guys?" There was that word again, "guy," this word we'd never heard before.

We were used to the word "boy." It was a word we had to listen to all our lives, and it came from the white men in our hometown and all through the Deep South. That word "boy" was the main reason we were there in that big city. Meanwhile, this big Black guy said to us, "You guys are not from around here." We said, "No, we are from Mississippi."

He said, "My name's Herman Lee Carswell. Did you guys come here with the pastor?"

We said, "Yes, we've known him for many years."

He said, "Welcome to the neighborhood. Most people around here call Pastor Jack 'Brother Jack.'" Herman welcomed us to Albany, and he too went back to the basketball game. Meanwhile, as they were playing, one of the other boys ran into the telephone pole and got a big knot on his forehead. Herman had someone go into the house and get a fruit can, and he started rubbing the knot on his friend's forehead and the knot began to disappear. Now that was strange to see. And he was all right, and they all went back to playing basketball again.

Afterward, Frankie Travis asked us, "Would you like to meet my family?" We said, "Okay." We went to his house; it was just down the street on Rensselaer Street. We took that short walk to his house, and he introduced us to his family—his mother and father, sisters, and brothers. The house had this strange odor. He said to us, "Would you guys like to stay for supper?" We said "Yes," and he said, "We're having spaghetti and meatballs." This was where that strange aroma was coming from.

His mother was very busy cooking, and his dad looked just like he did. This would be our first time having real spaghetti, and Frankie Travis was telling us his mother used real whole garlic cloves in her cooking; that was the smell we were smelling when we came into their house. And another strange thing: they had this loaf of bread that looked like a piece of wood. But Frankie Travis told us it was called Italian bread. We never tasted anything like this before, and it was very good; he said it was garlic spread all over it. Frankie said it was sent to her from the old country, Italy. And it was the oddest thing to see someone take a spoon in their left hand and twist and turn the spaghetti with a fork in their right hand. That threw us for a big loop. That was strange to see them do that.

Then Frankie Travis said, "We are Italians. My mother and father were born in the old country called Italy." Well, we'd never heard of a place like that. My twin and I began to stare at each other. The whole family all had jet black hair. We learned later in life that all Italians had jet black hair. Frankie went on to say, "This is the correct way to eat spaghetti; it's all from the old country." We had learned something new already. He said, "Go ahead, give it a try." We gave it a try the best way we could. It took a while before we could do it right. They also had some wine; we told him we weren't allowed to drink it. He said, "All my brothers and sisters, small and large, drink wine." He told us, "It's part of the meal." Everyone who sat at the  table must drink their portion of wine—red wine with spaghetti, and white wine with fish.

Well, my twin and I looked at each other. Frankie said, "Don't worry; you won't get into any trouble." This city was filled with Italian people, especially in this neighborhood. It was so strange to see so many dark-skinned white people. We could see them sitting and hanging in the windows and sitting on the steps, and they were very nice. We didn't know what to do or think. For one, it was a good thing. This would have never happened back home in our one-stoplight town. This was our first time and last time drinking this red stuff called wine in our whole lives; we wouldn't tell our mother. Why? It would be the belt or the strap to our bottom. We'd keep it a secret for a while.

Now it was time to head back home. Herman stopped us, "Hey, you guys, I saw you watching us play basketball. When things settle down, if you want to, I can show you around the city. Would you like that?"

We said, "Okay, that will be good, but we would have to ask our mom first."

He said, "My family lives over on Elisabeth Street, near Delaware Street; you are welcome to stop by sometime."

It was getting late, so we had to head back home soon or it's the belt or strap; it would hard for our mom to find a switch in this big city. We'd promised our mom we wouldn't stay out too long anyway. Our big brother was still working at Joe's Restaurant out on Western Avenue, and he'd be coming home soon, so we had to be there when he got home. And when he got home, we all shared some good news. He told our dad he had a job for him at the same restaurant. So, there were two people working in the family. Pastor Jackson didn't charge my mom and dad any rent at the time, so that was a big help. My mom prepared supper. I can still smell the aroma from the golden-brown cornbread and that tasty gravy, string beans, and mashed potatoes, with those golden-brown baked chicken breasts, traveling all through the house just like back home.

Everything was going well for the family in a brand-new place, a place we could call our home. All the memories from our two-room house were in the past, but I will never forget all the wonder and excitement that occurred there. I'm really sad those

*Figure 27 31 Red Wine with a plate of spaghetti*

days will stay with me for the rest of my life, and my twin brother will agree with me on everything I've talked about.

So, now my twin and I had to make and take all our adventures here in a brand-new city and its strange surroundings to boot. The next day, my twin and I asked our mom if we could go outside and play. She was a very good mom, the best ever. Again, she told us to be careful out there in those very busy streets. We went out for another adventure. As we played, we headed toward some screaming and shouting from down on Green Street.

We ran down there and saw all these little boys and girls. All the kids were the same size and age we were. Their parents had taken the top off the fire hydrant. Now that threw us again for a big loop and was a surprise as well. All that very cold water came gushing out. It was one way the kids could keep cool during this very hot summer day. For a long time, we just watched them play. It was exciting to see it as well. This would be impossible back in Waynesboro, because we had to go down to the Chickasawhay River with snakes and spiders to cool off on a very hot summer day. Another strange thing we experienced was the sound of sirens coming from the fire trucks, fire chief, police cars, and ambulances; they were all very loud to the ear, and it happened all the time, both night and day, almost like clockwork.

Most people who lived there had gotten used to those terribly loud sounds. To anyone who ever lived in or visited Albany, you had to stop at the one and only New York Bakery, located on South Pearl Street near Franklin Street. That aroma was carried throughout the area. The good thing about this bakery was that it was half a block from the church and three blocks from our house. We always wanted those big cookies with a two-tone color; one side was brown, and the other was white. You only needed just one bite, and it would melt in your mouth. Those soft brown croissants were heavenly good. That bakery seemed like it lit up the whole street with aroma.

We'd been here for a while now, and the streets were not as hard to get around. Our mom told us not to go any farther than State Street, which was to the north. The other direction was Lincoln Park, to the west. She told us not to venture down South Pearl Street—that was a bad part of town—because she knew her twins and how we loved to go on adventures. We'd been doing that since we were back home.

It was good we had learned our way around that part of town. Well, the summer had come to an end, so my mom took us all out for new school clothes. We called this our fun day. I do remember she bought all the boys' white shirts, blue jeans, black shoes, and some socks and T-shirts. The girls shopped on the other side of the store, and I can't forget the store. It was called Lodges Clothing Store, on the corner of Columbia and North Pearl Street. And the store is still there today; it is good to have a store that has good products for the kids and their customers, especially for young boys and girls. Meanwhile, our mom had promised the pastor that we would attend his church services at the Church of God in Christ. It wasn't too far from our house; in fact, it was about three city blocks away, the same distance as the bakery. The church was well known in that part of town.

That evening, Madea got us all ready for church service. We all got there on time. It was a wonderful service. It was a large church with two floors. This was a community church as well. It had a huge balcony in a circle design, and the downstairs area was large as well. On the other side, there was a large dining area with room to spare. There were two offices, one for Pastor Jack and the other for visitors with other business, like other pastors from other churches. It was a big church, and it had a very large basement suited for different functions. The best thing about it all was that it was just around the corner.

And one thing was for sure: we all will be coming back to Pastor Jack's church again. I thought Pastor Jack was a real man of God; he was an awesome man. The look in his eyes was something special. To me, he had a sense of caring for other people. I really think my whole entire family saw this in this man of God. The family attended the church service every week. There was a service every Tuesday and Friday night and three on Sundays. I really enjoyed all the services. Now that Pastor Jack had settled in Albany and given my family a good place to stay, we were all happy in this big city, our brand-new home. What a transition.

# TEN

## School #1

Now that the fall weather was here, it was time to get ready for school. Our mom got us ready. Us twins went to School #1. It was located on Franklin Street and Bassett Street; in fact, it was just around the corner from the Howe Library and a block and a half from our house. There we were two nervous little boys at school for the first time in Albany.

Figure 28 You are looking at the first school my twin and I attend, this is school #1.

Once we were inside our new school, I'd never thought I would be in the same classroom with both Black and white kids together. What a big change from the South. In our hometown, there were only Black kids in the class. This would take some getting used to. At least our mother had dressed us in some brand-new clothes, white shirts and black jeans, so we were ready for school.

But it wasn't too long before we had to change schools. The school was very small and there wasn't enough room for all the kids. What, when and where was our next school this time? We were told we were transferred to Geffen Memorials Elementary School, located on Schuyler Street and South Pearl Street. It seemed like each school got bigger and bigger each year. Geffen was brand new; we could see it being built over the course of several years. This school was fine on the inside, and it smelled so good throughout the whole building. We were pumped up and ready to start. That school didn't last very long, but we had lots of fun there, and we would miss this school, Geffen Memorial.

We were transferred to School #15, located on 75 Herkimer in downtown Albany. The school was an excellent example of advanced design for its purpose at the time. It was built in 1870–1871. It was a landmark building in the history of education in Albany. On February 5, 1980, it was distorted by severe fire damage. The building was demolished after the fire.

Now this was a huge school. It had these black stairs coming down the side of the building. Later on, we were told they were called a fire escape; we'd never seen anything like that before. It sort of reminded me of those plantation buildings back in our one-stoplight town called Waynesboro, Mississippi, but not as tall as the one here in Albany. Some good news: the pastor's two daughter's also went to this big school. I was so glad to see someone we knew. That made us feel a little more comfortable at this very large school.

This school had a big backyard at the rear of the building. There was so much excitement in the air. My twin and I found our room and met the principal and our teacher, and again we had to get used to seeing Black kids and white kids in the same class. Then it was time for recess. All the kids went outside to the back of the school. They were playing this strange game; it was called dodgeball. My twin and I had never seen or heard of this game before. We watched them play for a while; it looked like fun.

We were ready to play. They told us the rules of the game. "Are you guys ready?" my twin and I said, "Just words to us twins: we are adventurers from the Deep South, we are ready for this game called dodgeball. Any number of kids could play. Now the rules: one kid must stand next to the building facing the other kids, with the rest of the kids standing in the open area looking at the kid next to the wall. All the kids together would have this large ball. It was smaller than a beach ball. They would throw the ball at the kid next to the wall. If he or she got hit, they were out of the game. Let me tell you, this was a dangerous game, but we didn't care—it was the competition we liked. And when one got hit with this large ball, it really hurt, with a stinging sensation to boot.

At the end of the day, we had homework. Later on, during the school year, the weather turned colder. One morning, my twin and I saw snow for the first time; it had snowed the night before. It was amazing and very exciting with all the oohs and aahs—talk about a fantasyland. I could have never imagined seeing the whole city covered with this white fluffy stuff called snow. We saw all the kids on the block playing in the snow, so we said, "Madea, can we go out and play in the snow?" She said, "Yes, but be careful outside." My twin and I saw these boys hiding between the parked cars on Green Street. We watched them for a long time; they would kneel down and wait for a while, but here was the shocking surprise.

Once they kneeled down, they would wait for a tractor trailer to pass by. Then they would run and grab hold of the rear bumper of this tractor trailer, holding on for dear life and making sure their knees were slightly bent because it would make the slide of the ride much easier. This would give them a long sliding ride down the street.

Now, that looked like fun. Yes, you guessed it—it had some danger in it, but we were some adventurous little boys. So we would kneel down and hide behind the parked cars, waiting until the right time came when the first tractor trailer passed by. Now, this was our first time trying this dangerous game, but I guess danger was our business, because it came with us from down South. Danger and adventure always excited us.

Figure 29 The Angel of Death wreaked havoc in our family

"Are you guys ready? Here comes one, run and grab and hold on real tight!"

Down the street we went, sliding down the street, holding onto the bumper of this big tractor trailer on the snow. The other kids were yelling to us, "Don't forget, you must stay in the squat position!" We wished that could have lasted all day. Here we go again: boys will be boys. What was next?

They took us to Dead Man's Hill in Lincoln Park for another dangerous ride. There was plenty of snow. The hill was straight down and it was really scary, and a ton of fun as well. We would all stand on the top of this big hill, which was on Morton Avenue. We had those wooden and metal sleds, and we would run and jump on the sleds, and down the hill we went. It was so fast, everyone would wind up in the middle of the park. These were some of the scariest and most dangerous rides of all time, and they were for the kids with no fear. For us twins, this was right up our alley.

After going to School #15 for a long time, we got some news from the teacher in the front office: we were being transferred to a different school. But first, more bad news: the angel of death made another visit to our family, and we lost our grandfather, Vaden. We love you, Grandpa, and we will miss you very much. Not everyone could make the trip back for his funeral, so just a few of us made the trip. On the way, my big brother asked if anyone was hungry, so he decided to stop at a restaurant for some food.

We found a restaurant on the side of Route 11 South in a small town in Alabama. When we entered the restaurant, everyone stopped, turned, and began to stare at us. They were all white people, and it was a very scary feeling that sent chills down our spines. There were several guys in the corner, and they began to start trouble with us. They were screaming and yelling, "We killed your leader, we killed your leader!"

So my big brother grabbed us and said, "Let's get out of here now." We all headed for the door. That was one moment I don't want to experience again.

This was the same period that Martin Luther King Jr. was assassinated. There was lots of trouble going on in the South. Earlier, in 1963, President Kennedy, the thirty-fifth president of the United States, was assassinated. This was my first time crying. I cried over a white man; I cried in my sister's arms. There was so much going on in the Deep South.

We made it safely, attended the funeral service, and visited the family for a spell. Then it was time to head back to Albany. We would be attending a new school, and I wondered where it was located. Ervin, our next older brother, was attending this school. He said it was on the other side of Lincoln Park. We were here. I thought School #15 was big, but this school was so much bigger, and it too had three floors and a basement. Now we were in our new school, called William S. Hackett Junior High School, located on Delaware Avenue and Park Avenue, overlooking Lincoln Park.

We had heard of this school before. It was only eight or ten city blocks away from our house. We had so much fun back at School #15, but it was time to say our good-bye. We gave our mom the letter for the transfer. She said, "Boys, don't worry. *Everything will be all right*," and time passed. Then it was time for that very long walk, and most of the way was uphill through Lincoln Park. The school was so far away. We decided to take a shortcut through the park itself, but we had no idea what would happen next. There was lots of snow on the ground, so we started walking. All of a sudden, we both fell through the frozen snow and ice. Cold water filled both our boots. We made our way out of that cold field, but we had to go to school anyway, and we couldn't go back home.

I wonder what our mom would've done. There were no switches and no belts for us in the new city. Well, when we got to school, we told the teachers at the main office what had happened in the park, with wet socks and boots. They gave us new clean socks, and we went off to class. We would never do that again; we would stay on the sidewalk for the rest of the winter. It was a much longer walk, longer than all the other schools put together, and a very cold one to boot.

Hackett Junior High School was our brand-new school. It had three floors, and it was one of the largest buildings in the area, with those large steps and doorways in front. Our big brother, Ervin, was already attending this school. He was glad to see us. Now there would be three brothers attending Hackett Junior High School. We were excited and a little nervous. There were twice as many kids at this school, and my twin and I were ready for the big change. Our big brother met us in front of the school. He said, "Well, let's get started." We went inside to the main office for registration and placements to different classes.

But first, we had to take an aptitude exam. Well, at the time, my twin and I didn't know what that meant. The teacher told us what we had to do for the exam. We were placed in a different room and given the test and were told to let the teacher know when we were finished. Our big brother had to go back to his class. He told us, "You'll be fine; just take your time." Well, my twin and I didn't do very well on the exam. The teacher told us we had to be placed in a special education class. We asked, "What is this special education class?" We were told this class would help us in our academics and bring us up to par.

The assistant principal took us downstairs to the basement. It was a little cool and dark, and there weren't too many classes down there. It didn't look like other classrooms we'd attended in the past. We got closer to the classroom, and my twin and I heard some loud noise coming from this room. We entered the room, and we couldn't believe our eyes and ears. The principal introduced us to the teacher.

The principal said, "This is Terry and Jerry Williamson, our new students."

He said, "My name is Mr. Armstrong, your new teacher. I'm in charge of all the special education students here at Hackett Junior High School."

The assistant principal said, "I guess you can see they are twins."

He said, "Yes, and welcome to our school."

Then the principal went back upstairs. Mr. Armstrong told us where to sit, then he went back to his desk, sat down, and began to eat an apple and read the newspaper. Meanwhile, the noise got worse after the assistant principal left the room. Everyone was screaming, yelling, sitting on the desks, and making paper airplanes and throwing them across the room. There were boys and girls, and they were out of control. My twin and I couldn't believe this was happening. The teacher did nothing; he had no control of the students in his class. I used to think this would be a chance to walk and see the whole school. Well, that never happened in the least.

We knew this wasn't for us. This class was bad, and very noisy, and we didn't see anyone in the class with a book in their hands or doing any kind of homework—nothing at all. And this was our first day in class. Here is some bad news: they didn't even change classes. We stayed in this one classroom all day long, and there was never any homework passed out to us. We looked at each other, saying, "We don't want to be in this class at all." We couldn't stand the loud noise coming from all those rude kids. This was a big disappointment; we weren't looking forward to this kind of class.

Jerry and I told our mom when we got home. She told us, "Boys, don't worry; *everything will be all right.* Just focus on your work at school."

We told our mom they didn't give us any work at school. "Still, do your best to get through this. Remember what I said, stay focused."

The only time we left this noisy room was when it was time for recess. All the other kids went to the front of the school or the back, but we had to go to the side of the school and sit on the grass until the bell rang. Now that was weird. It didn't make any sense at all. Here is something you will not believe: my twin and I asked the front office if we could play in the mainstream classes with all of the other students in this school.

    They didn't want to hear that. "You are fine where you are. You just have to wait and see how things go for now, so you have to go back to your class." What a disappointment for the twins from the South, here in a brand-new city and school system. The only time we enjoyed ourselves was when we were heading for lunch in the cafeteria, but even then, the kids in the mainstreams looked at us strangely, pointing their fingers at us, laughing and giggling at the kids from the special education class down in the basement of the school. I called it the dungeon. They called us "stupid retarded kids in the special education class." Now that really hurt. We did our best to overlook what they were saying and screaming as we passed by. My twin and I just focused on the food served in the cafeteria, and let me say, it was so good, especially the sauerkraut and hot dogs. It was our first time eating this kind of food. We purchased two hot dogs with sauerkraut, and the taste was unbelievable. Two milks, white and chocolate, and it was some of the best-tasting chocolate milk; the white milk wasn't too bad either. We hadn't tasted milk like this in our old school back in Waynesboro, Mississippi. This time, our big brother Ervin was with us, and all three of us stayed together. Meanwhile, my older brother was transferred to a school called Philip Schuyler High School. We'd seen that building before; it was close to our church downtown, off South Pearl Street. Mr. Armstrong seemed like he didn't care for the kids. We found out later that when we were put in what they called "special education class," we didn't understand the special ed classes were for kids with learning disorders. My twin and I had thought we would be in the mainstream classes. We weren't in a special class in the other schools. Later, we went to the office to see what they could do.

Figure 30 This is Hackett junior high school on Delaware Ave

    Back to the noisy classroom. Our teacher, Mr. Armstrong, didn't appear to us as a teacher. It seemed as if he didn't care about the students. Well, there were these two students in our class. They were brother and sister, named Miguel and Anna Archibald. They were also in this special education class. They were white. I thought they were all right; we knew they were a little slow, different from the rest of the class, but they were okay with me and my brother. But the rest of the class laughed at them and made faces. They would call them stupid retards, and they were in the same class as they were. Something was wrong with that picture. It was like everyone was in a hole, and everyone needed the help from their fellow students. But the laughing and pointing fingers continued every day, and that was something we couldn't do.

Just because someone is different doesn't mean you should laugh at them and tease them all the time, calling them retards or stupid. I knew I had seen them before; they lived just down the street from us. We lived at 189 Green Street, and they lived at 69 Green Street, so we become good friends from that day forward. We walked to school together each day. I know for a fact they were much happier with us twins. We did all we could to try to keep them happy. They were so nice to me and my twin.

One other thing about this school was that the swimming pool was enjoyable. We loved to swim. They still didn't let us be part of the mainstream classes after going to the pool. We had to go straight back to that one large room in the basement. We felt like it was some kind of martial law.

We couldn't wait to get out of that school. Some good news for me and my twin brother: we had been told we would be transferring to a new school shortly. It was the best news of all time; it was a big move, and we were so proud it finally happened for us. The news came from the office. The transfer was to Philip Schuyler High School, and it was a long time in waiting. This would make our mom very happy with some wonderful news. And we didn't have to worry about the students in the special education classes anymore—all the noise and playing around and the loud talking, and most of all, the disrespect to others. We couldn't wait to get home and tell our mom the good news we received from the front office—our mom would be so happy. First, my twin and I will never have any faith in this school again. I hope there would never be any students going through what my twin and I had to go through at this terrible school. So, Jerry and I will take that long walk through the park with Anna and Miguel Archibald for the last time. One thing for sure, we will never forget how special they were to us. Personally, I will not forget this school ever. It brought tears to my eyes; this school made me so unhappy.

## ELEVEN

### The Angel of Death

Now that the school bell had rung, it was time to head home. We rushed out of school and ran through Lincoln Park. We said good-bye to Miguel and Anna Archibald. saying we'd see them tomorrow for school. We got home and quickly went up the stairs when we entered the house. My older sister and brother both had sad faces and were crying. My big brother had taken my mom to her appointment. This white man ran the four-way stop sign, and there was a big crash at the intersection. My mom was thrown forward, and her forehead hit the dashboard.

She was taken to the Memorial Hospital not too long after, and she was transferred to St. Peters Hospital. Then my brother got the news that our mom didn't survive the crash. This news devastated our whole family. I'll never forget that day as long as I live. All I could do was sit down and put my head in my hands and cry. My mother and father lost their last child at birth, a baby boy; now this was a second visit from the angel of death.

All the love and care she had for her twin boys was no more. It just tore us apart, those little boys of hers. This was the worst adventure we would ever experience in our lives. The words our mom told us, "Boys, don't worry, everything will be all right," were the last words our mom spoke to us as little boys before she passed away. Those special words our mom spoke will stay with me for the rest of my days. It was so sad for us all as a close-knit family.

My big brother Alvin took the accidental death of our mother personally, saying it was his fault. He struggled with the loss of our mom for a very long time. "No. Big bro, the man ran the stop sign—there wasn't anything you could have done; it was an accident." Unfortunately, no one offered any support to assess if my big brother needed to talk with a mental health specialist or counselor. I can only imagine how he must have felt on the inside . . . That's our big brother, our mom's first-born son, and it was really hard on him. The school gave us time off for the funeral services.

Pastor Jack came over to comfort us in this time of sorrow. The pastor, my big sister, and my brother discussed the funeral services. My mom wanted to be buried next to her family in Waynesboro, Mississippi, so they made plans for the trip back to our hometown. Alvin had his own car, so they used both cars for the trip.

My older sister Gloria took the train with my mother's body. I know that the train ride back to our hometown had to be a heavy weight on my big sister. It had to be very sad and emotionally draining from the devastation that hit our family. Although the service was beautiful, it was a sad time for us all. As I mentioned earlier, my other sister Geraldine was still living in Waynesboro. We all gathered around each other with tears, outstretched arms, and lots of hugs and kisses, and now as a close-knit family, we would keep our mother's legacy alive and strong.

Figure 37 My big sister Gloria Jean Williamso

What about my big sister, Gloria She was there for my mother during our upbringing during the hard times as a poor family in our hometown, with all the problems with the white men's nonsense and prejudiced ways. But we as a family persevered through those hard times. What's my big sister like? She would be side by side with my mom, just like two sisters, working and gabbing and enjoying each other's company. She was always there when my mom needed anything. That was the job for the firstborn of those newlyweds. Way to go, big sis.

Gloria Jean loved antiques in her house or apartment. She would display them in every room. She had a passion for fine art as well. Sometimes she would drive all around the capital district, looking for fine art. old photos, stuffed dolls, and strange-looking animals—she would have them placed in every room just like an art gallery, and all the small children were a little frightened when they came into her house.

I was so happy when I found out the story about Mrs. Mammie Russell. Jerry and I will never forget; it's embedded in the back of our memories, I asked Gloria Jean if she remembered everything and how she treated us. My big sister said, "Yes, Terry, I still remember how she treated you and Jerry when you were picking pecans for her." There many big pecan trees on her property. Anyone who lived or visited Waynesboro had to see her old Southern plantation house. After many years had passed, that old house is so dilapidated, and it still holds some bad memories for those twins.

Figure 38 This is what Mrs. Mammie Russell's house looked like back in the day- not the exact house.

We had to make another trip back to our hometown. Unfortunately, it was for a funeral. God's Angel of Death came with another visit. When driving through town, we passed Mrs. Russell's house. Gloria Jean said, "The house is empty! Stop, I'm going inside. That old dilapidated abandoned house has ghosts from the pass. Wait here, I'll be back in a few minutes." She stayed inside for a few minutes and came out with one of the most beautiful dining room lamps I'd ever seen. It had some strange drapes hanging from the lower rim. She said, "It's mine." Mrs. Russell will never miss it; besides the house is falling. I know she'll enjoy her old lamp; it is so beautiful. Now it was almost time for us to start preparing for the trip back to Albany.

She loves old new jewelry; it's a passion of hers. She would look for antique shops and look for hours. She gave me, her little brother, a sixteen-jewel, fourteen-carat gold pocket watch, with a beautiful gold chain to boot. Now that was unbelievable, and it was all mine. Oh, thank you, big sis. And just like my little sister, Vonda Joyce, Gloria Jean could sing with the best. She could really sing those gospel songs. Sometimes it brought tears to my eyes. The two of them were blessed with a good set of pipes. Besides, I should have listened to her some years ago.

Geraldine and her boyfriend Tommy Joe were still in Waynesboro. He promised he would bring my sister to Albany, but he never did, and we all wondered why. He didn't keep his word to our family. He didn't make the first trip up north because she was pregnant with their first child, but the baby was already born then. It was a baby girl named Sheila, so I'm a brand-new uncle now. I'd lost my mother and gained a niece; my sister would make plans to move to Albany at the first opportunity.

Good news always makes one feel better. Now for the long trip back home to Albany and the chance for my twin brother and I to go to our new school. I hoped we'd do well there, a real high school. Our brother Ervin did well when he went there. In fact, he made the newspaper all the time. He played high school football and had a chance to play with the Boston University football team. But there was a big problem at the time. I will give details later, and you won't believe the story. But now we were back home, preparing for school.

Pastor Jack stayed by our side. As a matter of fact, the last words our mom spoke to Pastor Jack were in her hospital room. She told the pastor, "Please take care of my boys." The promise he made was a true statement. He always checked in on us. By losing our mom, we didn't have anyone to really take care of us because my father moved in with his girlfriend, two months after my mom passed. She was our upstairs neighbor. Pastor Jack had his girls move back into the apartment, so my younger siblings were placed in the different homes of members of the church. My older sister was married by this time.

My younger sister and brother stayed with my other brother Ervin. Edward was the third from the bottom, and he stayed with my older sister Gloria. My twin brother and I stayed with Pastor Jack's son. His name was Sam—that's the name we called him—and his wife was Hellen. They were both really nice folks. They made sure we did our homework and were on time for school. Pastor Jack always had some work for us after school and on weekends. My twin and I had some hard work ahead. All we had to do was study and do our homework.

Remember how our mother always said to us, *"Everything will be all right!"* Those were the last words our mom spoke to us during our time in Hackett Junior High School. We thank you so much, Mom. We miss and love you dearly. Rest in peace.

For now, the rest of our family was spread all over the Albany area—some in Schenectady, others in East Greenbush, but all was well. We were trying to get our life back on track. Life without our mom was devastating. Jerry and I had just started attending our new school, Phillip Schuyler High School.

We had our class schedule, so now it was time to go to work. Though we were still adjusting, we were happy and expected to do very well in our new school. We both passed the placement exams and were told to keep a C average and that we shouldn't have any problems in our classes. Things were looking good for us. We had a job with Pastor Jack and the school was only three city blocks away, so no more long snow days walking through Lincoln Park. We had money for school lunches and school supplies. We took all the mandated subjects. Now it was time to hit the books.

As I said before, we loved going to church on Tuesday and Friday, and twice on Sunday was good for us. There was so much to learn about the life of Christ and his blessing. Not only was Pastor Jack our pastor and working boss, but he was also overly generous to us all. He owned several houses in Albany, and we worked in all of them. There was one on Ash Grove Place, two on Elizabeth Street, three on Alexander Street, and two on Delaware Street. His rent was less expensive than any other landlord's in the area. He taught us how to paint, hang and tape sheetrock, do some plumbing, and do some woodwork. He taught us all he knew.

He didn't want a pickup truck. He drove what they call a station wagon, so now he had a car and a truck all in one. He carried all his tools in it, and it was safe. Sometimes after work, he would be so tired he would park in front of the church and fall asleep. Later I will tell you a story that will blow your mind; working with him was inspiring to me. He used to sing special songs that would bring tears to my eyes and run shivers down my spine. It was real, and I loved it as well. So being in the presence of a man of God really made one think about right and wrong. I loved to be around him when we were working; he would work and pray at the same time.

There's another thing I would like to share with you. Pastor Jack told me two important things. He said, "A person can't build God's house with the Devil's tools." He also told me to take a large piece of wood that's really hard, then take a nail, and hammer the nail into this wood—don't hit it hard; just keep hitting it, and eventually the nail will penetrate the wood. It's true; he showed me that trick. This was a special man. I was so thankful to be in his presence. My big brother and my dad were still working at Joe's Restaurant, so they were doing well in addition to the rest of the family. We were regular members at his church and regular students at our new school.

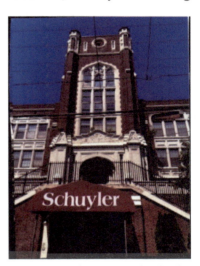

Remember the story I mentioned about my big brother Ervin who played football for Philip Schuyler High School? This didn't go very well with the rules of the church. The same was true for me and my twin brother at the same school. My brother Ervin couldn't believe what was happening; he loved football,

*Figure 39 This is my High School with a Big Heart*

and he was very good at the game. I never saw him play because I was doing school activities like study hall, music, band practice, or just normal everyday classes.

All my brother wanted was to play football. He made the newspaper all the time. He was so good; he played both sides of the game, offense and defense. And to top it off, he got offers from all over. The biggest offer Ervin got was to attend Boston University. From there, he was told he could have had a chance to play for the Dallas Cowboys. I always thought my brother could have been on TV playing football. So now I can feel for my brother Ervin and that big dream he never had that chance to fulfill, and it all started at Philip Schuyler High School.

"Phillip Schuyler, a school with a big heart!" That's our school. In fact, besides my twin and I, I had five other brothers who also attended this great school. Let's start with the youngest brother, Billy Wayne, then Edward Thomas and Dirome Shamon, the twins Jerry Webster and Terry Winfred, Ervin and Alvin. He and I were the only ones who had the opportunity to participate in high school sports. But it was a big letdown for us as athletes in high school; participating in sports was against the church rules during this time. It was viewed as "worldly." If only everyone knew how much we wanted to take part in this great opportunity. This was why I considered this a conflict between our school and church. Pastor Jack was only trying to keep us focused on the church and the creator of heaven and Earth. Ben Becker, the school Principal was concerned about everyone getting a good education. All in all, I'm doing fine in the church, and the school, and I can't be any happier.

In our school systems and our religious beliefs, as they always say, it was all good. It feels so good to be able to sit and write about all the good and not-so-good situations I went through all my life. This will give me strength to focus and carry on. My memories are like a jar of marbles. All the marbles are my memories, all my memories from the Deep South that carried on into the North. As long as the jar isn't broken or taken away from me, then and only then will I have a clear path to the future. That jar filled with marbles is my lifeline and future.

That future was just around the corner, and it would be my turn to walk across that stage with one of the most beautiful smiles you will ever see. From a youngster to a graduate from one of the most well-known schools in New York State, a school with a big heart. That smile would last forever. By then, I hoped to be driving my first car. Then, again, you will see that big smile on my face.

## TWELVE

### The Four P's

What's the significance of the four P's in my memoir? There were four wonderful people in my life. Their mentoring changed the course of my life. The first P stands for my school principal, a man of principles, an outstanding and caring individual, and my mentor.

The second P is for the Champ, the Olympic gold-medal winner in the '60s. He was the greatest of all time, and he was a preacher in the Muslim faith of Islam; Allah is their God. He was one of my greatest inspirations. The third P is for my pastor, a wonderful real man of God as well as my mentor. Finally, the fourth P is for my big brother Alvin, also a man of God and a preacher in the Christian faith. He changed the outlook in my life and for our whole family, from the South to the North, and he was my mentor. Now you know the Four P's. I will not do anything to insult the integrity of my school and church or the hard work of these four men who invested so much time and energy in to securing my future and providing support to my whole family to boot.

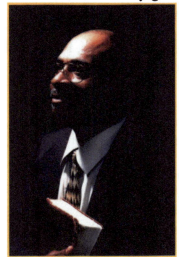

Figure 40 My big brother Alvin Earl Williamson, willing to teach others.

Now, for a recap in my trial sermon at my home church, located on St. Ferry Street and Franklin Street in the downtown area of Albany, New York. I think it's the best church in the downtown area.

The doors of the church were always open to the public. Pastor Jack was a pastor who would reach out to anyone needing help. One thing was for sure, I was so happy I was a member of his church. In fact, my whole family attended his church. There were three main services. Every Tuesday and Friday evening, services started at 7 p.m. and went to 10 p.m. Then on Sunday mornings, there was Sunday school, and next we would have what we called the "Young People Willing to Work" classes. Those would lead to the evening services. Now everyone could take part in a full day of church services, which is good for the heart and soul.

I had good news for everyone, especially my whole family as well as all the church members. Let's not forget our pastor. He'd told me weeks before that he would tell me when my trial sermon was to commence. said, "God is trying to tell you something. Just follow your heart and let God lead you. *Everything will be all right.*" Another déjà vu. Those were the same words our mom told us several times before she passed away, back when we attended Hackett Junior High School, that day we were on our way home to finding out the very sad news. Pastor Jack was a true man of God. It was as if a heavy weight was lifted off my shoulders, and it was all clear what God wanted me to do. Over a period of six months, Pastor Jack told me there would not be a lot of talking, just a lot of watching, and before long, I was in the church service.

I'll never forget this day, on a Friday evening. Pastor Jack was always preaching on Fridays. On this night, he just talked about the scriptures and other things concerning the Bible. Then he just stopped and turned and stared at me. I got nervous, thinking, "Why is he looking at me like that?"

"Here's our brother, Terry Williamson. He will be preaching his trial sermon on this special day." The actual date came later during that month. My heart was beating very fast, and the nerves were shooting all through me. Yes, I was very happy that Pastor Jack believed in me enough that he would let me become one of his young ministers at the Church of God in Christ.

Yes, this was my trial sermon. I'd been waiting for this for a long time. My subject was based on King Nebuchadnezzar. He was one of the greatest kings of the ancient time, during the period of the Babylonian reign out of the second chapter of the Book of Daniel. He thought he was equal to and as powerful as God, the Creator of Heaven and Earth. He had his sculptors construct a statue of himself. They had to make sure it was very tall. It had to be made with the best materials throughout the land, no matter the cost, because he was a very wealthy king and demanded the best: a head of gold, to show his riches; a chest and arms of silver to show his dueling ability; a belly and thighs of bronze, that they will always come in as one of the strongest combinations; legs of iron, which showed his bending and flexibility; and feet of iron and clay. Everyone had to bow down and worship this great statue made by man.

And it was placed in the middle of his kingdom so everyone could see, even from a very far-off distance. He would have his soldiers gather all the people in the same area where the statue was built. Then, he'd demand everyone to kneel and worship him. He didn't know God himself had already placed a prophet in his presence—the great Daniel, one of God's chosen prophets, who could interpret dreams. My sermon's title would be "The Three War Chariots," in which he attacked the holy people in Jerusalem, forcing them to leave their homes, taking their valuable items out of their homes. He just destroyed everything in his path, just to show them he was this great king. This is why I chose this sermon. I was a little nervous at first, but it didn't take long before I settled down. I wanted to do my best for my first time.

The sermon went well. I shared and delivered my message to the people. "Thou shall not put any other God before me." King Nebuchadnezzar at the end knew he couldn't compare himself to the one and only God. Pastor Jack was pleased with my sermon. He said he could see the sincerity on my face, and that pleased him very much. I was so happy that I didn't let him down, for he was a great man and a great teacher to boot.

I was more than happy. "Did you see that big smile?" As the pastor looked at me afterward, he began to speak. "We now have a new minister in our church." Everyone was clapping their hands showing their support. That was the icing on the cake, knowing he was our pastor, and he made all the decisions. My whole family was happy that I alone chose this path. All I had to do now was stay focused on the things at hand, to study hard and read my Bible and its references and always keep a sharp eye, and most of all, to not stop going to the house of God. The church is one place you can stay in close contact with God.

Now, my church and school were so important to me. I knew I must always stay sharp. When I returned to school, I couldn't wait to share my experience with my principal. He was pleased to hear the exciting good news from one of his students, and he was happy I wanted to share it with him. It reminded me of the time he stopped me in front of his office, telling me about the boxing gloves that hung on his wall in his office—a memory I'll never forget. Since I'm talking about my school principal, when he first came to Albany, New York, he was looking for a job as a school principal. His resume was outstanding in the fighting world, but he was looking for a change in careers. Well, it didn't pan out at first. The board of education wanted him as head coach for the varsity football team. That was a surprise to him. They knew he had experience working with younger boys in the past because of his boxing career, and they knew he was good at it as well, one of the best in the boxing industry. That's why he was chosen for the Olympic head coach. And look at what he did for this young boy named the Champ, one of his boxing students. My principal told the board of education that the job he wanted was his dream. He made his decision, knowing he must get his foot in the door first and see how things panned out. My principal took the head coaching football job and did a very good job with the team. But that wasn't his passion.

He wanted to start a co-ed athletic program, not just for boys but young girls as well. They too can become good athletes. He wanted to help build the future of all young people as athletes, and not just athletes, but the whole student body as well. It didn't take long before the facility and staff and the board of education offered him the job as principal of Philip Schuyler High School.

Figure 41 Minister Terry Williamson after my trial sermon

That was the news he'd been hoping for. His heart was filled with joy. And I can imagine how he felt now he had the job he'd been looking for, and it had worked out for him. As stated earlier, the boys and girls attending services at the church couldn't participate in high school athletic programs. Since this rule was passed down from our pastor, majority of the time I had to stay away from the school sporting events. During my studies in school, my main focus was all my classes; they came first.

Again, there were times I do recall going to the auditorium for the pep rally; for me, it was exciting being in the auditorium filled up with my fellow students. It was a mandatory event for all students. Anyone who was not in class or study hall had to attend the school's pep rally event. I didn't have a class that afternoon or study hall, so I made my way to the auditorium for the pep rally. I was part of the student body of this school, so I was going to the pep rally.

Besides, I didn't see any harm in sitting there listening to my fellow students scream and holler for their football team. It gave me the feeling of giving back to my school, because I'd learned and achieved so much there in that great school. It would always be a big part of my life. And I was a big participant

Figure 42 You are looking at the old Church I us to attend corner of Franklin

whenever I could be, and that made me feel so proud and happy. Those wonderful days in the auditorium were always exciting to me, listening to the packed house screaming for their team. They were every Friday afternoon when the football team was gearing up for battle with whoever was their opponent. The football team was called the Falcons. Seeing as I couldn't attend those events, I played my part during school hours at the pep rallies. I think Mr. Becker was more excited than most of the students. He was more like a cheerleader, saying, "Yay! Let's go team!" and he would scream out loud, "Who will win? I said, who will win?" and everyone would scream, "The Falcons!" The screaming came from a packed house.

Of course, Schuyler came on top most of the time. They only lost a few games the whole season. I didn't know much about the basketball team; they had a pep rally as well. After all the noise and screaming, everything got quiet, and Mr. Becker began to look at the student body. Then everyone began to sing our school alma mater song. "Schuyler High to thee we raise our voices loud and strong." This was back in my school days, but maybe one day I will see or hear from someone saying they know or have the words of that song. I knew all the words to that song, but there are so many verses I can't remember.

Now, here's the best news I've had in my life for many years, and I'm so happy to share it with you. I found my yearbook. I've been searching for my yearbook for so many years.

One day I was helping my brother Billy with a job he was working on in East Greenbush, New York, doing some renovation for one of his customers. He asked me if I would like to help with this big job. I said, "No problem, I'm here to help with anything you need. Besides, I'm not working."

One of the sisters from the church had my brother Billy doing some work on her house in Rensselaer. Her name was Mrs. Edna Thompson. We knew her for a very long time, from back when we were little boys. So my brother Billy asked me if I was busy. I said, "I'm not busy, let's go." After arriving, she described the job she needed us to do for her. As Billy gathered his tools, I went over to the area where Edna was sitting. I asked her what school she'd attended; her response was Philip Schuyler. I said, "You got to be kidding me." She said, "No, that's the school I graduated from. Wait here for a minute." She went into the house and came back with two books in her hand.

As she sat there showing me those two yearbooks and the dates on each book, my heart jumped. The date on the book said "Class of 1968." I let out a huge scream. "That's just like my yearbook! I lost mine many years ago and it was never recovered." She began to tell me, "Terry, the book is yours." I hope I didn't hug her too tight. With some hard work, I found the *Times Union* newspaper clipping of what happened that Tuesday afternoon in our school auditorium.

Now I was ready to start writing and preparing my memoir. The rest is history. Thank you so very much, Edna; you changed my whole world. And that's not all she had for me. Her husband Philip Thompson also attended Philip Schuyler high school. He graduated a year or so before she did, and he was a good man. I also knew him at the church. He used to teach the YPWW. I still remember his class from when my twin and I were small boys.

Here's one of the strangest and most wonderful things about him. During his years at Philip Schuyler, he was much older than his fellow students. Everyone knew that Mr. Becker was a very nice and understanding individual. So Philip went to Mr. Becker's office asking him for an unusual request. He felt if it was possible, he could have a sort of private graduation, because he was a man among kids. Mr. Becker knew just what Philip was saying. His response was, "Just leave everything in my hands, and you will be very proud you attended my school." Well, after Philip received his cap and gown, he knew what was next: that promise from his principal. Not only did Mr. Becker keep his word, but he also invited some other very important people to stand there with him: one state and one local person, someone from the entertainment world, and someone from the governor's office. Their names were mentioned, and their faces were well-known. I remember their faces; I've seen the photo. They were all there for Philip Thompson's graduation. If you

*Image goes here: Figure 43 Minister Philip Thompson, Graduation Day*

could see his face . . . Ben Becker kept his word. I knew he was a good man from that day he stopped me in front of his office. I was so happy to be a student at Philip Schuyler High School.

I was talking to some of my classmates about my memoir and how it was all about my school, church, and the Champ, and I told them how I would work, searching for answers for me in my yearbook. For example, my school alma mater song; it was a long time searching for that song.

I was hoping our school alma mater song—which goes like this: "Schuyler High to thee we raise our voices loud and strong"—was in the yearbook. I looked through the entire book and it wasn't to be found. It's a wonderful and inspiring song. I was overexcited with joy, but so far, no luck in finding my alma mater song. I've been looking for it for many years with no success. I also know my alma mater song from my junior high school, William S. Hackett Junior High School; it goes like this: "Oh hail to the Hackett high school with its colors, blue and gold." I'm still looking for both schools' alma mater songs. Maybe one day, I will find the words of both songs, and my journey will be complete, and I can feel the joy and excitement again. For now, I'd concentrate on what was at hand—my schoolwork and all the activities in and around the church. The pastors of the church here in Albany. I volunteered to do things around the church that needed attention, small jobs inside and outside of the church like painting the back wall, sweeping the sidewalk, or cleaning the windows. Anything needed.

Being one of his first young ministers, it was no problem fitting in; keeping the pulpit in order was something I enjoyed. Attending all the church services was part of being a young minister. I told him, "If you need me, I'm here."

I enjoyed it when he asked me to go for a ride with him to pay his bills. He said, "I need you to do the driving for me." That was no problem at all. I replied saying, "Yes, sir." I needed the practice; I only had a driver's permit at the time. For the last several months, Pastor let me practice my driving skills with his car—yes, the big, long, white Fleetwood Cadillac. I studied hard for my written exam, and I nailed it the very first time. I wish everyone could see my smiling face and how I feel about the results. The road test for my driver's license was next. I didn't pass the road test the first time. Remember, I took the test in this big Cadillac. What caused me to fail? It was the parallel parking.

I took it in Albany County the first time, so Pastor Jack took me to Schenectady County for my next appointment. The test was supposed to be much easier, and the streets ran differently. So I made another appointment this time and passed on my second time trying. That was great! I had my driver's license. The pastor said to me, "How do you feel now?" I replied, "Really happy; I'm a licensed driver now." I looked at him with a big smile saying, "What's next?" He said to me, "Let's go and look for your first car."

You didn't have to tell me twice. He said, "I will take you out first thing tomorrow." And that he did. First, he took me to DeNooyer Chevrolet out on Central Avenue. With no success there, Pastor Jack told me he would take me out at the beginning of the next week. It was getting close to Friday evening church services and the weekend. Meanwhile, there was some good news for our family.

Remember my sister Geraldine and her boyfriend, Tommy Joe, from our hometown? They couldn't make the trip the day we were leaving for Albany, but they would come years later, I couldn't wait to see my next oldest sister. They were married now, Geraldine and Tommy Joe Huntley, and their family was growing fast.

It had been a while since my twin and I had seen him. We both missed Tommy Joe with all his strange rituals and ways, like Tarzan or a cowboy. My sister and Tommy Joe had a baby girl. Her name was Shelia Huntley, and she was the spitting image of her dad. My older sister, Gloria Jean, would help her to find a place to stay here in Albany. For now, she would stay with my big sister, Gloria Jean.

Back at school, my favorite teacher Mrs. Miles stopped me in the hallway. She wanted to know if I was interested in volunteering for the Cerebral Palsy Telethon Drive. This program happened for one week there at our school. The Cerebral Palsy Telethon Drive was for the needy kids in the capital district area. They were looking for volunteers. I didn't think twice about it; I went straight to the office and signed up.

There was a good crowd of students there, all willing to help. They gave us some special canisters. I took two of them; I wanted to do a good job. They told me what to do and where to go for donations. After the instructions, it was time to hit the streets. We had one week to raise as much money as we could. We started from school at Trinity Place and Ash Grove Place and we went to North Pearl Street then to Livingston Avenue. There were two students in a group, and we made fun out of it as well. Within that week, I carried two canisters the whole time.

I raised just close to $68 over five days. Some days were slower than others. We did a lot of walking through the neighborhood, hitting all the stores and businesses of all kinds. It was a good success. Not bad for a schoolboy on a special day. Nothing is better than giving back to a worthy cause for all those wonderful kids. Now we were looking good for our school, and I felt great with the outcome and with everything that took place. I'm not sure of the total amount raised, but it was way over ten thousand dollars for that whole week.

Mr. Ben Becker was pleased with the large crowd of students who came out to volunteer for the drive. Thank you, Mrs. Mills, for asking me to volunteer for a worthy cause here at our school. I was looking forward to the same drive the next year.

Pastor Jack reminded me it was time to look for my first car. He asked me if I was ready. With a big smile on my face, I said, "Yes, sir." I began looking for my first car; I was not sure what kind of car. I had to see how things panned out at the next car lot.

This was our second trip looking for a car for me. This time, Pastor Jack took me to North Albany. Again, I was excited looking for the right car. In Menands, New York, on Broadway, we found this small car lot. It only had about twelve cars on it. There was this small black car that caught my eye from a distance, I said to the pastor, "Over there; I see it." I got out and went straight to this black 1961 Ford Falcon, a two-door sedan. If only you could see the smile on my face, and as an added bonus, the price was low—only two hundred fifty dollars, with tax and license and registration. That made me very happy. I was filled with joy. And I can say it was a very sharp car in my eyes, and my first. My car was jet black; in the photo the same car is beige.

Well, there was a small setback: my car was a standard shift, and the gear shift bar was in the steering wheel. Most standard shifting vehicles have their gear shift on the floor. I always wanted to drive a standard shift vehicle, but this one would be a challenge for me. I bought the car. It was mine and I drove it home. It was a stop-and-go process, but I did manage somehow to make it back to the house.

It didn't take me very long to learn how to handle the standard gear shifting in the steering wheel; in fact, it was a ton of fun, and now I'm a pro driver. Now there would be no more long, cold walks back and forth to and from school. No more slipping and sliding going to the store. I did have some friends at my school. I was not sure if I wanted to drive them around as a favor much. They didn't see and believe in the same principles and spirituality as I did, especially knowing right from wrong. Now when the church went on trips, I'd be able to drive my own car. It was a good feeling too.

Now I had my own transportation while still attending school. My father didn't have a driver's license, so now I could take him to places he wanted to go. He didn't work at Joe's Restaurant anymore. So there were now two car owners in our family. My big brother owned the first car in the family. He was working at another restaurant, and my father was working at the Inn Town Motel, next to the Greyhound Bus Terminal in Albany, New York. My dad got me and my twin brother a job there as dishwashers. After we filled out the working papers at the State Education Department, we were legally able to work.

Washing dishes wasn't a bad job, but those large stock pots were very hard to clean. We came up with a name for this job. We called it "busting suds." I liked the sound of that. We were both able to work. They had us work mostly on the weekends, and sometimes during the week. Working there, we never had to worry about something to eat. We were told to work, and when it came time to eat, we could have anything that was on the menu. To top that off, we were allowed to take the leftovers home if we wanted to, if there was some kind of big party or a wedding.

At the same time, Pastor Jack also had us work for him. I talked about the number of houses he owned in the downtown area; he was keeping the promise he made to our mom. Besides, we loved to work for him. He was one special person, and Pastor Jack, the pastor of our church. Again, if our mom could see her favorite two little bad boys . . . well, you know what I'm trying to say.

This was the first time us twins worked without our dad. Now that was a strange feeling. Well, at least he was not behind a horse and a plow. I was so pleased that our family was doing well. As I mentioned before, we owed it all to our big brother and the pastor. It was in God's plan. After work and supper, it would be time for church services, another part of my life I would continue to do. Remember what Pastor Jack said to me and Jerry before: "We can't build God's house with the Devil's tools." Now I could really see what he was talking about.

This was a good job for my dad. He'd come a very long way from sharecropping work back home. I knew that made him feel good, no more sunup to sundown work. This job would provide him with security for the family. And in doing so, he could now save money too. He had always been a hard worker.

Now we had two cars for anyone in my family who needed a ride. Well, it was time for school to put our noses to the grindstone and work hard for the best grades ever. I mean, way above a C average.

The secretary of our school said over the intercom, "I have some good news for everyone." Then Ben Becker took over the intercom, saying, "May I have everyone's attention. We are having a special guest come to our school in two weeks, no other than the light heavyweight boxing champion and gold medal winner at the 1960 Olympic Games in Rome, Italy—the one and only, the Champ!" I think the building shook from the roar of the student body. Can you imagine the excitement in the hallways and up and down the stairs? This would stay with me for a very long time. Again, could someone please pinch me? Now this was the greatest news ever, more exciting than my first trip to Albany, New York, and even more exciting than those football pep rallies in our auditorium just a week before. This was good news, and it would be so exciting to see him. I couldn't wait for those two weeks to arrive, and I could imagine the faculty and staff were feeling the same excitement in our school. This was going to be something great.

Until that day came, I would study hard in all of my classes and continue going to church and doing what was in God's plans for me—being a young new minister. I had to be always watchful. Pastor Jack told me his door was always open, no matter what situation arose. And he told me the most important thing I must do was read the Bible all the time, and it would pay off in due time, and not to forget to use the Bible references as a guide. The last thing he told me was, "Don't be afraid to pray a lot."

That's why I carried my Bible to school every day and was very proud to show my fellow students who and what I was all about. Yes, many times, my fellow students asked why I carried my Bible to school. I told them it was my way to reach my fellow students. I was trying to make a difference in someone's life. I was not the only one; my twin brother did the same things in life. Whether it was school or church, it was business at hand. One thing was for sure: I was not ashamed to let my fellow students and the faculty and staff and anyone in this school know that I was a Christian and a child of God. My principal knew all about me and my twin brother at his school. I always wanted to be someone and do something special in my school. Back then I didn't know what it was, but I felt it would happen for me there at my school.

My oh my, it was getting closer to the time when the Champ would visit our school. For the last week, all the students there at school had been in a strange mood. There was excitement in the air. Both the faculty and staff shared the same excitement about his visit. They were all talking with expectation. The one person who really knew the Champ was the one and only principal, Mr. Ben Becker.

This would be a historical event here at our school. Remember, it was a school with a big heart. One thing was for certain: I never had a chance to see him fight live. That was okay; it's fine. But on stage, a live event is unreal. I hope everyone felt the same way as I did.

People all around were talking about how good he was as a fighter. The word was out, and everyone knew he was trying to make the Olympic light heavyweight boxing team. At the time, there were three coaches, including Mr. Ben Becker. He was the head coach of the team. The other two coaches I had only seen in newspapers or on TV, but I still remembered their face.

Back then, we watched the fight on a black-and-white TV set. The room was packed wall to wall as the fight went into the later rounds. The fight was no contest at all. There was no need to watch and wait for the score card; we all knew the Champ would win the match.

This was the best fight I'd seen of him ever. It was special, and he wanted to bring the gold medal back to the United States of America, and with pride to boot. All my friends were screaming and yelling for him to win, and that he did in style, winning the Light Heavyweight Championship and the gold medal in that exciting contest. His whole life changed in an instant; everyone would know him now.

I couldn't wait for that day to come. All my fellow students were also excited. They too couldn't wait to see the Champ. Mr. Ben Becker and the faculty and staff were excited as well. This would be a very special day. I was so excited for my church and my school. I felt good about the way my life was turning out. I considered myself blessed.

It was Tuesday; the big day was finally here. I and all my fellow students at my school were ready. This would be a big part of history in the making. I went to my first-period class with a ton of nervousness. Then I got ready for my second-period class, and everyone got quiet and nervous. We could all feel the excitement in the air throughout the whole school. I was on my way up the stairs to my next class when the whole school got the announcement at the very beginning of second period. The announcement came from our principal, over the intercom: "Everyone, please assemble in the auditorium in an orderly manner." In my mind, I was trying to figure out what he would look like in real life, since seeing him on TV and in the newspaper was routine.

I asked myself what I was going to do or how I would react at the sight of him, and why I was getting so nervous. I had no idea at all. My afternoon class was on the second floor, so I didn't have far to go to the auditorium. It was between the first and second floors, and it was a large auditorium with a spacious balcony. I knew I had to rush through the crowd to find a good seat. I'd had good practice, as I had done the same in those pep rallies many times, rushing to find a good seat. I didn't think the teachers would mind if I ran through the halls; it was for a good cause. The light heavyweight gold medal champion was in the building. To me this was a lifetime event, not only for me, but also all my fellow students here at Philip Schuyler High School. I wondered what Ben Becker and the Champ were talking about at this time. Teacher and student finally meet again. There were three doors leading into the auditorium. It was always packed when we had our pep rallies for all our sporting events.

At this very moment, it was very crowded and loud throughout the hallways leading to the auditorium. Our special guest had arrived, and the atmosphere was filled with excitement throughout the building. I rushed through the crowd, looking for the best seat, something close to the stage if possible. The strangest thing occurred on my way through the crowd, heading to the auditorium. There were these two guys in the crowd, dressed in black suits and ties. They stopped me and began to tell me that today there would be some mashing and gnashing of teeth in the darkness.

I said, "What did you say?" He repeated it. I didn't know what he meant, or what he was trying to tell me. I had no idea why they stopped me in a packed crowd of students, faculty, and staff. I didn't understand what that statement meant. Besides, I was in a big hurry at the time, looking for a good seat. I didn't pay attention to what he was talking about. I replied, saying, "Wow, that's good to know." Then off I went to find a good seat. In the back of my mind, I kept thinking it was strange what he'd said to me.

I looked to my left and to my right for a good seat, then I looked up to the balcony, but that was out of the question. I spotted one seat near the front, so off I went over there. I found the perfect seat. Imagine finding a seat in the middle rows; this had to be the biggest blessing even outside the church, and it was the first seat in the third row. To top it off, it was in the middle aisle. It couldn't get any better than that.

I'd been waiting for this day for two weeks; this was my special day. I was happy beyond belief, thinking, "Maybe I should check my pulse. Someone please pinch me!" I was about to see my first real worldwide star ever in the sporting world. I was blessed to be in the presence of this magnificent individual who I admired wholeheartedly. He would always have my respect. I couldn't imagine how the rest of the student body felt.

I believe the faculty and staff must have felt the excitement in the air as well. The balcony was packed to the max; in fact, there was standing room only. The noise from the crowd was one sound I will never forget. It was almost as loud as the sports pep rallies in our auditorium before all the football games—all part of life as a high school student at Philip Schuyler High School. As I sat there gazing through the crowd, I was not able to control my feelings and emotions.

I looked to see who was on the stage. Well, our guest of honor, of course, the one and only the Champ, prize fighter, the light heavyweight champion, and a gold medal winner in the 1960 Olympic games in Rome, Italy. I watched that fight; as he always said in all his fights, "I'm pretty," and again the crowd went crazy with laughter and friendly gestures as well. It was exciting to see that. Next on stage was my principal, Mr. Ben Becker Next, the assistant principal Mr. Hunt and other members of the faculty and staff, about nine in all, sat on this large stage. Standing in front of the stage was the photography crew from the *Times Union* newspaper with the sports editor and chief. All photos were taken by the camera crew; I can still see the flashing from the cameras, flashing across the stage as if it was yesterday. I made eye contact with the Champ, he sat on the stage, and I took advantage of it. I still couldn't control all the nerves running through my body. This was another reason I wished my twin brother was still there at Philip Schuyler High School. I know he would have felt the same as I did. But I wasn't worried; he'd be coming back soon.

There was so much we had to do and share since he'd been gone. Mainly anything to do with the church and its duties. There was so much work to be done with Pastor Jack and the church marching band. I was excited it would be time to start practicing again. One thing was for sure: I would always be ready. Just bring it on. I was so excited. The whole school would be rocking, screaming, and yelling. The atmosphere would be filled with jamming students cheering, hands clapping, and the noise from the hardwood floors, especially in the balcony, Mr. Ben Becker always got the students revved up for the big game against, Albany High School. They were our rivals out of all the schools in the district, we came out the winner nearly 90 percent of the time. So the noise on this Tuesday afternoon would far exceed the pep rally sounds of excitement.

I was glad I went to church because it wasn't luck; I believe it came from the creator. I'm thankful for that. Now I had a bird's eye view of the stage, straight ahead. The auditorium was packed like sardines, and the stage itself was a little crowded.

There, the Champ, in person. I couldn't believe my eyes; please, someone pinch me.

The *Times Union* newspaper crew worked the front of the stage. There were still students trying to find a seat. It was a little unsettled at the time. They were waiting for the news crew to finish setting up their equipment, The *Times Union* sports editor was prepared with pen in hand, ready to write and copy all the important words spoken that afternoon. The photographer was there. He had at least four cameras hanging around his neck.

Then things began to settle down some. There were several spotlights about, as if it was a movie onstage. I was so happy they were in the building on this Tuesday afternoon. Otherwise, I would be in study hall or my typing class at that time, or on my way home from school. Mr. Ben Becker took the podium with a loud round of applause and a standing ovation. It was a day I'll never forget, with those goose bumps on my arms and running down my neck again. The Champ looked good up there. Mr. Ben Becker began to talk about the youngster from Louisville, Kentucky, That day was an exciting event for me as a young student, This would stay with me forever. Ben Becker talked with the Champ, telling him he was one of his best friends ever. The Champ looked around the auditorium and at the packed crowd in the balcony and all those who sat in the main aisles, I could see the joy and excitement in his eyes. As Ben Becker had mentioned before, the Champ was the greatest young man this country would ever know, and his gloves would back him up.

That was great, and I was in the perfect seat. I made eye contact with the Champ, I knew he'd had to see me several times at that point. I hoped he didn't think I was just staring; it was more than that. It was unbelievable. It was all I could do. He kept looking in my direction, which gave me the feeling of being overwhelmed with admiration and joy. Ben Becker walked to the back of the stage and the crowd got quiet. He came back with this big box, and all this time the crowd was wondering what he was doing. Suspicion filled the auditorium. What was going on in their minds, wondering what was in that big box he was carrying?

Out of this box, he pulled two sets of bright-red boxing gloves. Those were the same boxing gloves Mr. Ben Becker had shown me years earlier when I'd attended the school for the first time. The crowd saw them and started screaming and yelling, I could hear someone in the crowd yelling out "The fight is on!" to the point that everyone had to cover their ears. You could see flashes from the film crew's cameras as they moved around the stage. The news crew was just as excited, preparing to document every single moment.

Mr. Ben Becker reached in the box and gave the Champ his set of gloves, and the Champ started to put them on. Mr. Ben Becker grabbed the other set and did the same. After they both had their gloves on, standing there looking at each other, they both had some of the biggest smiles ever. Again, the crowd exploded with cheers and oohs and aahs as they were just standing there, face-to-face, with their gloves raised high. All that was missing was the sound of the bell. The strangest thing was that I could imagine that sound; it happened in all the fights. But there wasn't a sound to be heard—until the first punch was thrown.

Mr. Ben Becker threw the first punch, and the Champ weaved and blocked it then threw a left hook and a right jab. At the same time, he was dancing and smiling, and he kept saying, "I'm beautiful." The whole crowd went crazy, screaming and laughing. To see the Champ on stage with his quick feet was something special to see. It was unreal to the naked eye and another thing to see it live on stage. I never knew he could move so fast. Here, live on stage after everyone had been seated, the faculty and staff were enjoying it as much as we all were.

The Champ again had time to say, "I'm not ugly, I'm beautiful." That made the crowd scream with laughter, and they continued throwing blows. For a while, all I could see was the flashes coming from all the cameras. Everyone onstage was having a blast. Mr. Ben Becker and the Champ made it look so real.

I do admit, the two of them gave the crowd a really good show. All the time I could see the big smiles on their faces, looking at each other as if it were real. I had no idea it would affect me years later in life. One thing was for sure: this I could share with my own kids. And I'm so proud to be part of history, made here in our own school in a packed auditorium that Tuesday afternoon, and I had the best seat in the house and the best eye contact with one of the greatest, most world-famous people.

Yes, I know he kept on saying, "I'm pretty," and he said "I'm the greatest" to boot. To sit and talk with a person with that kind of status . . . the Champ, you are the best. And thanks for visiting our school. Philip Schuyler High School would now be a first-class historical site. And guess what— Terry W. Williamson was in the mix of it all because the world light heavyweight champion shadowboxed on the stage in our school, and everyone was so enthused. It was fantastic.

Those two bests friends enjoyed the boxing event of a lifetime. It was amazing and breathtaking as well, and it will be part of my memories forever. The excitement was so hard to explain. After the shadowboxing section was finished, Ben Becker put the boxing gloves back into the box and placed them on the back of the stage.

They walked back with a nice smile and gave each other a long, big hug. It could have lasted forever. That showed the love and gratitude and most of all the respect that they shared with each other for so many years. I witnessed every precious moment. Our principal was happy and excited. The student body and the faculty and staff Everyone stood up with a standing ovation. Mr. Ben Becker said, "Here's the one and only light heavyweight champion and gold medalist of the 1960 Olympics in Rome, Italy, and a great Muslim minister." The Champ stood there while Ben Becker continued to talk about him and his fights. I couldn't stop the chills from running all through me. I will always cherish this moment.

Mr. Ben Becker went on to say how he first met the Champ as a young boy and knew from the first sight that he would be something special in the boxing world. He also talked about how he was a very hard worker and how training was one of the Champ's strong points. Back when he was younger, he was a little shy somewhat; he talked very little, but that changed as he got older as a fighter. Ben. Becker was proud to be his coach for so many years. After he finished talking about the life of the Champ, and how proud he was of him, Ben Becker gave the floor to the Champ. He too received a very large welcome and a standing ovation. It seemed to last forever. The Champ stood there looking at the crowd from side to side.

His first words were, "I'm here in living color." The crowd exploded with laughter and cheers. I was so glad the Champ was in a very good mood. I could see the joy on his face, with a big smile. As he looked at the student body and all the faculty and staff, we were all excited. I could feel all the exhilaration throughout the building. Ben Becker himself had a hard time trying to stop laughing afterward. Then the Champ began to speak: "You must let the people know who you are as Negroes."

Well, I didn't expect to hear that kind of statement, but I did understand what he meant, seeing as we were both from the South and how the white man treated us as Black folks. Then the Champ went on to say, "I must tell all Black American Negroes: it's not about the white man's name. If your name is Khrushchev, people would know you are Russian; if your name was Ching Po, they would know you are Chinese, and if your name was Running Water or Chief Thunder Cloud, people would know you were an Indian, or if your name was Running Deer, they would know you are Indian. But when your name is a slave name, like Williamson, Jones, the Champ, Washington . . . the people don't know who you are as a Negro. This is why I'm here as a Black person, and the minority must do this—let the people know who we are. A proud Negro here in America."

This took me back to my hometown. My brother Alvin Earl and the Champ were one of a kind. They didn't let the white man push them around, that's for sure. Then he went on to say, "The reason I'm here is to give a message to all the Black boys in this auditorium. Don't be satisfied with your last name. It's a white man's name, passed down through past generations, and it must change." He also mentioned it was for all Negroes. But his focus was mainly on young Black boys. He talked about how he changed his religion to the Muslim faith and how he changed his name as well, and how Allah was his God.

"Allah" means "most high," and "Muhammad" means "worthy of all praise; the prophet and leader who they follow."

Ben Becker was the one who gave the Champ the permission to speak about anything he wanted, The Champ talked about the Muslim faith, and he focused on the Black boys in our school. I can recall here in this area how before the

Champ came to our school, we used to see many Black boys dressed in suits and ties, trying to get boys and girls to join the Muslim faith. They used to be on the street corner of St. Pearl Street and Ash Grove Place. I used to see them on my way home from church. They stopped me many times, trying to convince me to join the Muslim faith.

I told them I attended the church down the street, and I told them I was a minister at that church. My faith was different from their faith. I went on to say, "I believe in the one and only God, the creator of heaven and Earth. And Jesus Christ is the one and only son of God." Well, they wanted to stand there and try to debate with me about Allah, their God. They knew I was a strong-believing minister, and they couldn't change my mind. They stopped and headed the other way. At least they were faithful in what they believed in, and so was I as a young minster.

Now I understand why the Champ was speaking to the Black boys only at our school that Tuesday afternoon. He mentioned in his speech that day that he was planning a tour of the United States to educate the Negro people and to teach them how, what, and when he began to believe in the Muslim faith. He found the biggest crowd in our school auditorium that day. After a long speech to the crowd, he welcomed everyone to his next mass meeting. He really wanted the young Black boys, but all were welcome. It was to be held at the Ten Eyck Hotel, located on the corner of State Street and Chapel Street in Albany, New York.

When my family first came to Albany, as a little boy going to school at Hackett, School #15, Giffen, and, of course, Philip Schuyler High School, I passed by this hotel many times. Being a Christian, I couldn't participate in the Champ's mass meeting at the Ten Eyck, but I did hear it was a very large crowd of people. The one and only newspaper the *Times Union* covered this special event, and it was one of the biggest in American history at the time. I'm proud to have been part of it.

Now I can spend my days reminiscing about that fine memory. I'm one who appreciates the school systems and the education department for providing a momentous, special event at our school.

## THIRTEEN

## Schools and Education

Now back to school and all its classes and homework. I'm proud to say I was holding the recommended C average, and my classes and assignments were getting much easier. By graduation, it would be a C+ or better, with some extra class homework and long study halls. This may sound crazy, but I enjoyed walking the halls and climbing the stairs during the period changes. It gave me a sense of belonging to something greater than myself.

I wish I could personally shake hands with all of my teachers for their hard work throughout the years. Imagine if my twin and I were still at Hackett Junior High School. They were the ones who said we didn't have the skills to be placed in the mainstream classes during our time there. This is why I'm so happy about all that happened at Philip Schuyler High School. Everything will continue to reach new heights. After graduation, I was looking for higher education, like the Adirondack Community College, a two-year program with a certificate in commercial cooking. And by the way, I was accepted and made the college tennis team. I was the number three seeded on our tennis team, and we played several schools, like Herkimer College and Siena College, which were private schools, and the Hudson Community College. We won the nationals! Not bad for a kid from off the streets and self-taught. I didn't realize the sky was the limit.

I earned my associate degree in culinary arts at Johnson and Wales University. Remember the old saying, a mind is a terrible thing to waste? This was my main focus. For now, I'm waiting to hear the change-of-class bell.

It was time to get back to work. I was asked by my favorite teacher, Mrs. Mills, if I was interested in doing some volunteer work at the Schuyler Mansion. I would do anything she asked of me; she was the greatest teacher of all time. I could talk about her for days. I was to meet with her the next day before study hall. We didn't have to drive; Schuyler Mansion was only two blocks away from our school. This would be a short walk for all who wanted to volunteer that day. I was excited for this opportunity. Anything to keep me busy and focused on my education. Besides, if one looked at my school records, they would see I was one who gave back.

When something needed to be done, I was the one. She told me there was so much I could do there and around our school. Mrs. Mills told me, "There's always things to do at school, and there will be more opportunities in the near future." And she went on to say, "Remember what Mr. Ben Becker told all his students: Our school is a school with a big heart." Now that's a statement I will cherish and keep in my heart for a lifetime.

It was that time of the year again; Mrs. Mills asked me if I was going to volunteer for the Cerebral Palsy Fundraiser this year. I told her, "You don't have to worry about me." I was ready; she could depend on me for anything that came up. She posted the signs for more volunteers. The last year, I was one of the first ones to volunteer, and I collected close to $87. I would try to break my old record. One hundred dollars was a lot of money during this time; all those long walks door to door paid off. This would make a big impact on this year's Cerebral Palsy Fundraiser. It would begin tomorrow at our school. It would be a very big success for the little ones.

It's good to give back, because the rewards pay off in the end. Mrs. Mills told all the volunteers to meet at my principal's office for further instruction. After his small speech, we were all ready to hit the streets. This year, I took two canisters. I wanted to break last year's record. We went off down Trinity Place to Madison Avenue, store to store and house to house. There were two students taking part together. We talked all about raising the most for the whole week. It took us all the way to Livingston Avenue and back to the school. Both of my canisters were filled to the max—yes, no more room. That made me happy.

And I broke last year's record with over $100, and I was happy I was able to volunteer for the little children who were in need. There was a great turnout in the auditorium for the final countdown. All the volunteers, Mrs. Mills, and Mr. Ben Becker were very happy for the new record. The turnout was a record crowd as well. Now it was time to get back to my classes for the rest of the week. I was still on track; I wanted to make an impact there in my school, all the way to my graduation day. Like Mrs. Mills said, "There is always something to do here at our school." Now I understand the importance of school and church in my life currently. The same went for my twin brother. We received our course schedule, and we were excited to get started.

All the classes that were mandatory were complete—math, history, science, English, and gym. The extra classes gave us extra credit, like shop, pre-law, and art. So when we took our gym classes, it was a ton of fun. I made sure I did my best, looking for a good grade. My plan was to outdo all the other classmates. I noticed that at the end of all the exercises our teacher had us stop for the big run. Philip Schuyler High School didn't have a traditional track-and-field facility; there was no track and no football or soccer field.

So we had to run around the school, and not just the school, but the whole entire city block, which included that run out of the gym. We all ran down the stairs out of the gym through the basement, out to that tall black steel gate. We ran through that gate and onto the sidewalk. The first street was Trinity Place. We ran down Trinity Place close to the police station, made a right turn onto Arch Street, and ran up Arch Street to the corner. Then we ran up the hill on Grand Street and made another right turn on Ash Grove Place.

Then we ran downhill on Ash Grove Place to Trinity Place, took another right turn back on Trinity Place, then ran through the black gate and back inside the building to the gym. To me this was a challenge, as I was a runner. My plan was to always return to the gym in the first place, no matter what the cost.

This caught my gym teacher's eye. Mr. Emera told me, "Terry, you are very fast, and I had my eye on you for a long time. I want you to join my track team. This would put our team in a higher bracket in the district." That was good news, but I knew the answer already. I told him I couldn't join the track team. He said, "I don't understand why!"

"I must follow the rules of the church. I'm a member of the church here in Albany. We as Christians can't take part in school athletic sports. It's not part of the church rules and regulations, and we must abide by the church doctrine. By doing so, it makes one a strong church member."

Running was something I enjoyed doing, but I wasn't allowed to take part in school sports. In fact, this rule was mandatory for all the young boys and girls at the church. He responded, saying, "This don't sound kosher. I'll have a talk with your Pastor Jack soon." He said to me, "Where is your church?" I told him it was located on St. Ferry Street and Franklin Street. I was so happy he was concerned and wanted to help. He told me, "Don't worry; I'll see what I can do. You were given this talent for a reason."

I waited for weeks, but I never heard anything about the situation again. He told me this had to be handled by the principal, so we waited for an answer from him. He told me he didn't like it, but he had to respect the rules of the church. That was all I had to say about the situation, so it was swept under the rug. The church rules stopped me from doing something I really wanted to do as a senior student in high school.

I enjoyed running so much. One thing was for sure: going to my gym classes was part of the school curriculum and grading systems, so I continued my gym class through the years. This rule wasn't just for me, it was for all the boys and girls from the church. This was the same problem my big brother Ervin had to face when he attended Philip Schuyler High School, so now I understood what my brother was talking about earlier and what he was going through as a high school athlete and a young boy growing up in this new city. He was a very good athlete and one of the best in high school football. In fact, he played both sides of the ball, both offense and defense. I wished I had a chance to see him play. I was either busy with church services or making my way home from school. His name made the *Times Union* newspaper all the time. In the downtown area, he was the talk of the town, and he was good.

Ervin was offered a scholarship to play for Boston University. That was one step from the professional football rankings. I can see him now, with that big smile on his face. And he would tell everyone he missed the big opportunity to play in higher-ranking football. I can only imagine what was going through his mind and heart. It was so sad he had to turn it down because of the church rules; that hurt him both mentally and physically. It hurt so bad. He couldn't believe what was happening to a natural athlete.

Today he will not talk about it, not at all. On the other hand, he watches the game of football all the time. He said that was a long time ago, and he's trying to put it all in the past. I didn't have the opportunity like he did. I knew I was fast, and I loved to run. I ran all the time across the park, from school to home. It was so easy to me. Besides, I enjoyed it so much I could have made something out of it if the opportunity had come my way. Like my brother, it's a thing of the past. I wasn't in a position to be offered a scholarship. To become one of the Philip Schuyler High School track-and-field team members was just a dream for me.

But the rules were for all boys and girls who attended the church. For example, all the girls had to wear dresses and skirts below their knees, low-cut shoes, no jewelry, no open blouses, no open-toed shoes, and no makeup.

Gym class was part of the marking systems, so I continued to do my best in my classes—all of them. Mrs. Mills, my history teacher, was the greatest teacher I ever had. Everyone at some time always had their favorite teacher. She really knew how to get the attention of her students; she always got mine. She helped me in so many situations during my school days. I could go to her for anything that bothered me, from school and away from school. She was a beautiful, kind lady.

Driver's education class, which was offered for extra credit, really paid off, and it would have a big impact on my insurance now that I had my own vehicle. That discount would be a large help; I could use it. So I passed my driver's class, and it all panned out for me. The next thing was adding the insurance for that big break.

Mrs. Mills also asked me if I would like to volunteer for a special project coming up. I said yes. The first one was doing cleanup work at the Schuyler Mansion, this beautiful historical building site on this large hill on the corner of the two major streets here in the city of Albany, New York. Both streets were named after his family. They selected his wife's name, Catherine, so Catherine runs east and west. As you can see, it runs uphill from left to right.

The other street, Schuyler Street, they named after the lieutenant general, a military soldier. There was another street called Clinton Street, which was adjacent to Catherine Street and Schuyler Street. Schuyler Street runs north and south, parallel to South Pearl Street. I was happy to go on another volunteer trip with my favorite teacher and fellow students. Besides, this would look good on my school records.

We all met in the auditorium just before study hall. It was about twelve of my fellow students, along with Mrs. Mills. We didn't need a car, because the Schuyler Mansion was only two and a half blocks away.

So off we went to do some volunteer work at the Schuyler Mansion. Now for the long walk ascending the forty-five steps to that great building. We all were met by the caretaker of the property, who stopped Mrs. Mills in front of the building. They talked for a few minutes, then Mrs. Mills said, "Okay, everyone. Let's get to work." She divided us into three groups. We all did some cleaning around the grounds of this historic Schuyler Mansion site. Some of the students did some cleaning inside the building. All in all, everyone was happy with the outcome. It was a ton of fun for the students, helping with some very important work.

I have some very important information I would like to share with you. I enjoyed myself doing volunteer work at the historical Schuyler Mansion during my four years at Phillip Schuyler High School. To my surprise, those years were filled with happiness and sadness, because it had been a very long time that I had been away from this area. The other day, I was driving down State Street, heading in the direction of South Pearl Street. In the past, I'd taken this route many times, but this time it was different for me.

When I was driving, City Hall appeared to me, and it looked as if it were in the middle of State Street. That caught my eye. The closer I got to the building, I observed a statue, and I never remembered seeing it when I'd lived here years ago. So I stopped, parked my vehicle, and walked over to the statue. I found out one of the most astonishing and unbelievable pieces of information I had ever come upon in my life. I couldn't believe what I was reading and seeing. It was a statue of Major General Philip Schuyler. I found this out months after I'd started my memoir. My first thoughts were that I must go over to the state archives for additional information on Major General Philip Schuyler. What I found out was shocking and outrageous. I began to wonder if this Philip Schuyler, the general, was the same man my school, Philip Schuyler High School, was named after. Further in my research, I found out my school was originally called School #14 back in the 1930s. I began to think that all those days, walking to and from my home to school, my school wasn't Philip Schuyler High School. I was walking on my way to the Howe Library to work on my memoir, and I passed by my school every day. I'd never thought about looking up to the top of building. This day, I took it upon myself to look to the very top of the building, and to my surprise, there on top, I saw the words and numbers, "School #14." It was amazing to me. I went to this school for four years, and I always called it and knew it as Philip Schuyler High School.

Back to the archives for more information. Now here comes the shocking news. My school was named after a slave owner, and he also participated in slave trading as well, right here in Albany and other major cities close by. I attended this school for four years. At the end of those four years, I graduated from this great school. Back in those days, Philip Schuyler High School was well-known in the downtown area.

During the time of the Revolutionary War, the Major General was a war hero. They gave him special recognition as a general and changed the name of our school from School #14 to Philip Schuyler High School. This was a military decoration for an American icon. This took me back to the visit from the Champ that Tuesday afternoon when he came to our school. I wonder if he knew the school was named after a slave owner and slave trader? We all knew the Champ wasn't defeated with that kind of nonsense during his lifetime in Louisville, Kentucky.

There are so many people in America who don't know the background of General Philip Schuyler. I always thought slavery was only in the Deep South states. It was hard to believe it could be here in the Northern states, especially here in New York State. That huge building that sat on the top of this big hill was the home of General Philip Schuyler and his family. Most people don't know that the other building to the left of the main building, that smaller building, was the sleeping quarters for the slaves that worked for the general.

Now the two buildings are a part of history. I believe anyone who condones slavery shouldn't be allowed to accept any type of educational or military honors. All this was shocking and disappointing news to me. Now, today, it's in all the news how the people in the inner city of Albany want this statue removed from the City Hall building.

From what I heard and read, the mayor of Albany is trying to find resources to have the statue removed from in front of City Hall, and there are other organizations looking for this statue to be removed. They are trying to locate a company with the capabilities to remove it. It was said the statue was very heavy, made with bronze, concrete, and other metals. This ordeal was disturbing to me. Now my school alma mater was dampened. I used to enjoy singing the song, "Schuyler High to thee we raise our voices loud and strong." It's just not fitting anymore. I wonder who wrote this song, and if they knew the real significance of this song.

Now there are so many questions and very few answers. One day I will find all the words of this song. Then it will come full circle; I will still sing my school alma mater song. It's part of my life. Philip Schuyler was an American hero, and he deserves some recognition, but we must not condone slavery. Let's leave it in the past. The slave trade here in America was wrong and we must keep it in the forgotten past somehow. Today, there's another problem; it's all over the television and newspapers. Black is beautiful, yes, it's in most major cities here in America. There are kids, juniors, and adults trying to make an impact in the community.

They all should have the chance to live more fruitfully. Yes, we know the white man still has the upper hand on just about everything in all cities here in America. We as Blacks must not be ugly against each other and not be quick to judge others, both Blacks and whites.

"Black Lives Matter." Everywhere I go, I see or hear those words. The Champ himself tried to make a difference. It may or may not have made a successful impact. Now, people from all over are struggling, not only in America but the whole world. I personally don't believe it will ever change, and that's the way things are.

It will continue through the world. I'm so proud to say I made an impact in my school. People like my fellow students, the staff, and the faculty know how much I accomplished there at Philip Schuyler High School. I often wonder if everyone understands the meaning of "Black is beautiful." We should all make sure the words "Black Lives Matter" are something that will benefit us all as Black Americans.

Now I will continue to talk about my school. My favorite teacher Mrs. Mills asked me if I wanted to do some volunteer work at the Schuyler Mansion. Well, that struck a nerve in me; I would do anything for her. It didn't take me long. I was happy to help. Volunteering at the mansion was fun for me at the time. I didn't know about what went on back in the Revolutionary War days. Mrs. Mills had to know the history behind the school and Schuyler Mansion. For some reason, we didn't go near the other building. It was used for the slaves back during the Revolutionary War.

We did all we could, and it was time to go back to the school. Mrs. Mills said, "Okay everyone, it's time to head back. It was a good day cleaning the yard of the Schuyler Mansion." This was something I'd never forget. I did my volunteer work and was happy altogether. But Black people are still struggling.

My school principal, I will cherish what you have done for me through the years there at Philip Schuyler High School. The class of 1968 was a special and unforgettable year for me and my fellow students. Now it was time to go out in the world and experience all it had to offer. I had to remain steadfast and make good decisions and stay focused.

I'll never forget my school as "it's a school with a big heart." Let us not forget, today people are still crying "Black is beautiful." How many really know the real meaning of that statement? We as a people must strive for better success and be willing to work hard together. This is the only way to keep peace among us all.

I know Mrs. Mills would be very happy for those who volunteered that summer day. The next project was the Cherry Hill historical site on South Pearl Street in Albany. It was basically the same volunteer group from the Schuyler Mansion site. This time we needed a car, so the school had a van and a driver. Again, we met in the auditorium and headed out to the sidewalk where the van was waiting. We all climbed in and headed for the Cherry Hill historical site.

It was a short drive down South Pearl Street, just before the overpass. We were all there and ready to go to work. Mrs. Mills said, "Okay, everyone, let's get to work." We started taking care of the grounds in and around the site. There was so much I would have done with this lady. She was super, the best teacher of all time in my book. Thank you so much, Mrs. Mills. You are the greatest.

Here is another project I'm glad to share with you—again, more good news coming from Mrs. Mills. She said to me, "Terry, would you like to be a crossing guard for the school?" I jumped for joy. "Yes, yes!" I could remember back when my twin and I first came to Albany, we didn't understand why some of the kids wore those strange belts on their shoulders. Later, we learned it was for outstanding students who did special things in and around school. One thing was for sure: that belt looked good on them, with those bright shining colors. I also thought they were for police. Now, here in my own school, I had a chance to become one, to become a high school crossing guard with my special crossing guard vest and belt. I felt like a cop on the street. Everyone was nice to me as I stood there at the crosswalk, telling all my fellow classmate when and how to cross the street. Things went smoothly during the morning and the closing of classes at the end of the day. Now everyone can see why Mrs. Mills is so special to me, and if one could see that smile, she carried on her face, one would agree.

Out of all the classes I'd taken, history was my favorite. Mrs. Mills put so much into her instruction to the students in class. There was an announcement over the intercom, a message from my principal saying to all students and faculty, "Mrs. Mills is leaving our school." That was a quick turn of an unforeseeable event, and I couldn't believe what I'd just heard. Everything stopped suddenly and the emotion just took over me. I couldn't stop the tears from flowing down my face. I went to the office and asked Mr. Ben Becker if I could take the afternoon off because I was in no shape to finish the rest of my classes. He told me not to worry; she wasn't leaving until the end of year, so I would make the best of it—she is the greatest.

He knew how close Mrs. Mills and I were, together in everything we did both in and out of school and all those volunteer trips to different places. Everyone knew Mrs. Mills in our school. She was involved in so many programs. I remembered a few years ago, she'd invited me to her home. I had no idea she lived so close to our school. It was off South Pearl Street on the corner of Second Avenue. She always kept that pretty smile on her face. I will always remember all the different things she taught me throughout my school years.

I would truly miss her, and may God continue to bless her. She would finish the rest of the school year, and then it would be time to say a final good-bye to my favorite teacher, the great Mrs. Mills. There would never be another teacher to take her place. The closest person would be my principal—my principal and a man of principle. These two academic individuals were the ones who kept me on track in my education and future. I was so very happy my principal accepted us to attend his school. Everything really turned out great for us. I would continue to strive and do my best throughout the year and be one of the outstanding students in his school.

One afternoon, I was on my way to class. I was walking down the hall in front of my principal's office. He stopped me for a minute, and I thought there was something wrong. He said to me, "Young man, I see you come to school every day dressed in a suit and tie." I replied, saying, "Yes sir, me and my brother dress this way all the time."

I liked to dress my best there at my school and at my church. He replied, "Keep up the good work. By doing so, it's good for the rest of my students here at Philip Schuyler."

He began to tell me about his philosophy at Philip Schuyler High School. He told me, "Once in a while there are some of my students who think they are bad. I know how to deal with them; most of them don't dress like you and your brother." He said they dressed like ones from on the streets.

I said, "Thank you very much."

"Come with me to my office," my principal said. "I have something to show you."

The assistant principal looked at me as if I was in some kind of trouble. The office secretary and everyone in the office looked. So I followed Ben Becker into his office, and what did I observe? Of all things, it was a set of red boxing gloves. In fact, it was two pairs of them. Those were the same gloves him and the Champ used for shadowboxing earlier on. He said, "I don't use a rod or stick. I'm the disciplinarian here in my school. In cases like this, I'll take him or whoever down to the gym and give them the gloves. This is how I keep discipline in my school." I was so impressed to see what he was talking about. Now that's a good man; he always had my respect and attention.

At my school there were so many activities during and after classes. I did all I could to stay busy because soon it would be time for all the final grades for the year. Also, that big day, graduation, was just around the corner as well. So, I was taking part in all that was given to me and my fellow classmates. I will always have the greatest respect for all my teachers in every class and same for my principal.

## FOURTEEN

### The St. John's Nazarites

Another great man in my life is Pastor Jack. I give the upmost respect to my pastor. Everyone in our family was doing well. My twin and I were staying with Sam J., the son of the pastor. He was the one who helped his father drive south to bring us to Albany. So, Sam and his wife, Helan, were keeping me and my twin in line. I guess you know what two little boys can get into after losing their mother; we were still devastated. Well, we were not bad little boys. Helan and Sam spent a lot of time helping us with our homework. They were one of the nicest couples I'd ever met. In fact, all the people in the church were very good people.

All they wanted from us was to follow the rules of their house. They were very nice. I'm so glad they took us in. After losing our mother in that horrible car accident, my older brother Alvin was still devastated. He was driving the car when it all happened. The whole family was still trying to adjust, especially my younger sister and brother, Vonda and Billy. Sam and Helan were helping us to adjust to the church and the school and all they had to offer. Pastor Jack was pleased that we became members of his church. It had been a while since we joined. I felt good about the church.

We joined the choir. It's so nice to learn different things from other people. I'm proud to be a first tenor. Yes, I have a set of pipes, and I love to sing those spiritual songs. My twin is a second tenor, and he also has a set of pipes. Even to this day, I still love to hear him hit those wonderful notes. Everyone was so nice there at the church. The church members all welcomed us with open arms because they knew what all of us were going through—a new family in a brand-new city with all its brand-new surroundings. This was something we all had to get used to.

Pastor Jack said he had some work for us. Things were getting better all the time. We would be working in one of his houses. I couldn't wait for my first job, but first he had to see us work and learn hands on. Pastor Jack was trying to teach us all he could as young boys. Remember the promise he made to our mother, that he would take care of her boys? Now that we were willing and ready, it would be a regular day-to-day job after school. I took driver's education and started saving for my first car, no matter how long it took. Everything was looking good dealing with and around the church.

At this time, I would like to share a beautiful message with you about my pastor. Remember, the pastor was telling me about his dreams. The first dream was to own his first church. It took a while, but it finally came true. Now he owned two churches. As I said before, the one on Green Street was his second one. His first church was located on 7 Duncan Avenue, and now he owned the one on St. Ferry Street and Franklin Street. This was the church we attended all the time. That part of his dream was reality, and I knew he was very proud of how it all came together.

I was proud to be one of his many members, and I believe he knew that. I'm proud he kept my mother's wishes as he stood by her bedside. The other dream he told me about was so exciting. I really wanted to see it come true. God gave him this dream and a vision. He wanted him to search around and find someone who could tell him how to start a marching band. He searched for a while until he found this guy named Mike. He was a young white man who lived in Troy, New York. Mike played for one of the largest drum and bugle corps in the country. Pastor Jack invited him to the church, and he gathered all the young boys who were interested in learning how to play the drums and march.

It was a large group of boys who attended his church. I can see and hear Pastor Jack talking to all the boys. Mike was a professional drummer, and he would teach all of us how to play, and it wasn't cheap. It cost Pastor Jack a lot to hire him, but remember, God gave him this vision and this dream, and they would come true. So Mike introduced himself to all the boys as a group, telling us where he was from and how long he'd been living in the area. He began to tell us how he played in competitions all throughout different parts of the country and how he started at a young age. All he did was practice seven days a week until he became a first-class drummer, and people were looking for him to play in their drum corps. He also said it would take some very hard discipline to become a good drum player.

For me and my twin, this was right up our alley. We were adventurous boys from the South. I think I was more excited than anyone there. This was something I could do for a long time, and I would try to be the best.

Mike was so impressive to me. I knew I wanted to be just like him. He began to show us how to hold the drumsticks, and he told us the snare drummer holds the drumstick different from the tenor drummer. He began to play right off the bat. I knew this was something I was willing to learn. Everyone was stunned with amazement. I said, "Wow, that's unbelievable to see and hear. I can and will do this." He had everyone play a special beat, which would determine who would play the snare drum. The others would play the tenor drum, the bass drum, or the cymbals. I knew at that point I wanted to play the snare drum. It had the most beautiful sound, and it was hard to believe.

I was the one who practiced five days a week until I was the best. At some point, we all had to meet at the church, day in and day out, to practice the drums on the large table in the basement. I still had time to go to school and do all that was required for all my classes.

Now I was so excited for my school and church, even though there were still some misunderstandings concerning school sporting events and the rules of the church. At this point, I would try my best to do all I could to please both organizations: my school and my church. Both were so important to me and my future.

I think you will enjoy this statement: During the school lunch break, I would run down to the church, rush into the basement on the corner of South Ferry Street and Franklin Street, take out my drumsticks, and practice for twenty minutes, then run back to school in time for my other classes. I did this every day, and it was so much fun. I told Mike, and he was impressed. Mike was my mentor and hero when it came to playing the drums. Meanwhile, Pastor Jack was in the process of buying a whole drum set—I mean, a brand-new set. The name of the drum set was Ludwig.

The drum set included four snare drums, four tenor drums, two bass tom-tom drums, two sets of cymbals, and one bass drum, the largest of them all. This was a complete set, and it was all we needed to start playing and marching. Meanwhile, there were approximately twenty-five girls practicing for the majorettes. The pastor's dream was becoming a reality at last. Pastor Jack called all the members of the band. "I have good news. I will be ordering uniforms for all the marching band, uniforms for the boys and uniforms for the majorettes." It would take a few weeks before the order would be delivered to the church.

"I'll let everyone know when that day comes." He also talked about the color of the uniforms. He chose black and gold; that was part of his dream. So he had everyone line up to be measured for his or her uniform. I knew this was going to be out of this world. Everyone would have a complete uniform set, including boots or shoes. Of course, Pastor Jack had some help from Mike making that order for the uniforms. The big question for Pastor Jack was, "What was the purpose of this marching band?" It was his way to reach out and connect with the public and to all the young people in general in the downtown area and beyond.

The pastor's message was about God, and he was told by God to search and find people who wanted to know him, the Creator of Heaven and Earth. Remember the statement I mentioned earlier? Pastor Jack gave me two parables. He told me, "You can't build God's house with the Devil's tools." The second parable he told me about—he said take a large piece of wood that's very hard, then take a nail and hammer and start hitting the nail, not very hard, just softly. "Take your time and eventually the nail will penetrate through the wood," he said. He also gave an example; the parable was true. So now I understood what Pastor Jack was trying to say to the people. Make the right choice by choosing Jesus Christ.

I was blessed to have a job and was doing well in school. I was really excited about the things around the church. Things were turning out very well. One day as I passed through the hallway, there was a sign on the bulletin board that caught my eye. The band teacher, my music teacher, was looking for people to sign up for the school band. Boy, was I excited. If you could have felt my chest . . . My heart was racing so fast. What? They wanted me to be part of the band? That was unbelievable, and I was so excited.

The good news, just what I needed to hear in my school. Things were coming full circle. During study hall, I made my way to the music room. There, I talked with the music teacher. He introduced himself, and I told him my name and said I was interested in playing percussion in the musical band. I'd been doing this for some time now. There were other students there as well. He asked me if I had any experience playing the drums in a school band atmosphere. I said, "No, but it can't be that hard, and it shouldn't take me that long to learn." Besides, I thought I was pretty good as well. I'd played the drum for our church marching band and the drum set in the church services for a long time now.

Me and my twin brother had some experience and were willing to work hard and learn what it took to be in the best band. I know our mom would have been proud of us, being her favorites, those twins. We still miss her so much.

He said, "I can use you. Are you ready?"

Again, I replied, "Yes, sir."

He gave me my schedule and some music. "I'll see you in music class next week."

That was just what I needed: another big smile on my face. So now I was part of the high school band. I'd be playing the snare drum, the kettle drum, the tenor drum, and a set of cymbals. I practiced several times every day if it didn't interfere with my studies, or I practiced after school if necessary.

Can you imagine how I was feeling at that time and moment? But when there's good news, somehow bad news isn't too far away. One of our family members was talking about moving to Detroit, Michigan. It was my twin brother. Us twins shared and had all kinds of adventures through our lives. It was like trying to pull apart a closed fist into an open hand. Yes, there were some tears and some sadness that led to some uncomfortable feelings. As twins, we'd never been apart in our whole entire lives until now. This was an emotion only my twin brother could share; it was so real and at the same time it seemed like a dream to me. But on the inside, I knew something good would come out this move Detroit,

I had to respect my twin's decision. He had a dream of his own, and he got my support. Besides, it gave me a place to visit later. Our big brother Alvin had moved there some time ago, and he could help Jerry find a job at one of the auto plants there. My twin and I were talking about this for some time. There were several plants in the Detroit area. Alvin worked at Chrysler, Ford, Cadillic, and GM companies all over the metropolitan area, and Jerry wouldn't have to worry about a place to stay. Alvin had a big house, and he had plenty of room. I was told Detroit, Michigan, was a big and fast city. One day, I would have that chance to be with my twin brother again. Who knows—there might be more adventures for us. It's been wild.

But my twin would be coming back to Albany when the band started marching on the streets. Meanwhile, the uniforms for the boys and girls arrived. The colors were black and gold. The boys had black pants with a white stripe running down the leg and a loose-fitting golden shirt with a black collar as well as a billed hat with a plume on top and white patent leather shiny shoes. The girls, or majorettes, all wore pleated skirts with alternating gold and black stripes, loose-fitting blouses with a black collar, and white boots with white tassels. They didn't wear hats but carried silver batons. You had to see it with your own eyes; they were super sharp. Now the band was playing well, so the girls and the boys all practiced together as a unit. Yes, we were ready for the streets. We would practice as a group, and this would be the first time. The boys were ready, and the girls were ready; this would make us a real solid marching band ready for competition.

Remember, practice makes perfect! I would practice extra hard because it was exciting to me. I carried my drumsticks with me all the time, just like carrying my Bible and schoolbooks on my way to school. We used to practice the drum solos so long and hard. It was a beautiful sound. Pastor Jack used to sit down in his favorite chair, lay back, close his eyes, and listen to the sound of the drums. He loved to hear the different songs we performed, because this was one of his biggest dreams. This one really came full circle.

I loved him for his hard work. We gave Mike a well-deserved party for all the hard work he put in for the church's interests and for every boy who was willing to listen to his instruction. This was the beginning of a brand-new drum corp. I admit, it was a lot of hard work at first. We practiced five days a week and sometimes on the weekend. Pastor Jack told Mike to teach us at least six drum solos; this would give us enough space in between songs. Marching on the street, we needed many songs.

*Image goes here: Figure 49 The Nazarites are ready, competition.*

Mike taught us several marching songs. We had to march twelve or fourteen city blocks. That's because we needed that many drum solos. It seemed a little hard at first, but as time passed, we got used to the music. It became second nature. Well, at least for me. I worked extra hard. I wanted to be the best, so I put it in overdrive. I was ecstatic to be part of something so important. I had big thoughts; I wanted to take it to another level. Maybe one day I'd be playing in an international marching drum and bugle corps—one day soon. Mike told us we had to be ready for the competition. We were a very competitive young marching band.

Pastor Jack would be very happy to see what he'd started in a dream: his own marching drum corp. My oh my, how time passed. We were ready to give our best. Again, thank you, Mike, for all the help. Some wonderful news was that my twin brother, Jerry, was back in town just in time for our big march on the streets. It seemed as though he was gone for a long time. You know how twins are—they are always into something. Adventure was a part of our lives. That gave us all the excitement we needed. Those bothersome twins . . . Well, you know what I really mean. Those twins were church-going. God was looking over us, and we would carry this through to its fullest.

Jerry had returned back from Detroit; in fact, in the photo you can see on the right side is Ervin, and in the middle row those twins—I'm not sure which one is Terry or Jerry. If our mother were still here, she could tell the difference between those twins. And now our band was complete. Everyone showed up. We were looking good as a brand-new marching band. Our first big competition was here in Albany, New York. This I'll never forget—the parade started at the Armory building, that brown building on the corner of State Street and Lark Street. Each marching group got in formation and ready to perform. We all marched and played our best marching down State Street. It was shocking to see hundreds of people standing and cheering us on as we passed by.

Making a left-hand turn onto North Pearl Street, the mayor was sitting there looking and having a good time. I'm not sure of the count; there were so many different marching bands in the parade. I wish it was on camera. We were the only Black marching band in the competition. The competition ended at the Palace Theater. People were there from all over the state. Everyone was screaming and cheering for us; what a wonderful feeling. Could you imagine how Pastor Jack must have felt, seeing what he'd constructed from a dream and a vision from God?

Now the other marching band in the area would know who we were by our name. We were called the St. John's Nazarite. It fit well because it was a biblical word. All the hard work paid off, and everyone was happy. We started marching in different cities like Troy, Utica, Poughkeepsie, and all around New York. We were invited to play in New York City for this very large church. After getting there, Pastor Jack hadn't gotten the permit to march on the street, so they had us march inside the church. It was one of the most beautiful sights you'd ever seen, and the crowd went bonkers. In case you are interested in playing marching band music, you have to learn the twenty-six American Standard Rudiments. I still practice and play the drums today with the same skills. I was the leader of our band. All my hard work paid off for me there at our church thanks to Mike, our leader. In fact, that was how I was accepted into the high school band. Later on, during the year, my principal was excited to see how I played the drums. He told me, "Practice hard and long. It will pay off in the long run, and you will love it."

That was good news to my ears. Now it was time for our school concert, which was a long time in waiting for the band. Again, I was excited. This time I'd be playing in front of my family, friends, the whole student body, faculty, and staff, and most importantly, my principal, who will always be my mentor in my life.

The auditorium was filled with people from the outside. I could see all my classmates milling about, looking for a good seat. Now that the crowd had settled down, it was time for the commencement of the band. My music teacher had composed his own songs and music. He was one person who really loved music; one should see his music room. All along the walls were pictures of classical and conventional music, jazz, and some rock, and last but not least, orchestral music. He was a music lover at heart. He is someone who eats, sleeps, and breathes music. I could see it on his face when he was walking through the hallways.

My music teacher always wore a suit during classes, but when it was an onstage performance, he always wore a special tuxedo suit. He was a special music teacher and loved his work. What caught my eye was that he could play every instrument performed on stage. He wasn't the best drummer by far; he knew who were his number one drum-playing students in percussion. I was the best drummer he had in class. He always asked me to stay and go over some music with him. He had me practice all the percussion instruments: the tenor drum, snare drum, kettle drum, and Timpani drum. He knew I was his best student. I could play all the songs he composed, and the music list was long. This took me back to Pastor Jack and Mike from Troy, New York. They were the reason I studied and practiced so hard during and before class.

Mr. Ben Becker saw this in me. That's why he told me to practice. It would pay off—and it did. So I was the number one player, both in my class and at the church. I would carry this with me the rest of my life. I would be passing it on to my own boys. Drums are a nice form of music to play. My music teacher called me over to the side of stage with this cool look in his eyes.

He said, "This could be your big chance to shine as a drummer. Come with me."

We walked to the back of the stage. "Terry, can you play a solo song for me?"

I replied, "Yes, sir."

Was there someone who could pinch me? This made me feel so happy with a big smile on my face. My music teacher showed me the song list that was used during the year.

He said to me, "Just pick the one you like the most."

I had to pick one song before the band got started. I chose the song, "The Downfall of Paris." That was an exciting-sounding song, with so much rhythm. I started to choose one of the other songs. It was called "The Three Taps," but "The Downfall of Paris" was my choice. In fact, it was my favorite song.

Was I nervous? That's an understatement. It was something I couldn't control; the adrenalin was through the roof, filling so much excitement at same time. "The Downfall of Paris" was the best song of them all. The song was based on a battlefield where soldiers lost their lives, then all you could hear in the background was that victory song, played repeatedly for the victors of that great campaign. That was part of the reason I loved that song so much, and one thing was for sure—it would be a big part of my life. This song was so special to me as a drum player. It had so many different rudiments involved. There are twenty-six Standard American Rudiments, and I know them all. Our band played halfway through the concert, then I was instructed to walk to the edge of the stage, and all eyes were on me. I didn't panic, nor did I get flustered. I was ready.

I could see all of my fellow classmates showing their anticipation. I said to myself, "This is what I've been waiting for." With a quick look around the auditorium, I could see the faculty and staff's eyes in the distance as well. The brightness from the spotlight put me in the best mood. I was ready to play my best. I played and made the song as beautiful a piece of art as I could. After I finished, I gave a semi-bow, looking up at the crowd. It was the first time in my life that I got a standing ovation from a packed house. It was awesome and breathtaking throughout the auditorium. I'm not sure, but they may have also screamed "Bravo, bravo!" as well. It made me feel warm inside to see all the eyes from my fellow students on me for a short time. I'll never forget that moment; it brought tears to my eyes. After that, I was ready to play anywhere, anytime. Now it was time to join the rest of the band to make more music. If I wasn't working so hard on my memoir, I would stop and play another drum solo for you right now. "The Downfall of Paris" is my favorite song.

While I'm on the subject of songs, here are the names of the drum songs from the church marching band. The first drum solo was called "Jerry's," the second drum solo was called "Malachi," the third drum solo was called "Number One," the fourth drum solo was called "Number Two," and the fifth drum solo was called "Stick Beat." I still carry my drumsticks with me all the time; they are always close by. I wish somehow I could play for you. I think you would enjoy it. It would bring music to your ears, and that would make you smile. I enjoyed teaching others as well, especially the younger group. It was like giving back.

The concert was a big success, and everyone had a good time. I had to make my way to find my music teacher. He was very excited for the whole band, and he congratulated me on my drum solo. I gave him a big smile and he said, "Great job, Terry," and I said thanks. Next, standing next to the crowd, I said, "Where is my principal?" Over there by the stage, standing in the front row aisle.

I made my way over to where he was standing, I waited for the first chance to talk with him. He too complimented me on my performance. Now, that really made my day. Can you see me now, with the biggest smile from ear to ear? We all had a few cookies and some soft drinks, then everybody went their separate ways. All students had to be back in class on Monday morning. It was time to hit the books again. Our next gig would be the winter concert, which included the Skylarks singing chorus. I couldn't wait to hear them sing. I used to watch them practice after school sometimes; they were very good.

I would like to share another school activity with you before I move on to the church and the choir. One day in history class, I was wondering why the Skylarks were so special to our school. They performed in other schools as well and sang around the capital district all the time. They would be performing at our senior graduation ceremony that year. They had perfect harmony; I thought they sang just like angels myself.

My favorite teacher Mrs. Mills kept looking at me during history class. When class was over, she came up to me, telling me, "I would like you to try the typing class." It would give me two extra class credits. I said, "Yes, that will be great. I like working with machines." She was the greatest teacher ever. She said I could use that skill later in life. She was right so far in all the things she taught me. So I took the typing class. I loved a face-to-face challenge in class.

The typing class would be mostly girls, but anyone could type, making another skill for myself. It would pay dividends later in life. There were three types of typewriters: the Royal, the Underwood, and the Remington. I chose the Remington because it looked better. It looked hard at first, but I stayed with it until I began to understand the process and how to move my fingers. Once I learned this phrase, "It is the duty of all good men to work for jury pay," it was so much easier for me.

Before long, I was typing. I had fun with my typing, and the rest was history. My fastest speed was sixty-five words per minute—not bad for a beginner. So today, as I write my memoir, it did pay off for me. In my classroom, taking a class that gave us extra credit, I was willing to try something new.

In the pre-law class, I was chosen as the student teacher. My smile went from ear to ear. I was so happy to be recognized and chosen from my own classmates. So, as student teacher, I played the part of honorable judge. I picked one student to be a defense attorney and another student to be the prosecutor's attorney. A third student was the person on trial. Let's not forget the stenographer; this person would keep track of all records and activities during the court proceedings.

*Image goes here: Figure 51 My first*

Both attorneys began their arguments, and it was a blast, a day to remember. I did mention I wanted other fellow students in my school to know I was trying to do something special. I will remember it throughout my lifetime. I had conversations with my principal in the hallway that day, and he complimented me on my attire. I dressed my best in school each day. That was something my twin and I accomplished all throughout school. If we were setting an example, it was fine with us. My principal gave me his approval in the way we dressed, saying, "Keep up the good work."

I gave my response, saying, "Thank you. My principal, you are the greatest, and I will keep in mind what you are telling me."

So off upstairs to my next class, then study hall, and after that, it would be time to go home for the day. I sat there going over my homework and other work for the school. The rest of the time I would study my Bible before leaving for home. The whole school got an announcement over the intercom for the second time that day. My principal said, "We have some bad news concerning one of our well-known teachers, Mrs. Mills. She will be leaving us soon." I didn't know about the rest of my fellow students, but it was going to be very hard on me. She was the best.

Now she would see and hear all about one of her favorite students, Terry Williamson, a student she would hopefully not forget as well as the whole faculty and staff.

I have been talking about all the good and exciting things in my school for a while now. I must not forget another wonderful teacher, my art teacher. She was the art teacher for my twin and me, and she loved her job. She was not originally from the States; she was from a small country town in Swaziland. She spoke several different languages as well; I thought that was so neat. She reminded me of the women in Iceland. My art teacher was a fine art teacher, and she showed it in her work. She could draw, paint, sculpt—she could do it all. I thought she was so special. She taught me and my twin the finer things of art. She said, "The students don't make the art; the art makes the students." I didn't understand it at the time, but I learned later on during the art classes. The art class was on the very top of the school—I mean, the very top. It was like walking up into the attic. We had to walk on some long boards in order to get to class, and it was worth the trip. There were between seven and nine students in the class.

I think some of the students were there just to pass the time. I took the class because I wanted to see what I could accomplish, and it was the same for my brother. We both loved the art class; it was a ton of fun. My art teacher would stand and watch all the students, making sure they were on the right track. One day, one of the students put a thumbtack on her chair, and that didn't make her so happy, though she wasn't hurt from the tack. She asked the class who put the thumbtack on her chair. Well, there was no answer, and the class got quiet. One student said, "Maybe it fell off your desk." She said, "I don't think so, and it didn't fall off the bulletin board." I think someone wasn't very nice that day. She said, "I'm fine. Back to work, class."

I learned the finer things of art. My drawing and sketching improved, and my painting was doing fine, but sculpting just took off like a rocket. I loved working with the clay. First, the clay had to be kneaded to make different forms and shapes. After the shape had a good form, it was time to put the sculpture in the oven. My sculpture was an antelope. It had to be left in the oven overnight at a special temperature.

The next day, what a beautiful, silky-gray color it was. The painting was the last step. It gave the sculpture a very shiny glow. So all my art skills came from another wonderful lady, my teacher. I'm proud to have been one of her students. She really taught from her heart in a great school. In my school, there were my two favorite lady teachers and two men—my history teacher, my art teacher, my gym teacher, and, of course, my principal, a man of principle. All my art, music, and other subjects really made and shaped my future. Philip Schuyler High School was a school with a big heart, and I will never forget that statement.

Another great man was my pastor. Anyone who lived in the city of Albany, uptown or downtown, had to hear about the pastor, a.k.a Brother Jack, a man with a big heart. The people were Pastor Jack business, like the old saying, "The shirt off his back fit him very well."

I always called him "the pastor." If someone was looking for an apartment, they would look for the pastor. His rent was the lowest in the city. All his houses were in the downtown South End area. If you couldn't find him for an apartment, you could ask anyone on the streets, and if you needed him for anything, any type of religious concerns, he was always there. He was a great leader for mankind in all walks of life, and everyone was welcome to his church. By the way, it was the church in the downtown Albany, New York, area.

At South Ferry Street and Franklin Street, things were looking good for me again at school. I passed the driver's education class; it was a breeze. There were many students who didn't go as far as others. I took it in stride and made fun of it all. Pastor Jack took me to the DMV so I could get my learner's permit. I was still saving for my own car one day, since my big brother moved to Detroit, Michigan, and my father couldn't drive a car. He was still working at the In-Town Motel on Broadway next to the bus station. He worked hard every day, and at church he began singing again. He stopped for a while when my mother passed. It was good he was back singing again. Singing had been part of his life as long as I could remember. He was thinking about forming a group again. We must see how that panned out. At the church, the choir was going out of town to sing that weekend. Yes, I was in the choir. Like my dad, I loved to sing. For a long time, I'd been having these dreams that I was preaching in the church. I didn't tell anyone, but it happened over and over sometimes. I would wake up with tears in my eyes, and it happened to me all the time. I went to church all the time and I tried to be the nicest person possible and treat everyone with respect. I just wanted to do the right thing in my life, and I wasn't afraid of trying something brand new.

The dreams continued. Pastor Jack had always told me that if I had any kind of problem to come and see him. That was just what I needed: someone who knew God for a long time. He was my pastor. I was just a sheep, and he was my shepherd. Before I went home from school, I would go straight to the church and tell him all about my dreams. I ran down to the church—the door was always open—and when I saw him, this cool feeling came over me. I had tears in my eyes. "Terry, what is going on?" I sat down and told him about my dreams.

He took me into his office, and we sat down, and I began to tell him about all the dreams I'd been having. They were always the same dreams. It made me a little scared because I didn't know what to do. It happened mostly at bedtime when I was asleep, and I would wake up in a cold sweat and in tears. Pastor Jack said, "Don't worry; everything will be all right." Déjà vu. These were the same words my mom told me and my twin when we had all that trouble in school and classroom at Hackett Junior High School, the day we got home to find bad news.

The weekend was near, and the band would have a sample practice of the drum music. We would practice and play in front of the church on South Ferry Street and Franklin Street most of the day. It would likely bring a big crowd of people. They had to start getting used to the music around there. Pastor Jack would also have the girl's majorette team practice their routine. They could practice their marching on the streets. It would be a free show for all to see and hear.

This would get us ready to start playing and marching in other towns and cities. Now the bigger drum corps would begin to see the progress we made as a young marching band. Mike would be proud of us, and Pastor Jack as well. We all thanked him so much for his time and patience. Mike was a special guy, soft-spoken, and I gave him respect for all members of the church and the marching band.

At some point, we thought he would become a member of the church. Mike had been in competition for many years. He was a master at drums and drum solos. I could stand there and listen to him play the snare drum for hours. He was a competitive drum player and was willing to share his knowledge with all the young boys from the church. His fees were reasonable, but Pastor Jack paid much more than he was asking for.

We were a group of happy boys. If you could see the look on the pastor's face, you'd know he was proud of his brand-new marching band, a dream and a vision that came to him from God. Pastor Jack made some phone calls. The first church group that contacted him was a church in New York City. They wanted both the majorettes and the marching band to appear at their church in Manhattan. We had some time before we started marching. There was time to go for a short walk on the streets of Manhattan. We were told, "Don't go too far, and don't get lost." We all returned with a few items and some souvenirs from the big city.

Pastor Jack got us ready for the march. This would be our first official march. We all wanted Mike to make the trip with the band, so he told us to have fun and *break a leg.* I hope you know about that saying! We made the trip and were all ready for the big performance. But there was a slight problem; the church couldn't get a permit to march on the street. That was disappointing for the band. Pastor Jack couldn't believe what happened.

So Pastor Jack of the church said, "Let the band march inside the church," and that's what we did. We played the drums inside the church, down each aisle, and the people were enjoying the sound of the band's music. The majorettes performed their routine as well. With all those beautiful uniforms, we looked good. So the pastor's band was a great success for the very first time. I felt like I was on TV in front of a big crowd of church people. Now for us, the sky was the limit.

Let's go back a bit. Pastor Jack did the same thing as the Champ. They had the same type of path; they both went out to recruit men and woman, especially the young boys and girls, for the purpose of having new members to join their church organization. The Champ did the same, but in a different way, and for different reasons. The Champ was recruiting Black boys to become Muslim. As you know, that's what I had to deal with in my school that Tuesday afternoon. The pastor was recruiting for the Christian faith.

For now, I would continue to focus on my schoolwork and on that big day when I had to walk across the stage for that special rolled-up piece of paper with a white ribbon around it. Yes, my graduation. Now everyone was happy for the band, and it was time to load up for the trip back to Albany. You know I had to share our success with one of my favorite people, Mr. Ben Becker, my principal. He did what he always did and told me, "Don't stop playing your music. It will pay off."

I was so happy he was concerned and that he took time out of his busy schedule to give me some solid advice. What could one high school boy do to make himself a good student at Philip Schuyler? I didn't have to do very much; I had everything I needed right there in front of me. I would continue to study and work hard for good grades, which would make a brighter future for me. I was so proud to be a student at Philip Schuyler High School.

Like Mr. Ben Becker said to me, our school was a school with a big heart. I truly love that mantra, and it will stay with me the rest of my life. Pastor Jack also had a mantra: "One can't build God's house with the Devil's tools." Two powerful mantras I will carry with me all my days. My school and church both had done so much for me throughout the last four years. I was so happy to be part of it all. Thank you, Mr. Ben Becker, and thank you, pastor, for your hard work.

There was more good news for our family. In a few weeks, it would be time for our senior Snow Ball. They had been having this celebration for a long time. The Skylarks would be performing as well. This was something every senior would have to experience. It only happened once in a lifetime. Being a member of the church, I wouldn't be able to attend my senior Snowball with all the rest of my fellow senior classmates. This was something I would hold close to my heart forever, this special lifetime experience that would never happen. I called it a loss of a great opportunities in my life. There were photos in my yearbook. It was good, but it only brings sad memories. That was part of all seniors' lives before graduation. I would not be able to take part in this special event. Now it was up to my own sons to take part in that special presentation. I do remember seeing two of my fellow students who also didn't attend the prom night. We all were in church. Even that is just a memory. The church was all so important to us as well.

As I walked down the halls of my school, I could hear the Skylarks practicing, and they sounded good. They were practicing for the senior prom night. Can you imagine how a senior in high school who wouldn't be able to take part in their high school prom feels? Yes, prom night was the other event I didn't attend, because of my Christian beliefs. Thank goodness for photos in my yearbook; I would have those memories to share with my own boys. That's enough sad news; it's time for good news! It was graduation time—now that's good news.

Well, I didn't know how and what to expect for this huge event in my life. There was an announcement over the intercom from my principal's office: "All seniors, please assemble in the auditorium for a meeting concerning graduation." After the meeting, we were given all the caps and gowns. That really put me in a strange and sad mood. I would be among the hundreds of my fellow students getting ready for that big day on which our lives would change forever. They called it a walk. Yes, I would walk across the stage with one of the biggest smiles one could imagine.

*I Graduated from the Strand Theater uptown Albany of North pearl street.*

Once I received that special paper with that ribbon wrapped around it, I could say it was a long, hard journey with some ups and downs, but I persevered. Now I could say, "Mom, I did it." It was so sad she wasn't there to see the ceremony. All the senior class had their instructions. We all would meet at the Strand Theater located on North Pearl and Orange Street in Albany. Now today, it's just a large empty parking lot. All the families were there for their new graduates. There were people everywhere. Here I was with my cap and gown and that same smile on my face. Once inside, it threw me for a loop. My heart was racing to the max.

It seemed like a packed house; even the stage was full. The ceremony started and I waited with anticipation for my turn, listening for my principal to call my name. Now it's my turn to walk across the stage. Mr. Ben Becker stood there with a smile on his face. He knew we had made a connection in front of his office back some time ago. He gave me my diploma and shook my hand. "I knew you would complete it all." I said, "Thank you, my principal." Down the steps I went. Now the future was mine. A young minister and student did it all. I gave my greatest gratitude to my school and church. With my cap and gown on, I took a drive around the city to show off my accomplishment. And now the sky is the limit!

I received my notification from the United States Selective Service draft board. I was afraid to open the letter, knowing the outcome, because there was a major war in Vietnam. I was drafted into the United States Army. They told me, "This is our war, and we need all the troops we can muster." My Selective Service status was CO (Conscientious Objector). They tried to make me change my mind several times, but I kept telling them it was against my religion to take the life of another human being, because the Bible strictly says, "Thou shall not kill."

There was another young boy named the Champ who was born and bred in a town called Louisville, Kentucky. He and I went through the same nonsense from the United States Selective Service draft board. I have no idea how and when he got the letter from the draft board. The two of us had gone through the same, pounding orders from the officer of the US Army, telling the Champ he had to serve his country. The Champ refused to be drafted. He was boxing at the time. They told the Champ that if he didn't comply with the rules of the United States Armed Forces, he had to suffer the consequences. And he still refused to comply. So, they told him they had no other choice, and they stripped him of all his belts and took away all his titles, and he was facing jail time as well. He still stood by his words, "I refuse to take the lives of human beings." By doing so, the Champ lost so much time out of his life, years of his life, because of that decision. So we both were punished for not joining the armed forces of the United States. At the time, there were so many boys taking their draft cards and tearing them up. Some set them on fire, knowing it was a crime to burn any draft cards. Many young boys left the country and headed to Canada. In the city of Hanoi, Vietnam, they took the lives of so many US soldiers. General Westmoreland just had a job to carry out. Since my name was at the bottom, I was one of the last boys to leave the building.

All the officers kept on trying, but my mind was made up. For my final instructions, they said they had no other choice but to ship me off to Buffalo, New York, as a military punishment because of my religious beliefs. I had to work in a printing company for an undetermined amount of time. It's as if it was yesterday. I ran this machine called the multiset machine, making copies for a local magazine. Well, I did what I was ordered to do and went to work every day. It didn't take me long; I really enjoyed working at the factory. It turned out it was a good place to work. Within a year, they wrote me a letter telling me they'd decided to bring me back to Albany. There was the news I'd been waiting for over the last few months. Besides, I didn't like the city of Buffalo; it was a little bit too fast for me as a school and church boy.

Well, me and my little black Ford car were off, on my way back home. Now I could put 280 miles of road behind me. I was considered an honorable discharge status. I know it was a major war, and it took so many American lives over several years. It was on the news all the time. I thought it was sad for the lives lost. I hoped General Westmoreland would be happy that I did my part in the major campaign. I gained some valuable information to boot. I'd just finished high school, and that campaign didn't end until 1975. In that span of time, it took more than 40,000 to 55,000 men and boys' lives, some I knew personally from my school days. One of my best friends (I will not mention his name because of his family) went and came back with what they call "shell shock syndrome," and it was bad. I used to see him all the time walking down South Pearl Street. I'm not sure if he recognized me or not. I felt so sorry and helpless around him, but I didn't stop trying to talk to him. He was only one of so many all over the United States. Could you imagine taking the life of another human being?

God didn't intend for life to be so violent; that defeats his purpose. I would continue and try to put it all behind me. That trip to Buffalo was good for me; I learned a lot, and I will not forget that wonderful job. Since I did my time for the US Armed Forces, the Selective Services gave me, an honorable discharge. That made me feel some relief from all I had to go through.

I'm not sure about the Champ and what he had to go through. Well, I guess we both were happy it was all over. Now we could go on with our lives. Still, the war in Vietnam was still going on; there were so many lives lost in that terrible way. One thing is for sure: I will not forget what I had to go through. All the officers at the Selective Service building tried to get me to join, knowing it was against my religion. They said, "We need more men in this war; it's one of the largest campaigns of all wars that the United States has ever had to participate in over the years." General Westmoreland had thousands of young boys from schools and colleges drafted, making them become soldiers. I'm not sure, but according to the evening news, it was always thousands of men and boys killed in battle. I can't see or even imagine going overseas to any foreign county, trying not to get killed or taking the lives of other soldiers who fight for themselves and their own rights in their own country.

That's why I'm a CO. Taking the life of another is a sin unto God. It is stated in the Bible. "Thou shall not kill." Everyone, no matter what faith or belief, must know it's wrong to take the lives of other human beings. One thing was for sure: I would not go down that path ever. I was the one who was willing to take a chance to change the outcome. I was willing to do my best to preserve lives. Could you imagine pointing a gun at another human being? That's real scary; just thinking about that situation should change one's mind.

## FIFTHTEEN

### A Trip to Michigan

Back to the church and giving thanks to God. Now that I was finished with my school academics, I would go visit my twin in Detroit, Michigan, for a while. Alvin, our oldest brother, would be glad to see me as well. I'd be staying with him and Marceline; they owned a big house on the west side of Detroit. This will give me a chance to reminisce with my twin brother Jerry and his wife Olivia. Alvin owned his own restaurant, and he convinced me to stay and work for him as long as I wanted. I said yes because he needed someone he could trust in the kitchen. The restaurant was located on the first floor of the main building of the public library. I would be working for him for a while. I loved to see him work his magic at the stove. My favorite dish he cooked was small beef tips on wild rice. He had me work the line out front of the restaurant, and his place was always busy. I served the food to the customers and worked the cash register; it was a ton of fun meeting different people who work for the city of Detroit.

I worked for Alvin for a long time. I really enjoy the culinary arts and everything was fine until my big brother got a call from our sisters in Schenectady, New York. At this time, both Vonda Joyce and my older sister Gloria Jean lived in the city. The phone call was about our other sister Geraldine, who also lived there. She was missing, and no one could find her, not in Schenectady or Albany. Alvin said, "Give it some time; she will show up." It was all over the Schenectady newspaper. There were some concerns because Tommy Joe had treated my sister bad before. So we kept on working until the next day, when we got another call at work from our sisters. Only this time, it was devastating news that shook up our whole family. They'd found Geraldine dead, wrapped in her fur coat in the garage with wood stacked on top of her body.

*[ Image goes here: Figure 54 My big sister Geraldine.]*

Upon receiving the bad news, my big brother screamed in agony. I was working in the kitchen because we still had customers. Then suddenly, I heard this very loud scream coming from his office. I ran in and gave him as much comfort as I could from the loss of our sister. We all knew what that meant: another trip back to our one-stoplight town, Waynesboro, Mississippi. So Alvin and I had to make the trip to Schenectady to make the funeral preparations. Alvin knew this would happen to our sister sooner or later.

Alvin didn't trust Tommy Joe at all. Remember the big fight on our porch some time ago back home? My big brother gave him a good lashing. I had lived with my sister and Tommy Joe before, and I'd never seen him hit or fight with my sister ever until that last trip coming out of New Orleans coming back into Schenectady New York. I also knew he was a very heavy drinker, and his favorite drink was Southern Comfort whiskey. He told me, "Terry, if you drink, drink this, a real man's drink." He drank Budweiser beer as well.

Here's the story: Tommy Joe was very jealous. This specific day my sister and Tommy Joe had an argument, and this was where the alcohol took over. The kids were home at the time. But did not witness what took place in the basement. There, he took my sister's life. Tommy Joe was still in the house. Vonda stopped by; she said where is my sister?

Upon discovering she was missing from home Vonda began to inquire and started the search looking for her. He didn't give her an answer, so she screamed at him, saying,

"Where is my sister? Where did you get those scratches from on your face?" He tried to throw her off by saying, "Come with me into the basement," just to see if she noticed anything out of place. Vonda did find one shoe of my sister's. Again, she screamed at him, "Where is my sister?" So Vonda called Gloria. By the time she got there, Tommy Joe couldn't be found anywhere in Schenectady.

The kids were playing in the backyard. Yolanda, one of my nieces, was putting some things in the garage, and what she found in the corner of the garage, covered with some clothes and some pieces of wood, changed her life forever. She came screaming, there is a body in the garage she could not identify the body. After her brother went in to see he came out and identified it was my sister. "No, no, no, it can't be true, my mother is dead!" By then, Gloria had arrived. They called the Schenectady police, who came over quickly and canvassed the whole area. My whole family had to stand by while my sister was there in the garage. Tommy Joe was nowhere to be found. The story was that he skipped town, heading back to Waynesboro, Mississippi. Remember, we were all from the same town. Pastor Jack got the word, and he was there shortly afterward. All that was left was to start making funeral plans. The Angel of Death had visited our family again. Again, Pastor Jack said he would help us with the trip back south. For my big sister, Gloria, it had to take a lot of willpower to withstand the trip back to our hometown. There were only three girls in our family, and now one was gone to stay with God. We all hugged each other with love. This was the only thing that would keep us strong. Remember my mantra:

We all said our good-byes, which broke the hearts of my brothers and sisters. It was so devastating to us all. Geraldine didn't ever have a chance to see or talk face-to-face with our mom before she'd passed away. When she was still living with Tommy Joe years back in Waynesboro, he treated our sister so bad it was unbelievable. It hurt to talk about it with each other. We were all back in Albany, trying to put our lives in order again. I'd be staying with Vonda now that our sister was no longer with us. My twin was there for a little while, at least for the summer. He and I played a lot of sandlot football in the city park with other friends every Sunday afternoon. That gave us a chance to play some semi-pro football with the Green Jackets, our team in Glens Falls, New York.

We took the tryouts and made the team. I had played semi-pro before Jerry came to Glens Falls. His jersey number was 84; he was an outside receiver. My jersey was number 89; I ran the slot position, and sometimes the other outside as well. They didn't let him play as much. All we had to do was wait until half-time, and we would just change jerseys—that would give him a chance to play the second half. The coach couldn't tell us apart at all.

He used to call us "Heckle and Jackal." The whole team really liked us as fellow teammates. We did some traveling to other cities to play other teams, like the Binghamton Jets, the Watertown Red and Black, Troy Uncle Sam, the Scranton Eagles, and so on. We couldn't participate in our high school athletics during our school years, and we didn't understand why. As we know, they were the rules of the church. We couldn't break those rules, because we were good members. Now, many years later, we had a chance to play athletic sports, and there were no rules to be broken.

We played all the time, and we were on the road a lot. Then, and only then, we realized what we were missing back when we were attending school at Philip Schuyler High School. Those good old school days—we can't ever forget them. I hope you are sitting down. What I'm about to tell you will shock you to the max. One hot summer day, I left for Schenectady, and on the way, I stopped in Albany to see Pastor Jack, who talked about some work he wanted me to do that upcoming weekend. We sat and chatted for a while, and he told me to be at his house Saturday morning for work. Then I was on my way to Glens Falls for my football practice. We had practice on every Monday, Tuesday, and Thursday evening.

Well, on my way there was something wrong with the picture. An uncontrollable event happened on my way to Glens Falls, New York. My trip started on West Highway 90. I drove about three to five minutes on West 90, and I took the exit for the North Way, which would take me to Glens Falls. I observed in my rearview mirror flashing lights coming from a police cruiser. This cruiser was from the Albany Police Department. As soon as I saw the cruiser, I pulled over to the shoulder of the road.

I was driving my 1980 Dodge van, and before I came to a full stop, there were several other police cruisers all over the highway. There were other police cruisers coming down the wrong side of North 87. I got a little shook up seeing so many police cruisers stopping next to my van. When I did come to a full stop, all I could see were the black-and-white Albany police cruisers, New York State police cruisers, the Colony police cruisers, the Sheriff's Department cruisers, and the Schenectady police cruisers.

The next thing I knew, all I could see and hear was, "Let me see your hands." It seemed as if every police officer was pointing their gun at me. Could you imagine how I felt? I was still in my van. What would happen if one of those officers was a bigot? Who'd know if an officer had jealousy embedded inside of them for years? Prejudice is rampant in the Deep South. I know how it feels when someone has a gun on their side—it gives one a sense of control and power.

So I put my hands out the window, then they yelled at me, "Take your left hand and open the door." I did as they ordered, but before I could get out of the van, many of them rushed my van. All the officers had their guns pointing at me. One officer grabbed me by my arms, and another officer grabbed me by my neck. They slapped the handcuffs on me and threw me to the ground. I have a question for you—have you ever been pinched by a set of handcuffs? Well, it happened to me that day, and they didn't care at all. They dragged me to the other side of my van, that hard pavement, with the sand, dirt, and gravel, saying, "Don't you move."

All my life, I'd never seen so many guns pointed at me, especially by the state police and Albany police officers. After they threw me down on the pavement, I began to say, "Officer, what have I done? What's wrong? Why are you doing this to me?" Another officer yelled, "Keep your mouth shut." I said, "Officer, I didn't do anything wrong." They wouldn't let me say anything, with my hands behind my back in handcuffs, laying there on the ground. So I did as they ordered.

After they threw me down on the pavement, one officer put his knee on the side of my head, pushing my head into the sand and rocks. The other officer put his knee in the middle of my back, and all the time I was saying, "What have I done, officers?" They would only yell "Shut up!" They tore the shirt off my back and threw it in the bushes and weeds. Meanwhile, some of the other officers were going through my van. They were taking my van apart, both inside and out.

So I screamed, "What do you want? What have I done? What are you looking for?" They wouldn't tell me anything as they pointed their guns at me, saying, "Keep your mouth shut." I happened to overhear them talking. One officer said, "This has got to be the van they used for the break." They were talking about a prison break from the Schenectady County prison. I told them, "I don't know anything about any prison break, sir." They didn't let me off the ground. After a long time laying on the ground, they finally let me sit up. Laying on that hard, bumpy pavement was no joke. I told them I wasn't transporting a prisoner from a prison break and that I knew nothing about Schenectady County prisoners escaping from jail. I told them I was on my way to Glens Falls for football practice. They didn't believe me, and this was the result—stopping me and treating me like a criminal.

They still wouldn't allow me to say anything at all. When I saw many officers begin to rush to their cars, I knew then that it had to be someone else, not me. They kept me there; they knew they were wrong. I happened to overhear the two officers in charge talking: "This is the wrong guy; we can't just let him go. We must get him on something." So they told me they were sorry to say that when I was pulled over, I failed to use my turn signal. Of course, that was a lie. They took off the handcuffs and told me I had to appear in court in a few days.

I kept saying to myself, "This can't be happening." They said to me, "See you in traffic court." I said to myself, "What did I do to deserve all this bad treatment from all those law enforcement officers?" I thought all officers were here to serve and protect. That statement wasn't in my favor that day. I will not look at any police officer in a good manner ever again. It seemed like they took it personally. I was innocent of the crime they'd thought I had committed. From this day forward, I will try my very best to stay out of the way of all officers.

Today, I can see what Rodney King must have felt in 1991. It is so sad I had to go through that ordeal. Now I had to appear in traffic court. I made my court date and stood in front of the judge. He began to tell me what I was charged with. I said, "Your Honor, can I say something?" He said, "Yes." I began to tell him all that happened that day on the North Way. Before I could finish, he stopped me, saying, "Are the arresting officers present?" I looked around. I saw another officer standing there, but not one of the officers on the North Way that day of the arrest.

I did not see one officer who'd stopped and pointed his gun at me. There were no state, Schenectady, or Colony police officers in the court. The judge told me, "Get out of my court," because they were all wrong in what they did to me. I knew the whole time I didn't commit a crime. Now, every time I'm on the North Way, here comes that déjà vu. I will not ever forget what happened on that sunny afternoon. That was a traumatizing time for me. I always wondered if they caught the right person or not. So now, every time I see any law enforcement officer, that déjà vu quickly enters my mind and brings fear inside me.

Looking down the barrel of all those guns is enough to make a person go loco. I have a complex when I see any type of law enforcement officer in uniform. Now I know what caused the unfortunate incident with Rodney King. I really know how it feels in that tragedy. I learned my lesson when traveling on any state and local highways. I was only on my way to a hard football practice. This kept me settled down for the rest of the day. Besides, we had a big home game the next weekend against the Binghamton Jets, and it looked like another win for the Green Jackets football team. It's so hard to forget what happened to me, especially coming from a professional organization, which includes all types of law enforcement officers. It brings tears to my eyes whenever I see any police officers stop someone and throw them down on the ground and treat them like hard criminals; I tell you, it's really scary. I know this is a fact for sure—when giving any man or woman a weapon to wear on their side, they're given the power of controlling other people automatically. Some of those officers have itchy trigger fingers and feel the need to pull their weapon and point that weapon at another person, ready to fire at first chance. They mean to shoot to kill; they never think about hitting a person in the arm or leg. That's enough to stop anyone dead in their tracks. It doesn't have to be a target event or ending. What gets me is why do they always have to put their knees on the back of one's head and back? I learned my lesson, and I would try very hard to stay out of the way of any law enforcement officer, and I would always say "Yes, sir" to all officers when in their presence. That's the only way I know how to be treated like a person. Now I know how it feels looking down the barrel of a loaded weapon. Somewhere there are some good officers who will go the distance for any person who needs help. I have been in that situation before. It's the officers who don't care and just pull, point, and shoot. Then they attempt to ask questions, but most of the time there's no answers coming from any police officers, because wearing a gun gives that person power.

But at this time, I have a different kind of answer. Earlier I mentioned that I attended Adirondack College. There I met special young lady; I can't reveal her name at this time because of her right to privacy. We both lived and worked in the city of Glens Falls. We both had classes at the same school. My first time meeting her was at one of my football games. After the game, I approached her, telling her, "I want your phone number, address, and your full name." She told me I was fooling around with her, and I said no, I'm for real. She said okay and gave it all to me. I didn't realize my life would change forever. She wasn't happy that I lived in Schenectady, but I told her, "Don't worry; things will work out." I made numerous trips to see her. Her mom wasn't too happy at the time. The relationship lasted for three years. We had our own apartment on Glens Street all those years. We both had jobs in Lake George at the resort hotel. We did everything together for many years. She left school and joined the military—in fact, the US Navy.

I continued my classes; she was living at the time on Patuxent River military base. I finished school, packed up, and headed for the State of Maryland. There we promised to share our lives together forever. The first thing she said to me is that I had to get a haircut, and to me that was the first sign of being in control, but I didn't realize at the time because my concern was the two of us being together. We grabbed something to eat and headed to city hall in Lester Town, Maryland. There we got married; we raised our hands and made that solemn oath with those vows. We were cementing our lifetime relationship. I was one happy person, and the smiles went ear to ear. Now it was time to celebrate this special dedication. I received my welcome package from the base commander. The base was so large, with soldiers, men, and women all over the place with their military whites and their shining black boots. We had to look for a place to live out in town; she was still living in base housing.

We found a place in a trailer park; it was the less expensive at the time. I didn't work at the time, and we only had one car. I had to take her to work every day on base—that was fun, so I got to meet other people who worked at the same job. It was called V.Q-4 squadron. This was my first time being so close to so many airplanes and military personnel.

I would drop her off and pick her up from work every day. And I would have dinner waiting when we got home. Things were going so smoothly for us as a new married couple. Then she came with some good news—we were having a baby, and it was a boy—the best news I ever had in my lifetime. Well, bad news, it always happens when things are going well. Someone or something always throws a wrench in the mix of things. I found out I was not the biological father of our son. She kept it a secret for the whole nine months. What made it worse is that I knew the person she was seeing. He was in the US Air Force. They didn't meet at bootcamp; it was at a school, then they got their orders, one in the Navy and the other in the Air Force. They stayed in contact with each other all the time. I continue to be the best father for our son Stephen E. Williamson; *Figure 57 our first Son Stephen E. Williamson* in fact, I was the one who gave him his name. I will continue to be a good husband and father for my family!

## SIXTEEN

### Music Carries Words

I would like to share a sweet story with you about my little sister and how she was blessed to sing. I loved to sit and listen to her ring out those beautiful sounds of notes, lyrics, and rhythm. There were so many different songs. I didn't recall hearing her singing when we were back home in the South in our hometown. I'm a witness: she does have a set of pipes. I'm so proud to say I enjoyed lying in the grass in Lincoln Park as she rang out notes and rhythms from songs deep inside her heart. I hoped she saw me laying in the grass among the crowd, because that was my little sister reaching out to the people. Way to go, little sis.

My little sister Vonda J. Williamson was born in the city of Waynesboro, Mississippi, on April 25, 1954. There, she attended first grade. She started singing at the age of twelve with the local church called the Church of God. Pastor Jack was the presiding pastor.

There, she became one of his members, and a member of the youth choir. In 1977, at the age of twenty-two, she became a member of her first R&B band by the name of "Shakun." She was the lead vocalist in the band for approximately eight to ten months. In early 1978, she moved on to become a member of another R&B band by the name of "Samore" out of Albany, New York. She performed at various venues within the tri-city area, earning and winning a number of local talent competitions as well. I was proud and happy I could attend many of her gigs through the metropolitan area. Well, I'm happy we both sang in church choirs.

Figure 58 Vonda Joyce, Singing her heart out on stage.

Since we'd lost our mom in that terrible car accident, it had left a heavy weight on all of us. Vonda reminds me of our mom. The two of them have the same features, eyes, smiles, and body size and shape. Every time I think of the two of them, I can't help the feeling I get when I hear that song she sang when we were little. When we lost our mother, one thing was for sure—she and the rest of the family felt a great void in our lives. We never forgot how we were placed all over the city of Albany, living with different people and their families from the church.

Our dad was hurt more over my mom's death. My father did all he could to stay happy with the loss of his lovely wife. He took it hard. He just couldn't hide it. Later, he found a special lady friend who could give him comfort in his loss. This was something he really needed at this sad time in his life. So he did what he had to do to make himself happy. My little sister felt more abandoned than the rest of our brothers and sisters. Now she had no mother or father. It hurts my little sister when she talks about it with the rest of the family. She was a strong woman now that she had to raise three wonderful little girls all by herself right here in Schenectady, New York, and many years in Albany as well. I was there for support. We all had fun together, just one happy family. *"A strong family that lives together shares love together"* for sure. Those little girls were her heart. The oldest sister was or "Tea-boo." There was also (Kiki) and (Buppie).

Vonda Joyce, this strong woman, is the one who encouraged me to write and share my life story, which was an adventure and a journey in the form of words. I'm so happy for her input, and all the good times and bad times as well. Love is the only thing that keeps us bonded together. At this present time, all her girls live in Atlanta and are doing very well. Kiki was a world-class 60m hurdler and made the tryouts for the US women's track-and-field team. She made the 2008 Olympic team as an alternate.

Yes, she was very good. How good? I went with her to one of her practices at the SUNY Albany campus track-and-field facility. I knew she was fast, and I was fast as well. One day, I told her, "I think I can outrun you." She responded saying, "Okay, Uncle Terry, you can try." She got in the starting position on the rubbery surface of the track. I took my position on the grassy part of the football field, outside the track itself.

My sister Vonda started the countdown. Off we went. We both had a good start, and before long, all I could see was the bottom of my niece's feet. I knew then she was special, and to beat all. She said to me, "Uncle Terry, eat my dust!" To add insult to injury, I tripped and fell to the ground, trying to keep up with her to no avail. I did give it my best shot. She gave her Uncle Terry a track-and-field lesson that day. I was so happy for her. Now she's an attorney in Atlanta, Georgia. She also wrote a book called *Code Versus Code*. Athletes from all over the sports world would know how to choose the right agent in any sport, in all athletic sports and entertainment. She focused on helping all athletes with their financial situation as well.

My other nieces both have found jobs and are doing very well. Now you can see how their mother and uncle felt about those sweet and beautiful daughters. What's their mother doing at the time? Singing! She has the gift from God and a little help from our mother and father. I'm proud of her. I used to follow her group all through Albany, Troy, and Schenectady just to hear her sing. To me, it was fun following my sister in the metropolitan area, then she made a roundabout move—she joined another church in Schenectady.

There, she received her supernatural deliverance from a tobacco addiction. I know and Vonda knows that it's not the tobacco but the nicotine that causes people to have a smoking habit. She knows that's true and made up her mind. "I can't continue this path anymore."

She said she will never venture down that path again. I never saw her smoke ever again. I'm so proud of my little sister. It was a big problem with her smoking. I used to see her pick up cigarettes off the sidewalk, trying to find the longest cigarette butt in the ashtray both in Schenectady and Albany. I knew she had broken the smoking habit. I did support it at some time, because I'd bought packs of cigarettes for her. I'm happy she developed a strong will to quit smoking altogether that led to her seeking God for supernatural healing.

Now she has a strong devotion to and a spiritual relationship with God. Now we can share in taking part in the fruit from a giving, living God. My little sister is still singing now in the city of Atlanta, where she made several fine CDs singing praise and worship songs.

Remember the phrase, "boys will be boys"? I took my family on a long ride to a small town called Meadville, Pennsylvania. My twin brother Jerry moved there a while back, between Albany and Detroit, during and after our school years at Philip Schuyler High School. This small town, reminds me of your hometown back in the South. Remember, I talked about it earlier—it was the first time we as twins were ever apart. You know we'd been on so many adventures in our lifetime; there's no need to count them all.

You will not get bored in what they are. The excitement is still there to make us very happy. When he moved away was a very sad moment for me; we did all our adventures with each other all our lives. Now we could reminisce again, like we did back home the last time we were together. We arrived and I drove to the top of this big hill. There he had a very nice, big house. Here came all the hugs and kisses. It had been a long time since the last visit. I was shocked when I got inside his house. My own twin brother had all his guns. Now that was impressive to me, seeing as I love guns as well. But living on the military bases for all those years, guns were forbidden. I was happy to see so many guns.

He had two 30-06 rifles, pistols, pump shotguns—I can go on and on. It was impressive. I'd never seen so many weapons in someone's house before. Well, it was exciting to me, He hunted all kinds of prey—squirrels, rabbits, deer, and so forth. I wished I had time to go hunting with him while I was there, but time wouldn't allow it. You know those twins. I knew it would be lots of fun, Then, everyone knew our mom; those little boys were her favorite. Everyone knew we were some adventurous little boys. Jerry drove one of the largest cars I'd ever seen. It looked like a boat, just like the pastor's big Fleetwood Cadillac.

He married one of the most beautiful women I'd seen in a long time, Olivier Williamson. Even her name was beautiful. They have two wonderful girls. The oldest one is Ontwan Kiel, and the youngest is Angelita Williamson Davis. This made me a proud uncle of those sweet young ladies. Angelita is now the mom of two little ones, Arabella and Israel Davis. Now that everyone was fine, it was time to hit the road, making the long trip back to the Patuxent River Maryland naval base. It was a joint command; it's very nice on and off the base. We lived in base housing in a three-bedroom joint house. For now, it was just the four of us with the two boys: Stephen, our firstborn, and Tyller, our youngest. This was a three-year tour in Maryland, and the people were very hospitable.

Then we lived in base housing at 212 Hawthorn Road in Groton, Connecticut. Everyone was very nice in the neighborhood, and all the families had at least one child. There was always plenty of room for them to play. All the neighborhood pulled together as one.

Let's see, where are we going next? There were several choices. We didn't have to look very hard; this time the choice just popped out at us: Antigua, West Indies. This time we were traveling out of the country. Here came all those tests from the medical department, all kinds of shots just to leave the country. I'd never had so many shots, and they were all important; the whole family had the same treatment. I just felt sorry for our little boys. They just screamed and cried for a while.

All of this was getting us ready for the big trip to a strange country. They say it's a third-world country. That was my first time hearing about that kind of place. Antigua, West Indies, was another joint command military base. And the language was English, the same as here in America. For the most part, they were under British colonial rule back in the early-to-late '60s. I thought they were the same people as the Jamaicans. They had the same dialect and spoke the same broken language, and they lived on different islands. But first, we had to get settled in. The naval base wasn't too far away. It was located off the tip of Florida. They unpacked our furniture and all the things from those large wooden boxes. Now that we were finally settled in, it was time to live there for three years.

Our family was much larger now; we were blessed with two wonderful boys. Stephen was the oldest, going on six years. Tyller was our baby, and he was going on four years. They are a big part of my heart forever. I love them so much. I guess one could say Stephen has his mom's complexion and Tyller has his father's complexion—well, somewhat. He will never get as dark as me. I'm not really dark; just my normal skin tone.

We were all blessed with our health and strength. Our sons both grew up as little military boys. They weren't dishonest, and discipline wasn't necessary. The military environment paid off in dividends, and they didn't cause any problems, because the military has more to offer for the youngsters. The commanding officer welcomed us to Antigua. He said if there was anything we needed not to hesitate to ask.

One day the boys were coming home from school, and I could see the bus down the street. Stephen and Tyller got off the bus, and Stephen came walking with this sad look on his face after he got off the bus. This was the first day at school. He had one of the strangest sunburns, and I knew it had to hurt. So off to the base doctor; it was located in the quarter deck. This building was the only building built with steel and bricks.

He had a first-degree burn, but he was okay. There will be school tomorrow.

The other day, it started to rain, and it was coming down like cats and dogs. It only lasted for a couple of minutes. I went to the back door, and what did I see but a giant double rainbow, perfect in color. It was close to our building. The amount of space from the house to the ocean was about the space of a normal backyard. Out of nowhere appeared this beautiful rainbow with perfect colors. Except this one was double in close-knit colors. It two had the thick red, orange, and yellows. And the thick green, blue, and purple in close-knit colors. It was a double rainbow, the first one I'd ever seen in my life. What a beautiful phenomenon. One end of the rainbow appeared to touch the ground, and the other end of the rainbow appeared to touch the glassy still water. It was unreal to see with the naked eye. Now I know for sure all rainbows are round. What are you thinking about when you see a rainbow? It will always remind me of the great flood during Noah's reign. God will not destroy the Earth with water the next time. All this happened in the third-world country of Antigua. And it's a beautiful country to boot.

So after the short rainstorm, the sun came out for a while. But the very next day, there was a sound coming from the quarter deck. There was a bad storm coming this way. It would hit us within twelve hours. So we all got prepared for the storm. Without any warning, the storm changed course. It was upon us in no time—wind, rain, and water. It was a hurricane. The commander of the base had all families come to the quarter deck, because it was the only safe place on the base. We gathered the kids and headed to the quarter deck. Then it hit us; the wind and the rain were gushing all over. All the families were gathered in our building.

The building had those round windows. We could see outside, and it was bad; the palm trees were bending down to the ground. Things were flying. After about half an hour, the storm subsided. According to the weather report, it was heading toward Puerto Rico. They got the eye of the storm; it was very bad. This hurricane was called Hugo, a category 5 storm. It left the base in very bad shape. The tennis courts were destroyed. That really hurt, no more tennis lessons for a while.

The hurricane devastated Puerto Rico. The island was down for months. All this took place in September 1989. Now it was time for the big cleanup. We were up and running after two weeks. Now all we had to do was stay and wait for the next change of command. What was the next naval base? The other day, I had déjà vu. I was on a flight coming from California when I saw another perfect rainbow; this one was perfect in color. It still had those same colors. I couldn't believe my eyes. There was this guy sitting next to me on the airplane, and we introduced ourselves. His name was Dave. He played for the 49ers professional football team, and his position was tight end. He was big and tall, and that position fit him well. He looked at me and now I was a little frightened on the plane. He took it upon himself to make sure I got through the airport safely after getting off the plane. Otherwise, I would have gotten lost again like always. He also invited me to come and visit him at the State University in Albany. His job was a professional football scout for the New York Giants. I was thankful for the invite. I told him I was heading back to the naval base after my trip.

Each base tour only lasts for three years. To me, there was so much to do there on that base. Well, back to the everyday chores. As I said, time always flew by fast on each base. Now it was time to look at the dream sheet. This dream sheet would be the most wonderful set of orders of all. There was so much excitement in the air; this military dream sheet would take us to a country called Iceland. The military base was located on the east side of the country. It was called Keflavik, Iceland. We had to drive to New York City and then to Philadelphia International Airport for that long flight to a brand-new country. Now at this time, we had four boys, with two additions there: Jore'll, who was close to five, and Ryan, a baby at the age of two. Just a big, fun family, happy to be in our new home and in a new country.

The flight time was six hours. We had to fly over Greenland, and we could see it from the window of the plane. Then we arrived in Keflavik, Iceland. It seemed like it took no time at all. We all v climbed out of the plane and headed for the terminal. They had an escort waiting for us. From the airport it was a short ride to the military base and the quarter deck. It was a beautiful sight to see. There were several large buildings for military families. We all unpacked and took a short walk around the base, and the place was breathtaking. After we all got settled in, I got ready to do my job taking care of the little ones, all four boys, and we made every day count. When it came time for school, the boys got a little confused about what time it was. They would stay outside playing, knowing there was school the next day.

What was the problem? It was still light outside. It took some getting used to, having darkness all the time. It stayed dark outside in Iceland during the different times of the year. Here in fall, it would be dark outside for six months.

Then as the seasons changed, it would stay light outside nearly all day. The sun doesn't fully set for three months starting in May. The sun stayed high all the time, and it was hot too. Now we had to get used to daylight all the time. It was strange, and it took time to get used to the change.

We could go anywhere we pleased; there were no restrictions on the island. I have to share this with you: during the winter months and the school season, when all the parents had to take the kids to the bus stop—now this is very strange— all the parents had to tie a long rope around their waist, and each child had to hold on real tight so the strong winds wouldn't blow them away. That was how strong the wind was during the winter.

I took a job outside of the base to help with extra expenses. Being a certified sous chef, it was no problem getting a job at any restaurant. Not long after, I landed my own restaurant as a sous chef. It was called Chef Terry's Pasta Place, and it took off like leaping antelopes. The people on base were on the phone all the time looking for a good meal. My specialty was seafood and pasta, and it caught the attention of the Icelandic people. Another strange story: the military would issue each family six cases of beer a month. I kept mine in the house for people when they came over for a good meal.

One evening, four Icelandic guys got permission to come on base. They got their passes, knocked on the door for a good sit-down meal, and I was ready. I had a dish called the Volantes; it was stuffed with vegetables and chicken and covered with a bechamel sauce. I had breaded chicken cordon bleu, the zesty carbonara sauce, and a combination of different kinds of seafood. They all ate, and those six cases of beer I mentioned. They drank half of the six cases. So, I had to make sure they got off the base safely. I didn't forget about the black ice on all the roads; I hope they arrived home safely.

The northern lights in Iceland are spectacularly beautiful. It seemed like God reached out and blessed the northern part of the world. Iceland is one country I suggest that everyone visit; it would blow your mind. The island staple is of course fish. Keflavik, Iceland, is located on the west side of the island; it was located on the side of the island with jagged rock and volcanic ash carried by the very strong wind. Those inactive volcanoes were a sight to see. This gave me and the boys a chance to take a long walk down inside those volcanos. Now that gave us some real excitement.

The weather in the summer was around the high fifties sometimes. One could wear short-sleeved shirts and shorts during the day. Did you know all the swimming pools were outside in Keflavik? Of course, they were heated, and a ton of fun to boot. All the boys and girls swam at this pool. Now here was the strangest thing: all the kids had to climb up this large ladder in order to reach the top platform. Once there, the first kid would start out by pulling down their swimming trunks. This was done in order to slide down really fast, because their bottom would contact the sliding surface. When they made contact, it would give them a super ride. It was done by the boys and girls; there were no adults doing this technique. It was too embarrassing. Well, I know we wouldn't hear of this in America. And all in a very large pool, and you had to see this with your own eyes.

What was next? The ice cream shop. I must say, it was the best-tasting ice cream ever, and so smooth. Here was something that threw me for a loop: walking down the street on both sides of the street, you would see all these tall women with blonde hair. It looked like they were all sisters. No, I was told most of the women were blonde. I mean, on both sides of the street.

In the downtown area, all the mothers with strollers would leave them outside of the store while shopping, and there wouldn't be any problem with other people. Crime was practically nonexistent in Keflavik, Iceland. The police officers didn't wear weapons, just a nightstick, and the crime was very low.

Iceland looked as if it were close to the sky. Those breathtaking northern lights would blow your mind; it's so unreal to the naked eye. During the winter season, it gets really cold and windy. There was a problem with the black ice, and gusts of wind would make some unbelievable snow drifts. Those green trash dumpsters were tossed around like cardboard boxes.

Out in town, only four-wheel drive vehicles were allowed on the roads—that's how bad the winter was in this great city. Of course, their staple was fish, and sometimes when the wind was blowing in the right direction, it gave off a stench that was unbearable to the nose.

In my restaurant, I gave a cooking class for any military person who was interested in learning how to cook new dishes. My cooking class was televised on the local television station there in Keflavik. I always wanted to have my own cooking show on TV, and it was a big success. I was really pleased.

Figure 59 Sous Chef Terry Williamson tavern by the green

I suggest every American somehow take a trip to Iceland.

After Keflavik, our new orders were to the Groton, Connecticut, submarine base. This naval base was located close to two of the largest hotel casinos in the state of Connecticut. One was the Mohegan Sun Casino. This was the first casino in the area owned and run by the Mohegan Indians. I was one of the sous chef who opened it. They called it mark-night. Next was the Foxwoods Resort Casino; it was owned and run by the Foxwoods Indians. The Foxwoods Casino was the largest because of the square footage. I was one of the sous chefs who opened the casino; it was called the mark-night. The property was run by the Foxwood Indians. It was nice to know so many Foxwoods Indians. All the tribal Indians were very nice as well. I really enjoy working in such a big endearment. I'm happy my culinary degree paid off; this was a fine job, and I loved it.

One evening, the great Frank Sinatra was giving a concert, and he rented the whole eighth floor. He always made his way through the kitchen with his bodyguards. They would be carrying his favorite drink: Jack Daniels whisky. The night he was supposed to perform, he was too intoxicated. He couldn't make the show, so he had his son cover for him.

I had an opportunity to cook breakfast for the Blue Angels F/A-18 fighter jets. They gave an air show. People from all over were there. My job as a sous chef was to make sure they had a really good breakfast before their scheduled maneuver that special day. They were particular in how their food was prepared; they all wanted eggs benedict with a smooth, creamy hollandaise sauce.

Well, I really made their day. Everything went off very well. They even let me take a picture with them and let me and my boys take a shuttle bus to the runway to see them in the takeoff position. They were all in single file taking off one at a time. Now that was something very special to us all. There were seven pilots flying those fighter jets.

We all stood together with our arms stretched out around each other; that was an unbelievable photo. That morning was one I'll never forget. I love planes, all kinds, but the Blue Angels are my favorite. Then there are the Thunderbirds; they are from the Air Force, and they also fly F/16 fighter jets. Now, I can say without any doubt that my culinary degree took me a long way in the cooking industry.

I worked as a sous chef at the Tavern by the Green here in Groton, Connecticut. It's on the submarine base, and this base is located next to a very large golf course. The Tavern by the Green was mostly for the officers and was sometimes called the "officer's club." There, I was the assistant chef. This club fed approximately two hundred tables in one sitting. They held birthday parties, graduations, officer promotions, retirements, and decommissions of old submarines. I was second-in-charge in the kitchen; all I needed was a few hours at opening to complete all my meals plus my prep work. I went into the walk-in freezer and gathered all I needed to start the day, and I would have breakfast, lunch, and dinner all ready for the day.

We had a large dining room, as I mentioned before. Depending on the size of the party, I would do all the ice carving. I know you've seen them before. When entering the dining room, you would see ice carvings of dolphins, swans—carvings of all sizes and shapes. Well, that's what I did as a chef. Cooking for large parties will keep you very busy, but when finished, knowing it was a success was a great relief. I prepared a special chicken recipe, twelve-spice chicken. It made the local newspaper. Imagine cooking while the TV cameras are on you. What an accomplishment for me as a sous chef. I was happy I could cook any type of meal for different parties.

A world-renowned restaurant in Paris called the Cordon Bleu gave me so many opportunities after I graduated from Johnson and Wales University. That's what made me a sous chef. Preparing food is my specialty; that's all I know, and I got the best training from this great university. Studying the culinary arts, one would have the best opportunity in the cooking industry.

It was peaches and cream at first, but many times back and forth from Groton, Connecticut, to Johnson and Wales University was hard on me. I was a whiz in the kitchen. There were these two girls in the class, and they were very smart. They got an A on every single exam. Yes, I did struggle for a short time, but I made the grade. The two girls were lost in the kitchen during exam time, so when the instructor wasn't looking, I did all their cooking for them.
They were so happy to have someone to give them a hand; I was happy they did the same for me. Mixology was a very tough class that I passed with a perfect score. If one passed mixology, you were now a well-trained bartender, which would let you work in any well-known bar. A favorite of mine was butchering class. Everyone had to cut and carve the right part of a half cow; that was right up my alley. I love meat carving. It's all about being a good chef; that was my goal, and I think I did a good job.

The pastor's church members were giving him his golden anniversary party next month, but we wouldn't be able to attend because of the military's orders. There wasn't enough time left on the new orders. I would talk with him when that time came. He's one person I owe so much to, with all those trips to our hometown. My mom left some important things for him to take care of, and he didn't let her down. I will miss the program; I know it will be a big success. It would be good to see all the people from our church. Some were from the old days, and others were new to the area. It is good to see new faces. I'd have to wait until we returned to the States. It would be a big event. There would be churches from all over the state.

My father was one of the guest singers who would perform in the celebration. I couldn't wait to see the pastor; we would have so much to share about the last few years. I still owed him so much from the past. He gave my mother a promise at her bedside, and he made good on his word. He's really a true man of God in all respects, and there is nothing I wouldn't do for all his generosity throughout the years.

The celebration program was at the end of the month. I know Pastor Jack would be happy about the way things turned out. I still miss the old St John's Church on Ferry Street and St. Franklin Street, back in Albany. My, how time flies when you're having fun. There was so much to do here in this second-world country. Now it was time for new orders to another naval base somewhere in the States.

We were close to Albany, and we had family both in Glens Falls and Albany, so once in a while we would take a trip for a quick visit. It's all about a strong family. As I mentioned before, living on different bases, they don't last very long. It was about that time again. This time, there was a dream sheet. The choice was very easy. We chose San Diego, California. What person would turn down San Diego? I always wondered what it would be like to live on the West Coast with the beaches and sun. The average humidity was around 70 percent. There would be lots of things to do out west. The boys were overjoyed about the new orders; we would be moving at the end of the month. All we had to do was pack a few things we needed every day.

The Mayflower moving company would come and start packing by the weekend. It was part of the military moving package. The military also paid for all the gas for the trip to San Diego. The government paid a little more than $1,000 for the move we made ourselves. We were excited to drive across the country. We bought a brand new 2011 trailer from Home Depot and got a good price for it. With the truck and the trailer packed to the max, we were on our way to the West Coast.

The movers came and packed everything in the house. All we had to do was make sure the house was clean. The military was very strict about house cleaning; they would come afterward and do the white-glove test to see if the house was clean to their specifications. Now the moving truck was there; I can still remember this very large trailer truck. It had some very large words written on the side of the trailer: Mayflower Packing Co. We were packed into my truck and small trailer and ready to head off to the big West Coast. The packers told us it wouldn't take us more than three days to reach California.

I wish you could have seen the excitement in the eyes of me and my boys and the whole family. Seeing the beautiful countryside in every state was something unbelievable. On the way, we ran into some very bad weather in Oklahoma—a category 4 hurricane. It was devastating and very scary too. We were headed into the eye of the storm and didn't know what to do.

Figure 62 I'm receiving my certificate from the Capitan a member of the wife club.

So, I thought to myself, what shall I do? Stop and wait it out or continue to drive west? I decided to continue driving. I had to stop for gas. The gas station attendant told us to be very careful out there on the highway. He said, "Whatever you do, don't stop on the side of the road." That would be a very bad mistake, and it could be life-threatening as well. So, I gassed up, grabbed a few snacks, and hit the road.

Not knowing how things would pan out, everyone in the truck was shaken up. It was so frightening, this sort of thing; it's something one had to experience themselves. It was in the late afternoon and not long ago the sun was shining, but now it was really dark out. I kept driving into the eye of the storm, but I didn't realize it at the time. The storm produced very heavy, strong winds, and those dark clouds appeared out of nowhere within minutes. Here's the scary part: suddenly, it started hailing, and the ice cubes were the size of marbles. They were bouncing off the truck hood and windshield. They didn't cause any damage, thank goodness. I guess the ice was frozen to a real solid form.

It was as if we were in a movie. The truck and the trailer were moving side to side. I drove as slowly as I could, but I had to keep on moving. Most of the cars had pulled off to the side of the road. I was given a warning from the guy at the gas station—whatever happens, don't stop on the side of road. I continued driving forward. The storm couldn't last very long. So, I pushed on and stayed focused on the road. It was dangerous and very scary. There was debris and parts of large tree limbs flying across the road.

With a blessing from God, we made it through that terrible storm. Now we were on West Interstate 40; this was the longest road I'd ever been on. It was straight, and the gas stations seemed so far apart. This was one place not to run out of gas. There were so many beautiful sights, and the weather was getting hotter. It was 175 miles to Lake Tahoe. It didn't take us too long to reach the border of California. The next stop would be Sacramento. Now that we were here, it was time to find the naval base. It was called Miramar Naval Base, located off Highway 5 North. Base housing was about nine miles to the south in Tierrasanta.

It was a very large family setting, with lots of schools and parks for all the kids in the neighborhood. It had everything everyone needed—all kinds of stores and movie theaters too. All the boys were much bigger now. Stephen and Tyller were in high school at Sierra High School. Ryan and Jore'll went to De Portola Middle School. I made sure they all got to school on time. Their mother was already at work. I picked up a part-time job teaching tennis to adults, seniors, and small ones as well. It was located at the Tierrasanta Youth Center, a very large building for all kinds of activities.

On this basis, we all had a chance to see a lot of airshows, mainly the Blue Angels and the Thunderbirds. It was so much fun living in San Diego, the third largest city in California. Well, we would be there for a while before it would be time for new orders. I wondered where the next naval base would be the next time around. For now, we live and work in

San Diego. I do admit, it was like something I only saw on television.

## SEVENTEEN

### What's the West Coast Like?

You must see the size of the mountains; they are so breathtaking and unbelievable. They are a beautiful sight for all to see. There were 290 miles to the city of Monterey, California. We finally made it to Monterey, and now I could see what people

*Figure 63 Getting my granddaughter ready for tennis at the Monterey Tennis Center*

were talking about. Everyone kept telling us we would love this famous city. It sat right off the coast, and we could see for miles. It was unbelievable to see a city so close to the beach with its blue-green water. The further it goes out, the darker it gets.

It was a terrible trip altogether, but we made it in three and a half days. Well, we were here in Monterey. It used to be the capital, but years earlier they'd moved it to Sacramento. Here, we lived in a whole house in Marina, about nine miles from the base in Monterey. I still was the stay-at-home dad with "the Navy mom," doing all the cooking and cleaning just like all the other duty stations. We all had jobs. I had a chance to use my skills as a tennis professional, so I landed a job at the Monterey Tennis Center, one of the best jobs ever.

I was content working with kids, juniors, and adults at the Monterey Tennis Center. I was a tennis pro there; I gave private lessons. I restrung all kinds of tennis rackets. Restringing was my specialty, but also the hitting and teaching pro for people from out of town and locals who wanted to just hit or improve their game strokes and strategies for play. It was fun, and I loved my job. We had six tennis courts, and it was always busy. I will admit, it was a very good job. I never had to call out sick in the three years I was there. We lived off base in a smaller city at 112 Waldron Way Marina, California, about nine miles from the naval base. It was a three-bedroom house with a two-car garage, a medium backyard, and lots of flowers out front. Here, everyone there was ready to work.

Things were looking up for us—just one big, happy family. I was so happy to be in a situation where there was good news for a change. The weekend was here, so it was time to hit the beach. This would be the first time I'd ever had a chance to be on a real white, sandy beach. It was hot and we were having a ton of fun, and the weather was so beautiful. There was not a cloud in the sky. Here, the weather was always hot, around 70 on average most of the time. We were told that here you paid for the sun and sand. It's one of the largest cities in California, and oh, boy, it's very expensive.

This joint command was one of the largest in the military altogether. The base was called Monterey Peninsula Command Base off the 101. There was so much our boys could do in this beautiful city. The two older ones went to Sierra High School, which was a large school, the largest I'd seen in a while. The two younger boys went to middle school. And they were all doing well. Stephen and Tyller graduated already at Sierra High School in San Diego. Now there were just two more to go. What was next on that dream sheet? This time, it was the Groton, Connecticut, naval base.

Groton was close to New York, so we could visit Glens Falls and Albany as often as we wanted. So that was our choice. So now, where were the packers? We were on our way back to Groton, Connecticut, for the second time. This time, we would be living in the next city, the city of Norwich, Connecticut, in a brand-new house with two floors and plenty of room for parking. Stephen and Tyller had graduated early. Now it was Jore'll and Ryan's turn. I enjoyed picking them up from school. There were so many things going on there that I didn't like, but I had to bite the bullet. I didn't care for their school; it was called Norwich Free Academy. I couldn't wait until they graduated.

But before that could happen, the new order came; it was time to make another move. This time, it was back to Monterey, California. I was happy that we were heading back to California again. This time, we rented a Pinsky U-Haul truck, the largest one they had. Could you imagine driving this truck across the country? That was a big mistake. Never again. And there were three drivers: me, Tyller, and Ryan. Now this is a shocker—this truck was slow; the top speed was seventy-five miles per hours. We were in one of the slowest vehicles on the road, and we were on Interstate 8 West out of Chicago. Thats why it took us long to reach California. We all agreed never to drive a U-Haul truck across the country.

I'm a people person. I did it all, from teaching to stringing tennis rackets. I specialized in working with the small ones. I would always start with the four- to seven-year-olds. This would be my first young group. The second group would be nine- to twelve-year-olds, boys and girls, then all the junior and high school students. I would finish off with the college students. They would be able to engage in stiff competition in the college ranks and one day become professionals.

I had heard some great news: they were looking for volunteers at the Monterey Bay Aquarium. There was a special orientation process to be met if one expected to be part of this prestigious group: a clean police record, valid identification, community membership, three good references from the area, and a letter of recommendation from someone who worked at the aquarium. For me, I had no problem. One of the members of the church had worked at the aquarium for many years.

The job was a good experience for anyone who loves people and participating in neighborhood events. That was me. The name of the lady that gave me a letter of recommendation was Wendy. We both were members at the same church. I was one of two ministers there. She said she'd be happy to give me an endorsement letter. She also said her mother and father had worked for the aquarium for twenty years, and they were the reason she became a member.

I passed all the preliminary tests, and it was a really friendly group of people. So now I was an official member of Monterey Bay Aquarium. I was happy for that opportunity. The state of California was a super place to live—a little expensive, but you must pay for all that good weather. I was so happy to live and work in this beautiful state, something I never thought would happen in my lifetime. However, it wasn't long before the challenges would arrive and test the very fabric of our family's foundation, our love. Despite my best efforts, hoping and praying that my marriage stand the test of time, in the end it didn't.

My deepest desires were to live the type of life where all our kids could come home whenever they wanted to spend some R-and-R with their mother and father and grandparents as a loving family.

Not so in this case. Although I did and would always honor the vows in our marriage, things were not looking good for the family structure, we were falling apart. Our kids were in a state of shock when their mom decided she no longer wanted to be married to me and felt it was time for the boys to go their own way as well. There wasn't anything anyone could say or do to change her mind, it was made up. I had nothing to say about the situation. All our boys were shocked beyond belief; I was so devastated about her decision. I had to stay strong for myself and my boys. I will always be there for them, no matter what the cost. At this point, I had no idea this was coming. It happened out of the blue. Now I had to weather the storm and find a way out for me and my boys' sake.

Out of all the duty stations—Antigua, West Indies, Keflavik Island, the Submarine Base in Groton, Connecticut— the whole family was always involved in some kind of activity. *"A strong family that lives together shares love together."* All the boys took part in Boy Scout programs and church service programs. The biggest events were all the sports programs, and we did it all together as a family. Picnics and camping, fishing—we did it all. I didn't see the breakup coming; this was one way to destroy a really good family. Now I guess you're wondering why I didn't mention my boys' mother's name. It's because she didn't want to be part of our family anymore, or part of my story.

This night, I was in the front room watching a movie on TV. My youngest son Ryan came and told me Mom wanted to see me in our bedroom. I went to our bedroom, and all four of my boys were crying their eyes out. I looked at her. She was just sitting there on the bed, staring into space, with no care in the world. So, here it is in a nutshell.

"Well," she insisted. I quote, "We are two different people now." She went on to say, "It's not about me. You guys are on your own." I wished I could stop the tears from my boys' eyes. Her mind was made up. She stated, "We are going in different, and separate, ways as of now." At the same time, she had this cold look on her face; that was strange. She was totally wrong. She was still the head of household, and there was a legal document through the US Military, statements she signed herself as the legal head of household.

I believe a military person on active duty can't just throw her family to the wolves and act as if it couldn't cause some serious problems. I couldn't help but think, "Does she have any kind of conscience in this situation?" Meanwhile, what were my four boys and myself to do? There was only one conclusion I could come up with. Abandonment. This abandonment threw us for a loop, like something from a horror movie. All the sadness brought tears to my boys' eyes, and that was a terrible sight to see. I'm so happy I was able to keep my composure in this unforgiveable situation. An angry person can't solve any problems. Abandonment really hurt my boys, and we were about to experience the worst of it all.

Once someone becomes abandoned, it won't be very long before one is homeless as well. My oldest son Stephen said, *"I can't believe Mom is doing this to Dad."* He couldn't believe what she was doing to all of us.

Stephen moved to Minot, North Dakota. There, he got settled and went to law school. He was doing well with his studies.

My second-oldest son, Tyller, had a place of his own here in Monterey a year earlier, so he was fine where he was. It was a very nice place. He was the Monterey city councilman; this made me very proud. So, he was okay.

Jore'll also had a fine job at the Lexus car dealership as a detailer; this was one job he really loved. All he talked about was detailing cars. At the end of his shift, he had to find a place to park and sleep for the night. Most of the time, he would park by the small lake off Highway 101, next to the Home Depot store.

My son Jore'll was hurt the worst of all my boys. I found out he was so devastated he didn't know which way to turn. He couldn't keep the negative thoughts out of his mind. He couldn't withstand the strain it put on him, being abandoned by his mother. Living in his car was something that drove him a little crazy, if you know what I mean. He found it terrible trying to sleep in his small car with those long legs. He was around six feet and four inches tall and was still growing.

Every night, he made his way down to the lake next to Home Depot. There, we could see a big crowd of homeless people sleeping in their cars, vans, and mobile homes. If one were homeless, this was the place to go, and the police didn't bother the homeless people as much there. Ryan and I parked next to Jore'll in my truck. The three of us made it as comfortable as possible. One thing was for sure: I was happy they had jobs. I had a part-time job at the tennis center.

Jore'll was so upset about the outcome of his mother's decision. That was so terrible; she shouldn't have put everyone out on the streets like animals, without a care in the world. There are just coldhearted people, and that is what she was. She didn't give us a second thought. Jore'll just kept it all inside. But I looked at him and knew it hurt him badly. It got to the point where it was so unbearable, he posted it on social media. He was reaching out, desperate for help from anyone.

As his father, I didn't know this was taking place. He was reaching out to someone who could give him some comfort and hope. He knew I would always be there for him, and he also knew I was in the same predicament as him, Ryan, and the rest of my boys, Tyller and Stephen. That's a father's responsibility, looking out for the offspring. Yes, I was there when all the trouble started. I remember when he told me he had found a place to live with a friend he knew from work.

I was happy for him. I took my truck and helped him move in. If only you could see his face. I wanted all my boys to be happy. I didn't know all this about Jore'll until I got a call from my sister Vonda. She told me what she read on social media, how Jore'll was so upset about being abandoned by his mother. That was concerning to me; they are my boys, and I would do all I could to help him stay safe and as happy as possible. I never thought a mother could be so cold and cruel. I had no other choice but to leave this situation in God's hands. He would take care of me and my boys.

Ryan, my youngest son, was working for a welding company part-time, and he was attending school at Monterey Peninsula College. He too had to sleep in the same place that Jore'll was sleeping. He slept with me in my truck. I gave him the back seat because it had more room, and it was much more comfortable. He was really upset, and I could see it in his face. That made me feel bad. I slept in the front seat. It was strange, but we were doing fine. The three of us learned how to adjust to being abandoned and left out in the elements.

My boys were devastated at how things turned out. I told them we'd be fine. Sometimes I slept at the Tennis Center Pro Shop. We did what we had to do to survive at this low point of our lives.

I'm a Libra, and I will go the distance for the ones I love, no matter what it takes. I will go even farther for the ones who share and return the same love. It is strange how one life changes in the flash of a moment, without any warning.

I would not let the abandonment alter my way of living; life is too short, and wasting time was no option. At this junction, I would not let this unravel my way of life. In the end, I would receive greater gifts, and that gift came from the one and only God. He would take care of me and my boys. God would never let us down and would always be by our side. I carried the fear of God in my heart. I was thankful for my boys; they were doing well. My prayers would always be with them because they were the joy of my life, even though someone tried hard to disrupt our relationship. I would continue to work hard for the better things in life. I think everyone you meet is fighting some kind of battle in life. Sometimes it's a battle you know nothing about, but we as a people and as a family couldn't let this stop our way of life.

There are some things in life you wish for, and maybe some things you can't have. It hurts more when you can't have them, and even more when you are poor—I mean, really poor. When there is a struggle, don't fight the uphill battle. I would focus on making life more pleasant for my boys and myself. Now I had a different battle ahead; it would be in a court of law. This took place in the city of Monterey, California, at the Monterey Supreme Court. I don't have to go into details—all divorce cases pretty much have the same outcome. Someone wins and the other loses. The presiding judge weighed all the evidence and made her decision. In my case, it was in my favor, because I was considered the party who was believable and honorable and sticking to the vows of our marriage.

Now that this shocking news had destroyed our family, we all needed to find a sturdy place to live. Stephen and Tyller were doing well. Ryan and Jore'll moved to San Diego. It was a fine place there in Monterey, but I had no other choice but to move back to my hometown, Waynesboro, Mississippi. I lived in a small trailer home; that didn't pan out well at all. The hurricane was a category 5—one of the most dangerous land disasters that one person could ever encounter. I couldn't ever imagine living in a small trailer in the middle of a category 5 hurricane. The wind and rain with heavy thunder all sounded like a freight train ripping and tearing things apart. I had to come up with another plan of action. I was not sure where to go from there.

Well, some good news: our father was rich in years. He reached a milestone of one hundred years old, and our whole family was so very happy for all the hard times throughout the years. They gave him a large celebration. The mayor of Albany gave our father a proclamation, letting the people of Albany know about this man who'd lived a good life and a very long one as well. I talked with the mayor; her name was Kathy Sheehan. I talked with her secretary; she mailed me a copy of that proclamation, with gold letters on some fine paper. Good news is food for the heart. For now, I would move to Detroit to be close to my twin. He owned his own business called J&O Salvage Company. I really enjoyed working for and with him. It was amazing to see him work the business.

I tried it for a while. It was still difficult at times. We did a great deal of traveling from state to state. I found a small house, very reasonable. It was okay, but I had no furniture. Well, all I needed was a place to sleep, to shower, and to cook some good old-fashioned meals. Some years earlier, I used to drive a shuttle bus for the Detroit Metropolitan Airport. This would give me something to do at night. They were glad to see me. I got the job and drove for eight months. I'd been gone for such a long time that I totally forgot about the rough, treacherous, hard winter coming down from Canada. I made sure I stayed busy during the winter.

It seems when things are going well, something will spoil our family's happiness. The Angel of Death had visited once again and made that happiness become another devastation for us all as a close-knit family. The only difference with my father's death was that the family would not be making that long trip back to our hometown. It was very hard to swallow for the rest of the family. As you know, he was born and bred in the state of Alabama, and he raised his family in the state of Mississippi. We wanted his body to be placed next to his first wife, our mother, reuniting the two lovebirds that eloped across the Choctaw County line.

Since he was married, they laid him to rest with his second wife in Albany. We all had mixed feelings about the outcome. One thing was for sure: they gave him a beautiful homegoing celebration. The sunrise and the sunset all came together for a great hardworking man. We all would miss his special songs he sang so often. The whole family was there to see him leave in the arms of the heavenly Father. May God continue to take care of our father. One thing was for sure: we all were there to see our dad, as his life was rich in years. It was a blessing to be with him on his milestone of living to one hundred years. Even his siblings called him Dad, but his friends and my mother all called him Neshia.

Some good news: my two younger boys, Jore'll and Ryan, had moved from San Diego to Glens Falls, New York. As soon as the snow melted, I'd made my way to South Glens Falls to be close to them. They would be looking for a place for me, now that the winter has passed South Glens Falls. I couldn't find a place for a long time, so I looked in the Albany area and, with some good fortune, found a place in the downtown area, in fact, at South Pearl Street. It only took a few weeks. This was the break I really needed—a place of my own, just like in Detroit. I had no furniture at the time, so the landlord was very nice. She asked if I needed anything, and she gave me a beautiful king-size bed with other furniture to go with it. I was overjoyed with her kindness.

It was on the fourth floor—not too bad. It could have been on a higher floor. That meant all those stairs to climb, if or when the elevator wasn't working. The parking lot had security cameras all around the grounds. It felt good to be close to my boys. I tried to take a trip to visit them at least three or four times a month. It was okay for a while, but now the gas prices had skyrocketed. When I first arrived, the price of gas was $2.80 a gallon. Now it was $4.60 a gallon. Everything had higher prices now that I was closer to my boys, but I could visit them even more now.

## The Assault on South Pearl Street—February 22, 2022

I fear walking the streets of downtown Albany. I had to walk to the library to continue working on my memoir. It was about three blocks from where I lived at South Pearl Street. People began to stare at me, as if they were looking for something. That scared me something awful, but I told myself to just keep on walking and not to look around as I walked. Sometimes I would walk down Grand Street, but it was the same as Pearl Street. So I tried walking down Trinity Place. It was the same area where I was living. It didn't have the same violence like South Pearl and Grand Street.

When I did walk, I continued to look around to my left and right, and occasionally I looked behind me, just to be safe and have that awareness. When I had to go outside, I made sure I used the back entrance. Sometimes I use the side entrance, but altogether I tried my best to just stay inside and leave the trouble on the streets. The real trouble was out on the streets, and that was where it should stay.

My younger son Ryan was upset, and he wanted me to move out of the area. So, I was in the process of moving as soon as I got the okay from the housing office. The way things were here, any place was better than Albany. I didn't know where to start; my son wanted me to move up north, to places like Boston Spa, Saratoga Springs, or Hudson Falls. My son lived in South Glens Falls, so that was the first place I looked when I first arrived here from Detroit.

One other thing: I didn't have a great deal of faith in the police department. They were supposed to protect and serve. I also lost faith in the court systems. I was just a number among thousands of other citizens who lived in the metropolitan area. I couldn't understand how a person walking the streets of Albany could be assaulted and robbed, and they pretended they had a gun. I didn't know that at the time, so my heart was filled with fear. I was told by the police nothing would become of that. Where was the faith in our law enforcement officers? Things would get better as time passed, and then I could put it all behind me. It would be just a dull, memorable thought.

My family had just gotten over the death of our father. Now, the Angel of Death came with a swift visit to my older sister, Gloria Jean Williamson Koonce. My big sister was our mom's right-hand helper in that two-room shack in our hometown. She was our mother and father's second-born child. She carried a pretty smile all the time. I'll never forget the gold she had put in her mouth, between the two front teeth. When she smiled, the gold would glitter. What's happening to our family was in God's hands, and there was a reason for it, and his plan was to strengthen our family. My big sister was a fighter. She was in the hospital for a while. Things changed for the better, but then she took a turn for the worse and had to go back in the hospital. There, she fought hard for some time. And the Angel of Death only doing God's will. I guess when one family find their family member is place in hopes is a shocking moment. We all knew it was a matter of time.

As I mentioned, we are a close-knit family. We stayed there until she was told, "Relax, don't fight. You are in God's hands." Then and only then, she gave a strong look and God took her with him to a place where there was no more trouble, pain, and heartache. I've mentioned this so many times, but we had another long trip back to our hometown. This would bring our family much closer. That's why I tried so hard to get our family to take heed to my mantra: I stood by my mantra. I also reached out to other family as well.

Now it was time for some fun and good times with my boys who lived in Glens Falls. This would help me to clear my mind from all the trouble in Albany the last few weeks. We would go and do some bowling, and maybe a few games of pool, just to share time with each other as father and sons. And like I always said, they had good jobs. That was all I wanted to hear. Now that the weather had changed, spring was around the corner.

Now I could really do things with my two boys, like biking, mountain climbing all over Lake George, and most of all, some serious camping. I bought a new tent and other camping gear. Well, this one day, Ryan and I decided to go camping at Lake George. It was hot, and there was good weather. We drove up the mountain and found a good spot to park, and off we went into the woods.

We couldn't believe what we'd discovered: a freshwater running stream. We pitched the tent, put away all the food so the bears couldn't get into it, and went for a hike up the mountain overlooking Lake George to the highest point on the mountain, looking down on that huge lake. We made the trip back down the mountain to our campsite, had something to eat, and prepared for the night. We got comfortable for a good night's sleep. The weirdest thing is the stream made one of the most beautiful sounds, as if we were under a rainstorm. It was so cozy and peaceful that we had no problem sleeping.

The next morning, we awoke and had breakfast—nothing like cooking in the woods early in the morning. Ryan had to go down the mountain for an errand. I told him I would stay here and relax with the sound of the rushing water. Within hours, it started to rain, and the tent started leaking. I thought the tent was a sure deal not to leak. I grabbed all I could so it wouldn't get wet, but it got worse, so I tried to call him. Well, there was no cellphone service on the mountaintop. I didn't know what to do, so I said to myself, "I will flag down the first car that passes by."

It took a while, then one car came by. I flagged it down; it was a single couple. I said, "Please, could you help me? I have a hole in my tent and my son just left and went to Glens Falls. And there's no cellphone service here on the mountain. So can I give you my two my son's phone number?" They said, "That will be fine with us." I told them to call either one of my sons and tell them the tent was leaking and I was getting wet and to please come and help me before we lost everything—our laptops and tablets, and so forth.

That was a good plan by stopping the first car that came by. Not long after, Ryan came running through the woods, and we packed all our things and headed down the mountain. And we will make plans for the next adventure. I stayed in Glens Falls for the weekend. I slept in my truck every night. Let's not forget what happened back in Monterey and the devastation I and my boys endured and what we had to encounter; it threw us for a loop. Yes, that was an underhanded situation, and I still believe it was a dream or nightmare of some kind. Like I mentioned before, I will not let anything stop me from seeing my boys—they are my heart. Their mom didn't understand what it meant that *A strong family that lives together shares love together.* Her plans to start a new family didn't pan out.

Afterward, I headed back to Albany. The next trip would be riding our mountain bikes. That was a ton of fun. Just about every weekend, I did a ton of things with my sons throughout the whole summer. I missed my granddaughter; she and her mom were in Germany. My daughter-in-law was stationed there; she was in the Air Force, and they planned to visit later that summer. I couldn't wait to see them. She was getting close to the last years before returning to the United States.

For now, it was just me and my two boys. We would always find something to do; having fun in the outdoors . . . it couldn't get any better than that. Now it was getting close to the end of summer and the season would be much cooler. In the last year, we lost family members. This would make us stronger and keep us looking to the hills from which come our strength. The Angel of Death once again came to visit our brother, Edward Thomas Williamson, one of my younger brothers. He pretty much went through the same thing as my older sister, Gloria Jean. He too was a fighter, spending time in the hospital for a long while. As usual, we as a family were there for him. He was placed in hospice, a sign we knew meant it would only be a matter of time. Just like my father, he was married, and his wife was still living there. She wanted him laid to rest there in Albany. The family was there to support her and the rest of their family. All in all, God was still with us all. We needed to look to him for strength. Now there was one girl left and six boys out of ten children, all from my mom and dad all the way from the Deep South.

So now our family was trying to put our lives together and look for strength from God. He said, "In the time of sadness and sorrow, don't worry, I will be by your side. And keep your eyes looking toward the mountain; there you will find me." Well, I'm happy to say there were good times in our future, and it would be happening in a few weeks. This time, it would be a special celebration. We would all be heading back to our hometown real soon.

The whole family was having a special going-away celebration for our big brother. It was a well-organized trip back to our one-stoplight hometown, Waynesboro, Mississippi. This time, it was well-deserved, and a long time coming to boot. The entire family was putting their resources into the trip, with both financial and moral support. We were giving my big brother Alvin Earl Williamson a special homegoing celebration on his eightieth birthday. Not only did he want family, but all those who knew him in the past and present.

This is for my big brother and my mentor. He's one of the main reasons I'm writing my memoir in the first place. There are a number of reasons—in fact, four in total. One, Alvin Williamson; two, the Champ, three, my principal; and four, the pastor. And so many more important people are the reason as well. I was inspired to go take this journey, which is an adventure in the form of words that bring peace and happiness, and other times they bring tears and sadness.

They are all put together to bring out this wonderful and entreating story. I consider myself blessed as well, and I'm so thankful for life, health, and strength, which are the most important things in life. This is what my big brother had been wanting for such a long time coming. Now it finally panned out, and his decision made me very happy. And I see the glow all over his face; it shows in his footsteps as he walks. There will be family from all over—Michigan to California, North Dakota to Louisiana. I love you, big bro.

We'd all be gathering in our hometown once again. One thing was for sure: the Angel of Death would not appear to take another member of our family today. There would be music, all kinds of food, swimming, games—just a ton of fun on this special day. I looked all around, and all I could see was joy and happiness through the crowd. This took place at the City Hall, at an unbelievable price. The families all had a wonderful time, with music and very good food. It lasted for a good part of the day. It ended, and now everyone was heading back to the church. There, we all would participate in prayer and thanksgiving, music, and videos. I was pleased that everything came out so well.

Now it was time for everyone to prepare for those long, different trips back to their homes. My trip would take us back to Albany. This time, it was a trip during which everyone shared love and peace, and everyone had a ton of fun all around. Meanwhile, this gave my twin and I a chance to reminisce. It had been so long since the two of us had time and the chance to tour our hometown.

Where shall we start? Let me see. We will take you to the place where our house used to be. This was a shocking surprise as we stood there looking at each other, saying, "This can't be true." All the property where our house sat on back then seemed to be so large to us, and the house was very huge as it sat so close to the train tracks. Well,, we couldn't believe how the terrain had changed so much. Today it is so very small. and to us now it is unbelievable to the eye. We looked at each other in amazement.

The train tracks seemed so far away from the house. That old, dusty dirt road seemed so small. Now, it was paved with blacktop and stone. To us, there was plenty of room to play, and there was room for a small garden, a water pump, and clothesline. We just looked at each other in disbelief, saying, "Our house was on this small piece of land." Yes, I know— time and space had changed things. So we continued our tour around town. The next stop was Mrs. Mamie Russell's house. Remember the plantation-looking house that sat on the corner? It wasn't there anymore; my twin and I will always cherish those memories, even though Mrs. Mamie Russell cheated us all the time when we picked pecans for her back in the day.

She thought we were two dumb little Black boys and that we knew no better. Only if she really knew how smart we were. We could still see the huge pecan trees that sat on this large piece of property. And let's not forget that Confederate flag on her back porch. We guessed she was a rebel; that's what we thought back then.

Now that our old grayish house was no longer there, my twin and I wanted to walk across the property, but we thought it wouldn't be a very good idea. It would be better if we just looked from the road. We were still in the one-stoplight town. The next stop brought tears to my eyes; it was the spot where we saw the train T-bone this white car owned by the white man, in which he didn't survive. It was as if it was yesterday, that terrible, horrifying accident in which a man lost his life. There were more scary and dangerous events. Don't forget, we were adventurous little boys back then.

The scary old train trestle—this time, we were both in deep sadness and had to fight back the tears. When we were little, it seemed so big and tall, and it put fear in our hearts and minds. And it was a very dangerous trestle as well. It was still huge and really frightening, and all those memories came rushing back to our hearts and minds.

And I couldn't believe we played on this trestle. Those crossbeams were coated with blacktop to preserve the wood, and the wood was very sticky, but this didn't stop us from climbing the trestle. The surface made our hands black, dirty, and sticky. We made sure our mom didn't see us with all that black tar and dirt all over us.

Many times, I can remember our grandmother telling us to stay off the trestle, because many people had lost their lives on it. Well, you know those twins—we had to climb it, we had to walk across it, and we did it many times when we were little boys. That was the adventure in our lives; just look back and you will see all the troublesome and scary things we got into.

The trestle was giving us an invite; it was saying, I'm here, and that was all we needed to hear, with so much excitement. The real danger was on top; there wasn't any side railing to keep people from falling off. We had to climb through the crossbeams. This photo shows the water level is shallow. When we were younger, it was much deeper back then, and scarier.

The rushing white water was very strong at that. We could fish and swim in that cold and clear water, and those huge rocks were very slippery. We could have fallen in at any time. So this was our away-from-home playground, knowing we could have gotten the switch or the belt if we got caught. Well, we decided to go ahead anyway. I guess we were too young and innocent to have that kind of fear.

Could you imagine two little boys standing on this big trestle when the train was coming? Next, I talked about the backstreet burger shop in town, owned by the Cooley family. We were told that the backstreet burger shop was still there in the same spot. So we looked at each other, my twin and I, and we decided to give the backstreet burger shop a visit. Back in the day, when we were little boys, the road went to the left only. In the front of Cooley's restaurant, there was a door for the white people entered the restaurant. All Black folks had to enter at the back door, just like all homes through the area.

There was a big sign on the side of the building that read "Cooley's Burgers." That sign was new to us. It was always called the backstreet burgers. The burgers were so delicious that I could eat at least four or five all by myself, but today in 2021, they didn't taste the same.

I could only eat one and a half burgers, and Jerry could only eat half a burger; he didn't like them at all. What happened to that good-tasting hamburger from when we were little boys? Mr. Cooley was the person cooking all the hamburgers, and he also owned one of those Confederate rebel flags flying out front. Now his son was the owner, except there were some changes.

The burgers didn't taste the same anymore. Yes, he was one of those good ole' boys. One thing we didn't forget was how he cheated our mother and father at the Cooley's car dealership back when we were little. Now that his son oversaw the restaurant, the hamburger was not that good, and they were much smaller and very greasy. It was because the second generation took over. I guess they didn't stick to the original recipe; those good-tasting hamburgers were a thing of the past.

The other stop we made before hitting the road: The Chickasawhay River in our hometown. My twin brother and I were at that river today, and it was still scary. It took the lives of so many people. We both stood there looking at this dangerous river with tears in our eyes, knowing it could have taken one or both of us at any point. We reflected on how Tommy Joe used to take us there, so many times for so many years.

I came close to death that one hot summer day in my hometown, there with my sister Geraldine and her family Tommy Joe, Shelia, Walter, Thurnell, Yolonda, Rene JR., and Antionette, with my youngest sister Vonda. This is my story: we all were there for a visit in Waynesboro, and it was very hot that day. Tom said, "Let's go for a swim," so we all went down to the Chickasawhay River. We all walked on the cool brown sand, looking at this dangerous river. We all looked and said it looked scary, and let me tell you, I was scared. Suddenly Tom ran and dove into that scary river. He swam to the other side with ease, climbed onto the bank, turned, and yelled, "Terry, what are you waiting for? Come on over."

It was the adrenaline that took over. I looked and with no hesitation dove into the water. I had good strokes and was swimming with ease. I got to the other side, climbed out, and chatted with Tommy Joe for a moment. Then he again dove back into the water and swam back to the other side. Again, he yelled, "Terry, come on," and into the water I dove, swimming with good strokes. Then before I got halfway, I saw this huge spider swimming toward me—that's all I remember. I was on my back laying in the sand. My sister Geraldine gave off a very loud scream that prompted Tommy Joe to dive back into the rushing water to save my life. I'm blessed to be alive and able to talk about it. And the memories still bring tears and a chilly feeling all over me, those chills that make the hairs stand up on the back of your neck and on your arms. It was so unbelievable, and so eerie to boot. This dangerous river isn't as large as the Mississippi River, which is three times the size. On the other hand, it's still a large, dangerous river, and I swam in it.

It took the lives of so many young people. It runs from Jackson, Waynesboro, Mississippi, to Lake Pontchartrain in New Orleans. One thing was for sure: I would not venture down that path ever again. Now it's time to get back on the road. Us twins knew all the celebration and fun had come to a close. We must make that long trip back home, the 1,800-mile journey back. It would take us about twelve hours to get to our destination.

My younger brother Billy and I would stay in Detroit at my twin brother's house, then we would make the trip back to Albany and start prepping for the Fourth of July 2021 celebration in a few days. My granddaughter would be coming back to the States from Germany for the summer with her mom. We all couldn't wait to see them. She and her mom had been gone for a long time. They would be in North Dakota for the whole summer. Then in September, they would make the trip back to Germany. My youngest son Ryan made the trip to visit them. I would do anything to visit my granddaughter; for now, I had to stay away until she came to New York. The problems with my sons' mother continued, so I couldn't make the trip to North Dakota, but I would see my granddaughter in August, just before they made the trip back to Germany.

I couldn't wait to see my granddaughter; she was so big and beautiful, our grown-up little girl, and she was growing so fast as well. Her mom had a few more years left before she came back to the States for good. I couldn't wait for that day to come. At least I could FaceTime her while she was in North Dakota. She made me feel so happy this Fourth of July, my one and only granddaughter.

I bought all the camping and hiking gear for us. When she arrived, this would be her first time ever spending time outdoors in the woods with her grandpa. I couldn't wait to get her back on the tennis courts; she'd loved the game of tennis since she was four years old. We always had a ton of fun as papa and granddaughter. She had so many stories to tell me; the best one was the story about the lifestyle of a shark. I just love to see her face when she's talking. She's so serious.

Imagine the time we would have, when she was back in the States for good. Until then, I spent time with my two younger sons, Ryan and Jore'll. There we'd do some mountain biking, hiking, tennis, and, if possible, leave room for some freshwater fishing. This summer, the sky was the limit. I was so happy for my two boys; they both had good jobs, and they both were hard workers. It will pay off in the long run as they get older.

Maybe one day soon, I'll take them back to visit my hometown, so they will know their roots and share it with their children one day. This will continue to build the family name, just as me and my brothers did for my father in his later years. Jore'll didn't make the trip to North Dakota to visit his niece and her mother; he had to work.

Ryan made the trip to North Dakota to spend time with his niece. She would have so much to do with her Uncle Ryan. I knew he would keep her busy there in the flatlands of North Dakota. So when Ryan made it back to South Glens Falls, the three of us would spend some father-and-son time on the mountaintop at Lake George. Ryan raced motorcycles, and I just loved to see him ride. He really looked good on a motorcycle, and he's a safe rider. He wanted me to start riding. Well, I'd see, maybe later this summer. For now, I enjoyed watching him ride.

He was out riding now, and when he got back, we would both watch the motorsports GP races on TV. It was our special time to share the fun of watching and riding. I couldn't wait to see him giving his niece a ride on his motorcycle. I can see her now: "Uncle Ryan, one more time! It's fun!" My two sons and my granddaughter had the whole week in August to share and have tons of fun, because soon she would have to return to the Air Force base in Germany by September and continue her schooling there.

I know she would miss her new friends and the new surroundings. Pretty soon, she'd be home for good, in less than three years. And Papa can't wait for that day to come. I love good news: there were three days left before my granddaughter would be in South Glen Falls. She and her mom would be here for a week, and it was time for so many fun things. She'd be going on eleven years old now. In fact, September 2021, my granddaughter would have a brand-new birthday celebration. Well, there's some sad news unfortunately—she'd be back in Germany on her birthday that year. Thanks to the new technology, we had FaceTime and Facebook on our phones, or texting. And another good thing was that she had her own cellphone at the age of ten years old. We'd celebrate her birthday in fashion. For now, we were off to the pool. She swam like a fish; she loved the water. Those traits came from her dad and Papa. There would be tennis, biking, camping, and a whole lot of other fun and games. For now, I was blessed to have one granddaughter, but not for long; soon, A. D. W., my daughter-in-law, would be having my other granddaughter.

The new baby would be here soon; in fact, it would be around December 22. My granddaughter was so happy about the good news, so now her Uncle Ryan and Uncle Jore'll and Uncle Tyller would have another niece to love and play with. I don't have to say anything about how I felt as her Papa. Now I could say I have two granddaughters. I was so very proud that Tyller, who lived in Monterey, would be able to make the trip to New York to see his niece. I knew he was very busy with his job; he was the Monterey city councilman, and he'd held that position for more than three years, Right now my son is preparing and working hard to run for mayor of Monterey County. That was very good for the family, and as always, we would continue to give him our support for his campaigning success.

Good luck, my son, in your run for mayor of Monterey, California. For now, with my two other sons, Ryan and Jore'll, I couldn't wait for that first week of August to come rolling in and to spend some special time with their niece. The weather would be great, with just a few days with no chance of rain. Anyway, we were ready for the outdoors and fun, which would bring all kinds of happiness. That's what life is all about.

Until that time, I'd continue to work hard on my memoir. It's really like a full-time job. I made the trip to the Howe Library on Schuyler and Clint Street six days a week— Monday and Wednesday from twelve to eight, Tuesday and

Thursday from ten to six, and Friday and Saturday from twelve to six. I want to express my gratitude to the staff for their dedication. I had no idea that writing a memoir would take so much out of you physically and mentally.

This was a real nine-to-five job, and I was excited that it was working out very well. I was blessed with the foresight and ability to put these words and thoughts together. I would continue to strive for dedication in recording my memoir.

## EIGHTEEN

A Strong Family That Lives Together Shares Love Together

This is my granddaughter. She was in Glens Falls, New York, for one long week. And my oh my, look how she has grown. Like my son Stephen said before, she was growing up before our very eyes—a very tall, slim, beautiful, sparking-blue-eyed young girl, and let's not forget the curly blond hair to boot. She screamed that wonderful word I love much, "Papa"—that brought sweet music to my ears. We both ran toward each other with outstretched arms to share a special, big hugging moment.

Look at you; I miss you, and I love you. "Me too, Papa, as well." Now it was time to gather all the camping gear; it was all ready and packed. Let's hit the woods for fun and games. Then we'd make our way to Crandall Park to see if my granddaughter still had those tennis skills.

She loved the game of tennis; she'd been playing since she was four years old in San Diego and Monterey. I will play with her as long as she wants. I'll always be there for her. Kids learn so fast as they grow up and develop those good tennis skills.

They didn't have tennis for her in Germany, so this would be a long, hard practice for her today. "She said, what's next Papa?"

"Hmm . . . let me see. How about some soft-serve ice cream?"

"Oh, thank you, Papa!" So off we went for some soft-serve ice cream. After a short drive across town into Glens Falls, we were there, as I held her little soft hands.

"Okay, little girl, what do you want?"

She said, "Papa, you make the order."

"OK, my little girl."

"Two banana splits please, the works—vanilla, chocolate, strawberry, whipped cream, peanuts, and a maraschino cherry on top. And don't forget the napkins."

"Mmm . . . that was good, Papa. Okay, Papa, it's your turn. I know—let's go to the movies! What's playing Papa?"

"The movie *Nope*; it came out this July."

She said, "Can we go and see that one Papa?"

"Sorry, baby girl. It's rated R," I said. "Instead, let's go to the outlet mall. There you can leave with a bag filled with lots of new things. Then afterward Papa will show you how play the drum. I know you will love it. I'll teach you how to play the tenor drum so we can play together. I'll play the snare drum."

Now that was fun playing with Papa, an unforgettable moment in our lives.

These are the things I enjoyed so much with my granddaughter. We had one solid week, and we would make sure she left with joy and happiness. The last day, what could we do for fun?

My son Jore'll said, "How about rock climbing?"

"Well, for your niece, and my sweet granddaughter, it's not that safe. Besides, it may hurt her little fingers and toes, and she could get blisters."

Ryan said, "Hey Dad! What about ziplining? You know she will really enjoy that."

Well, off to the North Way 87. What a place—it had a nice ride throughout this part of the Adirondack Mountains. Now that we were there, it would be filled with tons of fun and excitement. It was so much fun, and what an adventure. How time flies when you're having fun. We stayed there almost five hours, and even then, my granddaughter didn't want to go home.

My oh my, that one week went by so fast. Now it was time for her to get ready for that long flight back to Germany. Her mom had a little more than a year and a half to finish her overseas tour in the Air Force, then it would be back to the United States. As her Papa, I can't wait until she's back in the United States for good. Imagine the fun we would have then. Here come the hugs, kissing, and tears of joy for now. I was told by my daughter-in-law it would take between eleven and fourteen hours to fly back to the Air Force Base in Germany.

My daughter-in-law and my granddaughter had to make one flight change in Amsterdam. When they landed and got settled on base, there would be one more visit from my daughter-in-law before her tour ended this next August of 2022 to early 2023. She had one of the most amazing, exciting jobs for a female soldier. She works on, of course, the one and only C-5 Galaxy. This plane is a workhorse; the payload for the C-5 is 281,001 pounds, the C-17 payload is 170,900 pounds, and the B-52 bomber payload is 70,000 pounds. My daughter-in-law worked on all three planes, and she knew them all like the back of her hand.

Every time I talked with her, she always talked about her job. Her stories fascinated me, and she always took the time to tell me what I needed to know. And she would answer all my questions. I'm fascinated with military planes. My first fascination was the Blue Angels F-18 fighter planes, and Fat Albert, a C-5 Galaxy with its rocket busters. My second choice—the Thunderbirds F-18 fighter plane, they performed at the Sacramento joint command base; these planes are from the US Air Force squadron. And the others are from the US Navy squadron. Now that my daughter-in-law and my granddaughter are back in Germany, we all miss them so much. I can't wait until she comes home for good.

Me and the boys would have to stay in contact with them by social media and Facebook, or by FaceTime. We will always be there for my granddaughter, and their nieces. I could focus now on my two boys in Glens Falls, New York: Jore'll and Ryan. I will visit them mostly on weekends. They both had good jobs, and they didn't have any problems with hard work. Jore'll was saving for his favorite car, the GTR twin-turbocharged 3.8-liter V-6, manufactured by Nissan. It would cost him more near $70,000 for his dream car.

Ryan owned two motorcycles. One was the BMW 1000 r, the other a BMW 1000 rr–M. They are some of the most powerful machines of the line. The BMW rr–M was his favorite. He uses the BMW r for commuting back and forth to work and around the city.

Look at this wonderful bike; this was one of the bikes he had his heart set on, the BMW rr–M. He took it for a test ride, and it would arrive around the first of April. I can see him now with that big smile that stretches from ear to ear. Well, we both would be happy. But first, let me tell you a few exciting stories about my son Ryan and his adventures with his first motorcycles.

It all happened back in Monterey when the three of us—Ryan, Jore'll, and I—lived in Seaside, California. We did a lot of mountain biking, and Ryan was much better than I was. But he wanted more adventure. He asked me what I thought about motorcycles.

I told him, "I don't know Ryan; they are a little dangerous."

He said, "Dad, it's all up to the rider. Come with me; I'll show you the bike."

I went with him. One of the guys from his job had one for sale. We stopped over at his house. Ryan knocked and he opened his garage door, and there it was. He took one look at the motorcycle—if one could see the look on Ryan's face and the glow in his eyes! The guy took it out and Ryan got on it, started it up, and just took off down the street. I thought he would fall or crash. He got to the end of the street, made a large circle turn, and headed back up the street with no problem at all. I had mixed emotions— he did a good job riding for the first time. I knew he had to do some research first, and he showed signs of a good rider. The rest was history. Now I love to see him ride. I looked at him and said, "Well, maybe someday I can give it a try." That day came quicker than I thought. I bought myself a motorbike; this would give me some time to practice riding. It was a Honda 150-G. It weighed 275 pounds and it was a ton of fun and easy to ride. So, 2022 has been a good year so far for us all. This bike ride will be a ton of fun. I know it's also dangerous, and I have the scars to prove it. I will go for a long ride to Troy, Schenectady, Delmar, East Green Bush . . . just having fun on the road. It's so peaceful, and I always stick by the rules Ryan taught me and wear the right gear. The color of my bike happened to be the same color of Ryan's bike and Jore'll's car. So now we were a threesome team. Now we could all ride together on the crooked road in South Glens Falls. They said, it will be so much fun, and I couldn't wait for a group ride.

Now there was a big change in the weather. I could feel it in the air; soon it would be September, and then cooler weather. *September*—that's my granddaughter's birthday. Happy birthday! I love you. I'm so happy that my whole family has been blessed by the Creator of Heaven and Earth, from all corners of the Union: Monterey, California; Lathrup Village, Michigan; North Dakota; Atlanta, Georgia; and the metropolitan area of Albany, Glens Falls, and Warren County. It's the end of August, and it had been a good summer for us all. It was time to prepare for the cooler weather ahead. September would bring the beautiful change of colors in the leaves, all throughout the northern parts of the state. I couldn't wait for the NFL season as well. Yes, I've been watching football for many years, and now it was time for the regular season kickoffs. At this point time I don't have a favorite team; I'll wait until the season starts.

This, too, would give me extra time to spend with family and friends around the TV. Now September had come and gone, and it's October. I wondered if my granddaughter and her friends would share Halloween on the Air Force base in Germany. Once Halloween had passed with its cooler weather, to my granddaughter: *Trick or treat!* Look what I have for you: a big heart of love! The leaves had changed their colors, and they were so beautiful. One thing was for sure: it would also bring some very cold weather here and about. Which holiday is your favorite?

Everyone enjoyed good news: my twin brother and I would get together for the first time in a long time. We didn't share our birthday this year. It seemed to pass by so fast. Yes, we are Libras. Hmmm . . . what shall we do on this special day? I know! I'd take a drive to Detroit and give him a big surprise. It was only twelve hours to Detroit through four states: New York, Pennsylvania, Ohio, and Michigan. This would give me some R-and-R time to myself.

I knew there would be a lot of competition against each other. There would be chess, tennis, and throwing the frisbee; who do you think the winner would be? Then, off to Belle Isle for some fun with the grandniece and nephew, Isabella and Israel. Last but not least, back to his house for a small snack and then the big football games on TV. My two boys in South Glens Falls would go out on the town as well. We shared lots love joy and peace. We all were happy and blessed. Meanwhile, we will take a long ride here in Michigan to capture the beautiful changing colors of the leaves here as well. It is so special; no two leaves are the same, just like one's fingerprints. Ryan was in Monterey with my other son Tyller who was campaigning to become the mayor of Monterey.

I wished I could be there with him at that very moment. He was doing a fine job. At the time, he was the Monterey City councilman. We all couldn't wait for election day on November 8th. Afterward, he would come to visit us in Albany and South Glens Falls. For now, I'd give my twin brother a surprise in Detroit and have some fun on Belle Isle. This was one of nicest places in Michigan to visit. It was about ten miles from my twin brother's house. It was unbelievably beautiful, with all kinds of wild animals all through the very large national park. They get people from Canada as well, and it's so pretty during the wintertime.

Before it got too cold, it seemed we were on the road a lot in the last few years. It's all about family. Love—it can't get any better than that. After a long ride up the North Way, looking at the beautiful changing colors of the leaves was something I couldn't miss. It wouldn't be a long before the trees would all be bare. That's when we know winter is around the corner.

Now it was November 8th, and it was time to get ready to scream and yell for my son in Monterey. On this special day, he was running for mayor. Bring out the Champagne; it was time to celebrate. From city councilman to mayor of Monterey—I like the sound of that.

That's the way to go my boy. We all were so proud of his accomplishments over the years. I know his niece and my daughter-in-law would be so happy in Germany with the good news. I know we all were blessed. So far, the weather was very good—not a cloud in the sky. It didn't look that good the next week. It would be in the low sixties, which was good for that time of the year. I was really blessed; in fact, my whole family was sharing the blessing from above. There was so much happening on this day. There were some ups and downs and so many disappointments, and some hard times as well, that brought the shedding of tears.

The Angel of Death had visited our family so many times in the last couple of years. We had to keep our faith and hope in God's hands. This would make our family stronger.

Remember my mantra: The Angel of Death will always be around, but that's the will of God, and the Angel of Death is only a message from God, no bad news this time. I was heading home from the library after a long day working on my memoir, and when I got home, I'd call Monterey to check in on my son Tyller, the city councilman. At this time, I knew he was working on his campaign. I made a call and talked with Ryan, my youngest son. He was helping Tyller with his run for mayor of Monterey. They were busy and said they would call or FaceTime later.

But Tyller did say he was winning with 50 percent of the votes, and his opponent had 30 percent of the votes. That was very exciting to me, and he said they would call me back later on. Well, I didn't get that call. I kept watch on my phone for a time, but there were no calls. I stayed up as long as I could, waiting for that call. I couldn't fall asleep; I tried many times. I was up all night. I couldn't help thinking that maybe his opponent with 30 percent of the votes came back and took the lead, and I was afraid to call and check on the stats on this momentous occasion. Well, I was on my way back to the library, but I couldn't concentrate on my work, because I thought my son had lost his percentage of the votes.

I was so sad and afraid of the consequences, and it kept eating at me. So, I put my computer in hide-my-screen mode and took a walk outside to my truck and just sat there, staring out into space, wanting to call my son about the results. But I just couldn't bring myself to do it. Instead, I called Ryan and asked him what was going on with the campaign. He said "Hi, Dad. You have to talk with Tyller." That was not what I wanted to hear, so I was very nervous about what he would say to me.

I held the phone for a short time and then began to dial the number. Tyller picked up his phone saying, "Hello Dad, I tried to call you."

I said, "I was nervous and afraid to call you; I wasn't sure of the results."

He said, "I understand, Dad, but I couldn't reach you. Anyway, I won the election."

There was no sense in trying to hide it. The tears came running down my face. It took me back to when Tyller attended the Naval Academy Prep School. There I felt the same then. I tried to hold back the tears, but by doing so, it made me so hoarse I couldn't talk. At that point it also hurt. Tyller began to say, "Dad. I made history as the first Black person in Monterey to become mayor."

I said, "Don't forget, you were the first Black person to become Monterey city councilman as well."
"Yeah, Dad, you are right."

So now I could relax and get back to my work. I was looking forward to making that long trip back to Monterey.

The weather was very cold outside, but I was so excited that I couldn't feel the cold. When I got home, I'd be on the phone for some time, and I wouldn't forget to pinch myself. Yes, I knew it was so important, a great significance for the whole family, and it would help build the future for us all. This would take me back to the Naval Academy and the Naval Academy Preparatory School and how it made me so proud of my second-oldest son, Tyller Wendell Williamson. I gave him that name. I got it from one of my favorite movies called *Greased Lightning*, starring Richard Pryor. He was Wendell Scott, a famous Black racecar driver.

Back in the late '60s and early '70s, Wendell Scott's toughness and tenacity earned him a place in the NASCAR Hall of Fame Class of 2015. My son Tyller was on his political path and endeavor. His last words on the phone were, "Dad, I'm not finished yet. I'm going to become the President of the United States." You are my son, Tyller. That's my boy.

I was sitting there writing my memoir, knowing that in less than a week, I'd be on the plane on my way to Monterey for his swearing-in on December 6, 2022. It would be a memory in the back of all our minds forever. For now, we all had to prepare for Turkey Day. Thanksgiving was a special time for us all; we were blessed to give thanks to God and his blessings over the last years and looking for many more to come.

And we would have a ton of good food, with pies and cakes, cranberry sauce, turkey, mashed potatoes, and gravy. I was so happy God blessed us with our health and strength, seeing and celebrating another Thanksgiving, and the same for my granddaughter and her mother in Germany at the Air Force base. Remember, they will be back in the States within a few years. Now that Thanksgiving was behind us, we were all waiting for some good news from my oldest son Stephen and his wife A. in North Dakota. When would the new baby be here? The family didn't have to worry anymore. We all got the call the next day.

The baby came early. In fact, she was born on November 20, 2022, at 5:18 p.m. Isla Truth Williamson was my new granddaughter! God was looking over my family. She was twenty inches long and weighed 7.9 pounds. My daughter-in-law and my new granddaughter were doing well. Here was some good news for us all. We were blessed twice. We all knew Tyller won the election in Monterey, and I was one very happy and proud father. Way to go, my son. What's next, the president? It is not out of the question.

In a few days, I would make the trip to his swearing-in on December 6th. This would be a monumental event for my family. There were mixed feelings; it was something I couldn't explain, and it was hard to control. I would try to put a finger on it when I got to Monterey. There were a few days before the ceremony. There's history in the making; I can only imagine what was going through my son's mind and heart as the days got closer.

All that hard work through the years all paid off. Now we could all sit back and see him as a leader throughout the community in the city of Monterey. I was so proud as a father for my son, as he went to high school on the Reserve Officers' Training Corps, and he was a full-fledged Boy Scout. In fact, all my boys were Boy Scouts. They all started as Boy Scouts in the states of Connecticut, Maryland, and California. They were all good military boys. It can't get any better than that; Tyller attended the Navy post-graduate school.

Then he went on to the Naval Academy. I knew he felt special, and I did also as his father. And I made sure I let everyone know that this was a special young man. "Way to go, my son." Well, I'd be making my way to the airport for that long flight to Monterey. I called my other son, telling him, "Don't forget the time you have to take me to the airport." He said, "No problem, Dad, I won't forget." I arrived on time, waited for the flight, boarded, and relaxed, then off we went.

We all met at City Hall. There was a very large crowd of people.

The swearing-in was on December 6, 2022. It was a thing of beauty. I talked to and knew many people in the crowd. Okay, it was time for the photos to be placed in our memories, then a small celebration that included some music and good food and a special time with the family before heading back to the airport. On the way back, there were only two layovers before landing at the Albany airport. What was next? Back to the Howe Library for more hard work. I was working so hard on my conclusion; the way things were going, it would be a big success, for me and my family as well. It was almost the middle of December, and we had our first snowstorm.

There were 6.6 inches of snow yesterday, according to the Albany airport, our first snowfall of 2022 between Thanksgiving and Christmas. I felt good about my memoir at this point. I felt the conclusion was not far off. This was Christmas Eve. All my family was getting ready for a healthy Christmas. All the presents were all wrapped, and it was time to share them with each other. Today was Christmas Day, and I'd be spending all my time there in my apartment alone; that's something I had to get used to. I had some special food I'd set up for later. I would give all my boys a special call, and a text message to boot. It was a long list: Tyller in Monterey, Jore'll and Ryan in Glens Falls, Stephen and A. in Minot, North Dakota, and to all my other family members, wherever they were. My granddaughter would be sharing Christmas in Germany with her mom. This was a time for sharing and giving thanks. We were all blessed to live and see another Christmas and were looking forward to a brand-new year.

If the weather permitted, my younger brother Billy and I would be taking a trip to visit my twin brother in Detroit for the New Year in about a week. I knew Jerry would be glad to see his younger brother and his twin.

There's something I would like to share with everyone. To anyone who comes in contact with this book in any way, remember earlier in my previous statements when I mentioned how much it hurt and how devastating it was to hear my twin tell me that he had planned to leave Albany and that he'd decided to try his own adventure in Detroit? We did and shared things together all our lives. I felt lost without him walking through the school; there was a void that echoed throughout the building. It hurt so much that I had to go and talk with our principal about it, and like he always did previously, he gave me the best encouragement and advice about anything during my school years. "Don't worry; he's only a few states away, and I know he will come to visit his family." That was earlier during our school year, but today, in about four days, it would be time to share a brand-new year: 2023. And oh, how it came so fast.

And a Happy New Year to granddaughter back in Germany; Papa loves you. So, Jerry and I would share a ton of things together with family for the New Years. I knew we would continue our competition between each other when I got there. At first, I would try to beat my twin this time in billiards, the game he taught me a long time ago.

And I still couldn't beat him. He also taught me the game of tennis, and I think I can't beat him. There would be all kinds of games we could play. And there would be a ton of fun the whole time we were there in the Motor City, Detroit. I was fascinated with that great city back in the day; I'm amazed how my twin could go anywhere with ease. I never experienced him getting lost on the east side or the west side.

There were countless times I had to call him because I couldn't find my way to his house. He would say, "Tell me, what do you see around you?" Once I gave that information, he would be there in no time at all. I call Detroit "the city with thousands of expressways." I never saw him use the regular streets—always the expressways.

There's a question out there that people are looking to get answered: what do twins have in common, and what is life really like being a twin? Well, I'm a twin, and I think it's something very special in our lives.

"Do I know you?"

"Have I seen you before?"

"What's your name, is your name Jerry?"

"No, my name is Terry; Jerry is my twin brother." We get this from people all the time.

We have an unbelievable connection between each other. For one example, our voices. When I talk with other people, all I can hear is my twin's voice, and it's unreal to me.

Standing in front of the mirror, I know it's me, but when I look hard, I see my twin. We both are sentimental from the heart, and we are Libras—not that we believe in the zodiac signs. If it was true, remember that statue that hangs in every city courthouse, letting the people know this court is well-balanced and fair to all the people? That's what we are: a well-balanced set of twins. We hear some of the strangest things being a twin; don't let us enter a store at the same time. All faces and eyes will turn and begin to stare at us.

That's not a bad thing; it was surprising to see two people looking the same. It's always the same question: "Are you guys twins?" We would smile and say, "Yes, we are." My twin always said, "It's our dad's fault." People would always laugh. Well, I have to throw this in: "Here come those two bad boys." We didn't see it that way. You know, "boys will be boys"; there's never any actual harm done in any respect, you know what I mean? Earlier, I mentioned us twins both have a lifetime scar on our right leg, due to not listening to the ones who were older than we were, like my big sister Gloria and our mom and dad.

We knew us twins were a special gift from God. We did and shared everything together. Here's the biggest and saddest time in our life: Jerry told me he'd decided to move to Detroit, Michigan, during our school year at Philip Schuyler High School. That was our first and last separation until we both got married. Even then, it was still hard being apart.

Everything he knew, he wanted me to know and to share those thoughts; the same was true for me. One other thing: I have a short note for you. Living on the military base, I didn't need to drive from San Diego to Detroit for my driver's license renewal, all I had to do was send my driver's license to Jerry in Detroit, and he would take it to the Department of Motor Vehicles, which was the secretary of state. He would take the photo pay the bill, then mail my new driver's license back to me in San Diego. That's what twins are for, to look out for each other. During our lifetime, our dad could never tell us apart. He would always say, "Which one are you?" The same was true for our grandparents, Mary and Vaden Davis.

Not true for our mom; she could tell us apart anywhere, coming from school or going to church. That's why she always dressed us alike. I have no idea how at all; maybe it was a mother's intuition. That's why our grandmother called the two of us Twin–Twin for Jerry, and Twin for Terry. This was fun for us; when we visited our relatives, the little ones had a hard time telling us apart. They would stare and just look at us. Here's another surprise: all our teachers had the same problem. It's all about those twins. Boys will be boys. Do you have a twin?

Even though we sometimes had to shed tears together, it was part of being twins. Last but not least, we still and always did believe in God, the Creator of Heaven and Earth. Some years ago, when I lived in Schenectady, New York, I went to the market for a few things. I'd written a check, and they took the check to the office and looked at me. Before long, the police were at the cash register saying, "You are under arrest." I said, "For what?" They said, "For writing a bad check." I told them I'd never written a bad check in my life. They took me out back and showed me the check.

I said, "That's not me, and that's not my handwriting. Look, this is how I write my name." I also told them I was a twin. So they had no other reason to hold me, and my twin got it all straightened out when they made a call to Detroit. It wasn't a bad check; there were some numbers missing. Well, for those twins, that was a close one. We're not really bad twins; we are just a little adventurous once in a while, just getting into some scrapes like all boys would do.

Wait, there's more! Jerry was a good pool player. He was shooting pool against this guy for twenty dollars a game. It was called Nine Ball. Jerry beat the guy so bad. I had left to change clothes—we lived upstairs from the pool hall. When I came back downstairs, there were four guys waiting for me. The guy who Jerry beat in the pool game was the first one to punch me, straight into my chest. I fell back against the wall. I said, "What's going on here? Who are you guys?" The guy Jerry was shooting pool with said to me, "Who's the bad one now, Mr. Super Pool Shark? There's no pool table out here on the streets! And what are you going to do now, here on the streets?"

And before long, I was surrounded by four more these guys, "thugs" looking and waiting to beat me to smithereens; that's one day I didn't want to be pulverized. One had a small baseball bat in his hands. Was I afraid? I was beyond frightened. All the time, I kept wondering, what can I do to stop these guys?

"Where is my brother? Where's Jerry?" He was still in the pool hall, and I didn't have time to call out to him or start running for the door of the pool hall to get him. So I was surrounded by five thugs off the streets. All five were going to beat up on me, and I didn't know what to do. I couldn't run, because I didn't know the streets of the city at the time.

I tried to talk my way out of this bad situation, but that didn't pan out at all. Just before they began to wallop on me, this girl came running, screaming, "Stop! He's not the guy, you have the wrong one. He has a twin brother." Boy, what a relief. I thought I was a goner. All because I'm a twin. But I wouldn't change a thing, because God gave my mom this special, great gift. Those twins . . . what would our mom do at this point? "Hey, get away from my boys."

We were special to her. It was all about those twins. Last but not least, we still, and always will continue to, serve and believe in God, the Creator of Heaven and Earth. So which one is me? That's the big question! What about those twins? What connection do they have with each other? Seeing is believing. There are other things we have been through; it would shock you.

I must save a portion for you for later. For now, here's the big question. Which one am I? It will appear again and again in my memoir, and in my conclusion. Let me be the first to say, this memoir is to everyone who was involved for the long haul throughout the last twelve months with some ups and downs. Sometimes I felt like giving up, but there were so many people around me that gave their support and input.

The last thing I would do is let them down; that's not kosher, not at all. I will keep my head and hands to the grindstone. I finally got rid of that dark cloud that's been hanging over my head for more than six long years, which were depressing, and heartbreaking to boot. Now I can celebrate with tons of joy and happiness. I know there's a brighter future waiting for me. Things will come full circle. I only have the support of my four boys.

My older son Stephen E. Williamson is married with his wonderful wife; she's an assistant professional and he's an attorney, and they are living in Minot, North Dakota. I'm looking forward to a grandchild one day—I hope sooner. Next, there's Tyller. We all know he's the mayor of Monterey, California. There's Jore'll Ryan Williamson. He's working for a very large pharmaceutical company, and he loves his job. My youngest son Ryan Michael Williamson will be graduating from college with an engineering degree real soon. That means another trip back to Monterey soon—in fact, before the New Year. I hope things will be much brighter this time around. Let's not forget my wonderful granddaughter; she's my heart. This is why I want to share life with them all the time. They are my family, and I love them so much. May God continue to bless each one of them every day. For now, for me and my boys and my granddaughters: the sky is the limit, my little ones.

Don't forget, keep looking toward the mountain; that's where all our help comes from, and may God continue to bless my family. Now we are living in the city of Marina, and everyone is doing fine. Here we're all enjoying the sand and sun. There are always things to do here. The weather is always around the low to high seventies, and there are a ton of places to see and visit. For me, I have a part-time job teaching tennis to adults and juniors and the little ones.

One day, I came home from work. Everyone in the house had good jobs. We were living in Marina, California, about nine miles from the base in Monterey. She was an active-duty military personnel in the United States Navy as a yeoman. This day, I had to work longer than usual. I got home and made my way to the front room to watch TV and to relax. All four of my boys were in the house; I could hear them laughing and talking in the back rooms. So everyone was in the house, including their mom. She had come home much earlier; she was in our bedroom, watching TV I guessed.

Just a normal day at the house. I got comfortable sitting there, then Ryan, my youngest son, came to me saying, "Dad, Mom wants to see you in your bedroom." I didn't hesitate and proceeded to my bedroom. When I got there, all the boys were crying their eyes out.

Jore'll was sitting on the floor with his head in his lap. Ryan and Tyller were standing in the hallway, both in tears. Stephen was in the doorway, also in tears. I said, "What's going on? And why are the boys crying like this? I don't understand why the boys are crying like this." As I looked into her eyes, I got this strange feeling that this wasn't the same woman I knew all those wonderful years traveling in the military. She just sat there on the bed, staring out into space, then I called out her name. Then she said, and I quote, "We are two different people now." She went on to say, "It's not about me, you guys are on your own. We are going in different ways, and as of now, separate ways." My boys were devastated with this shocking news, as was I.

I'm a Libra. I will go the distance for the one I love, and I will go even further for the one who shares the same love. It's strange, knowing how one's life can change in a flash without any warning whatsoever. This shocking news was a big blow to my boys, and even worse for me as their father as well as her husband and a military spouse. I couldn't understand how she changed overnight. At this junction, I would not let this unravel my existence and shatter my dreams.

So now what were my boys and I to do? All this happened in Marina, California. I thought things were on the upswing for our family. Everyone had a good job, there were no family problems—we were just one big, happy family as far as I could see. I worked at the Monterey Tennis Center as a tennis professional. There, I gave private lessons, working with small children of all ages. I worked at the pro shop and did all the stringing for all kinds of tennis rackets. In all, I loved my job. My oldest son, Stephen, was in the Air Force and doing very well.

My next-oldest son, Tyller, was working on base after attending the Naval Academy. I'm proud of his accomplishments. Jore'll landed a good job at the Lexus/Toyota dealership as a detailer and earned a very good pay. Ryan was still going to school and working for O'Kelly's auto shop. We all didn't understand why she was making this terrible decision with no warning in sight. We all thought she would let us continue paying the monthly rent and staying in this big house. It was a nice place—three bedrooms, with a two-car garage. She went to the landlord and cancelled the lease. Remember what she said, "You guys are on your own"? I wondered what the main reason was for this shocking news coming from their mom. We all knew what was next: finding a place to live.

To add insult to injury, we helped her clean the house. And she just sat there out front and had a huge garage sale. There was no place to go at this time. We all lost so much, and a ton of personal items to boot. She went on her way, and what were we to do? We all were abandoned with no place to go. Stephen, my oldest son, was hurt and shocked, saying, I quote, "I can't believe Mom is doing this to Dad." He was hurt badly. Shortly afterward he moved to North Dakota; there, he could continue his military career.

Tyller had found a place here in Monterey before all this commenced. Ryan was the one who was affected the most; he was still going to school and working at the same time. Now for Jore'll, Ryan, and myself, we had been abandoned, and now would be homeless as well. No one saw this coming.

The only thing left for us to do was live in our vehicles. Jore'll owned a nice car. Ryan didn't own one at the time, so he and I had to sleep in my truck. I slept in the front seat of the truck, and Ryan slept in the back seat of the truck. Going to school, he needed more room to get his proper rest. Now all three of us were officially homeless people. What a terrible feeling; it was like being lost in time and space. And help for us was so far away. Most of the time, we had problems from the police and other people walking on the streets, so we had to move to different locations all through Monterey.

Jore'll found a parking space next to this lake by the Home Depot. There was a crowd of homeless people living and sleeping there. Tyller wanted to help, but he had one bedroom for two people. Stephen had already moved to North Dakota. The abandonment lasted for some time. Jore'll was hurt more than the rest of us. It got to the point that he didn't know what to do. He couldn't sleep; he just tossed and turned through the night sometimes. So, he put what he was going through on social media and Facebook to let everyone know what happened to him and his brother and myself. It's no joke sleeping in your vehicle throughout the cool nights. Jore'll was the first to find a place to stay; it was in Monterey. I was so happy he found a place to stay for a while. It wasn't the best neighborhood, but at least he had a bed to sleep on for the first time in a long time.

It was one of his friends at the Lexus dealership. I helped him move his things that were left from our house. The apartment his friend had was a nice place, with plenty of room, and he was happy to do all he could. I thanked him for helping my son. Ryan knew someone from school, a friend that rode motorcycles like he did. Again, I helped him move. It was a place in Pacific Grove, California. His new apartment was nice as well.

He wanted me to stay with him, but the landlord was against it. Well, I was so happy my two boys were happy and had a good place to live. That was what was most important to me. At this point, I really felt bad—hopeless and depressed. Not being close to my boys was heartbreaking for me. They will always be part of my heart. One thing is for sure, I pray they never let go of their dreams: I will never forget or abandon them. I will do what it takes to make them happy. Now it was just me and my truck. It was my place of residence for most of the summer. That being said, I had no legal address. A person can't receive any mail without a legal address from the United States Post Office. So I had to purchase a post office box, and it wasn't cheap. The process was easy, but it was expensive as well.

After purchasing the post office box, I still couldn't receive mail from the government. It had to be a legal address, which I didn't have. For a long time, I couldn't receive my mail. My boss at the Tennis Center said I could use his business for a legal address. That was good news, but I was still living in my truck. Now what was I to do at this point, sitting here in my truck in the parking lot by the seaside? Most of the people living there were homeless for many years.

They were used to moving from place to place to get some rest and sleep. I felt like I was a stranger there. No one had ever seen me before. They stared at me as if I was the police. They looked like in a way they were saying, "What are you doing here? You are not part of this homeless neighborhood." I felt ashamed but had no other choice; I needed a place to sleep and rest.

It was so sad that it was hard to keep the tears from flowing down my face. It hurt mentally and emotionally. All I could do was lay down and try to fall asleep. That was a big problem, trying to find a place to sleep. Yes, it was in Monterey, California, but sometimes it gets a little cool at night. It became a routine. I found an area for people who owned RVs, so that was a big break for me. They were very nice to me—I guess it was because I drove a pickup truck. I felt more comfortable there. It became a small community for homeless people. I often looked at them thinking, "Am I like them? Do I have that homeless look the way they do?" Sometimes it looked as if they didn't have a care in the world. That's the way I wanted to feel. The area where the homeless people lived was down by the shores by the ocean in the city of Seaside, California. There, people could wash their cookware and boil water for cooking on hotplates, taking life as a day-to-day routine. The Catholic church came by every Sunday, giving away bottles of water—one case per family. By being part of the homeless and abandoned people, I had a sense of peace. Well, for every good thing that happens to you, there's always something that will go wrong.

People who lived in Monterey County weren't happy with the people living by the seaside, so the mayor of Monterey made it forbidden to camp or live in this area. The Catholic church tried to intervene with no help. So they commenced a breakfast in the city park. There had to be close to fifty or sixty people there for breakfast. This was about seven in the morning—yes, it was early, and I was hungry.

There were homeless and abandoned people there. So there I was, in the mix of them all. I tried to make myself feel part of the crowd. I hoped they didn't reject me, because my clothes weren't dirty, and I had clean shoes. I could use a nice hot breakfast. I used to walk the street just to pass the time away. During the night, most of the time I had tears in my eyes, thinking, "There must be someone who can help me." My boys came by once in a while to see how I was getting by alone. I observed the way they were looking at me. That made me feel as if I didn't do my job as a father.

I always told them my concerns were their health and welfare. Since there was no real place to sleep, it became more difficult for me. I got sick and tired of the police; they were always knocking on the window of my truck, saying, "Hey, are you all right in there?" I would reply by saying, "I'm okay." The people walking on the street always bumped into the truck, talking too loudly. Then, a blessing from the almighty. God was looking down on me and had me in his plans, and I was happy.

My boss Allen at the Monterey Tennis Center came up to me saying, "Terry, don't be ashamed. I feel for you. I talked it over with my wife Leasa. We decided that if you want to, you could stay in the pro shop. There are two couches, this big TV set, and enough room for you to stay there. One problem: it's only for a few weeks." That was the best news I had had in a very long time.

"I can't believe your wife abandoned you and your boys like that. It was an underhanded act against you and your boys." He couldn't understand how she could do this and still work for the US armed forces. I told him some people don't care; they only think and care for themselves, and family doesn't matter.

All the time, I couldn't help thinking about those unpleasant words that came out of my boys' mother's mouth: "We are two different people now." To me, it hurt to the very core; those are some cold words to hear from someone you knew for so many years. All that being said, now it was time for that battle in a court of law. A divorce was pending, and there was nothing anyone could do about it. I tried so very hard to avoid anything that involved legal action, and I really tried in different situations to resolves the misunderstanding of what was causing the problem in this marriage. It takes two to commit to a marriage. On the other hand, it takes one to destroy a marriage between the two of us. You can take a horse to water, but you can't make it drink.

Again, my boys were devastated with the very sad news about the divorce between their mom and dad. If you could see the disappointment on my sons' faces . . . It really made me sad as well. All those days back and forth to the courthouse took a toll. I had no problems, not at all, because I knew I did all I could do to save the marriage. She couldn't wait for the final dissolution, but I would fight to the end.

Now that I couldn't save the marriage, I just let the situation take its course. Right now, my concern was for my boys and their health and happiness. After many months and weeks, we got the final decision. In the end, I received a greater gift, a gift from God.

God will never let me down and he will always be at my side. He has prepared a special place just for me. And I carried the fear of God in my heart. I'm thankful for my four boys; they are doing well. My prayers will always be with them because they are my joy in life. Even though it seems someone tried hard to disrupt our relationship, I will continue to work hard for the better things in life.

I think everyone you meet is fighting some kind of battle in their life, maybe it is a battle they know nothing about, so stay focused. This will make or break your outcome. There are some things in life you see and maybe some things in life you can't have. It hurts more when you can't have it, and even more when you are poor—I mean, poor. When there is a struggle, don't fight an uphill battle.

Here is that negative moment; "We are two different people now." This will always be in the back of my mind forever. That statement devastated and destroyed my immediate family; it was the most unpleasant comment I've ever heard in my lifetime. It's strange how one person can alter the course of someone's life and cause them to go through so many changes in their life. That deep feeling inside of me hurts so badly. I tried to make an impact by being there for my boys with the best support I can muster, but all she was doing was destroying their lives. For now, all I can do is make sure my boys are doing well and see that they are happy and have a good, healthy life. I will continue to ask God for his blessing for my four boys, and myself as well, because my boys are my heart. I really want them to be able to look up to me as a father who will go the distance with them.

It will make me very happy when I can say, "Look at them now." Today, they are strong and healthy. All four have very good jobs. To me, it looks like a promising and bright future for them. This is what every father and mother should want for their children, and I will continue to teach them right from wrong. This is for you, my boys. I will stand by my words. Yes, I'm a Libra. As I mentioned, I'll go the distance for the ones I love. This is the way I was brought up as a child, and it continues into manhood. There's an old saying out there that everyone should know: *"Make someone happy."* It can't be wrong because I've been trying to do this for years.

All I'm trying to do is to share what I believe with other people. If so, I certainly can't go wrong with my suggestion. I learned this by being around other positive people. That's what I taught my four boys, and now they can pass it on to their nieces and nephews and to my granddaughter, and the new granddaughter on the way—in fact, this December.

It's what life is all about for our family. Now everyone can see what kind of person I really am; that's why I have shared it with the readers. May there be peace and love and happiness in everyone's lives. Now that Halloween, Thanksgiving, Christmas, and New Years have passed, the year 2023 will bring nothing but happiness and bundles of joy to my whole family. I want everyone to remember my memoir. This is my resolution for my family. This has been a super great journey in the form of words. I want to thank everyone who took this journey with me. Thanks for your support, and my deepest gratitude is extended to everyone. I'm so thankful, and this will be a wonderful and exciting story, so enjoy! I'm looking forward to hearing from you in any kind of response.

Take a second look at your family. Look at the little ones—that little boy in the corner playing with his toy soldiers and the little girl sitting on the couch playing with her two dolls. Your mother and father sitting together on the couch, maybe watching television or reading the newspaper. This is what a whole family should look like. Please remember my mantra: I guarantee you will see a large difference here and about.

That's the way my life was in the past. I'm strongly looking to be able to share those good days again with others and family. It may take some time, but I have a strong amount of patience, and I'm willing to take that chance on life again. Life, give me your best shot, I'm ready bring it on.

Thanks, everyone, for taking this adventure in the form of words with me. I'm overwhelmed with joy and peace and the fulfillment of happiness. Now I can say I really completed my memoir. It was a long, hard road to travel, an adventure that traveled so fast, moving all these words as they began to form before me. Thank you so much, my readers. May I say, it has been a superior journey—not too fast, not too slow, but just enough rhythm and momentum to carry on. This will bring some unbelievable events here to the hearts and minds of so many. And don't forget my mantra: Stay safe, and may God continue to bless us all.

T.T.F.N.

Conclusion

It has been a hard and long journey. It was so wonderful traveling back in time; it's like being in a teleportation machine operating out of the Deep South, taking my whole family to the North, with tales of love and sacrifice, making my family stronger. To all the people and organizations I owe my gratitude to, thanks for your support. I have lost six of thirteen members of my immediate family: my mother Velma, my sister Geraldine, my oldest sister Gloria, my brother Edward, and my father Andrew. Sometimes life is easier with help coming from someone other than family. Thank God for my sons, Stephen, Tyller, Jorell, and Ryan: as you know, they are my heart, along with my beautiful granddaughter. I was blessed to raise four healthy boys into manhood. Stay focused, be kind to your fellow man, and sons, don't forget my mantra: "*A strong family that lives together shares loves together.* I'm reaching out to other families as well. You are building a future for yourselves. Remember, stay focused and stay safe, and may God bless.

T.T.F.N. I'm your father

## Acknowledgments

I'm thankful for the New York State Archives staff, for their assistance in helping me find the rolls of microfilm, which were important to me. The Howe Library was great for writing that changed my life forever. I met the one and only, the sport legend in the world of boxing. This individual held three different titles in the heavyweight division. He also won the gold medal at the Olympics in Rome, Italy. Also, l thank the *Times Union* newspaper staff for covering that great event, the photographer and the editor-in-chief; it all happened at my school that special Tuesday afternoon. It changed my life forever. I'm so grateful, and I thank God for all he has put before me.

T.T.F.N.

## Special Thanks to the Five Females in My Life

To my mother, #1, *Velma Davis,* who God blessed to bear those two twin boys that kept her on edge so many times. She took charge and created a wonderful life of love, sacrifice, and survival in the Deep South. It wasn't easy to raise seven boys and three girls in the sixties; thank you, Madea, for your

dedication. #2, my big sister, *Gloria Jean Koonce:* I should have listened to her; #3, my sister *Geraldine Hundley,* murdered by her husband; #4, my *sweet granddaughter*, she's my life; and last but not least, #5, *Vonda Joyce Williamson.* She told me, "Don't quit, Terry! Stay focused." You are the last sister in our family—Love you, little sis. And keep on singing those wonderful and beautiful songs. You look good with the mic in your hands; I see you don't have any stage fright.
T.T.F.N.

## About the Author

I'm a Libra, a twin, and I am a well-balanced person; it's not that I believe in astrology, or the zodiac signs. I'm happy to share with you the amazing life story—it's all about my family having a hard time in the South. We had to endure at the hands of the white man the prejudice, jealousy, and injustice toward all Black folks. It's hard living in the white man's world. Thank you, Mom and Dad, for our upbringing. They ensured a good healthy life and education for us all. I've loved the outdoors. Breathing the fresh air is a sign of freedom. I am a kind-hearted person, and I love the company of other people. I love music. Teaching others is my way of giving back. Playing the drums is a passion of mine; I can spend hours playing the keyboard. Climbing a mountain is breathtaking. After finishing a long bike ride in the park, riding my motor bike through the countryside is joy and freedom; yes, I'm a thrill-seeker! I am sous chef, and I love cooking and tasting the best cuisine. I love movies and TV shows; here are a few of my favorites: *Gunsmoke*, *US Marshals*, *Sanford and Son*, *The Andy Griffith Show*, *Transformers*, and last but not least, *The Bible* series on TV. Most of all, I love God, and I'm thankful he has allowed me to start and finish my memoir. I'm one happy and proud person reaching out to all families. God bless and stay safe.
T.T.F.N.

## Gratitude to the Following People and Organizations

Edgar Perez, Vonda Joyce Williamson, Amani Franklin, Caren Hicks, Latisha Williamson, Gloria Jean Koonce, Andrew Williamson, Lewis bond 2on, Edan Thompson, Velma Williamson Davis, Aaron Caesar, the Howe Library, Tanisha

Fraser Emily Thomas, Alvin Earl Williamson, Trisha, Kimberly H., Stacey B., Kelly H., from the South Mall Towers. Olivia Ruth Williamson. Krystyna P., Angelita Davis, Ontwan Kiel, Jerry W. Williamson, Ellakisha O'Kelly, Walter Huntley, Amar Parikh MD, Trish C., and Olly B., Dirome S. Williamson; my sons Stephen E., Tyller W., Jore'll R., and Ryan W.; Albany Archive, Ervin Williamson, State and Local Library of Albany, Kira I. MD, Barbara Daley, Sandra Williamson, Harold Borton, Eve Williamson, Joe Auto Repair, Krystyna Polglase, Billy W. Williamson, to all of my family, wherever you are, thanks. Geraldine Huntley Williamson, Edward Thomas Williamson, Aaron, Johnny, Mary Haney Davis, The South Towers, Vaden Davis, Barbra Daley Williamson Roney Williamson. *A strong family that lives together shares love together.*"
T.T.F.N.

**Appendix**

# Formal Recognition/Citation

Silvest, Tyler. Username KansasScanner "BNSF 7112 Leads NB Baretables Olathe, KS 12-26-17". Taken December 26th, 2017. Uploaded to Flickr Decemeber 28th, 2017. Retrieved January 28th, 2024.

Hauser, Cyprien. Username Cyprien Hauser. "Tunisia, Ksar Hallouf - Working the drylands with horse and plough - May 2010". Taken May 7th, 2010. Uploaded to Flickr May 26th, 2020. Retrieved January 28th, 2024.

Username j van cise photos. "Why did the turtle cross the road? ~ Huron River Watershed". Taken May 3rd, 2018. Uploaded to Flickr May 12th, 2018. Retrieved January 28th, 2024.

Nunnally, Robert. Username gurdonark. "Nine-banded armadillo". Taken May 12th, 2013. Uploaded to Flickr May 12th, 2013. Retrieved January 28th, 2024.

Auckland Museum Collections. "Pot, three-legged". Taken May 14th, 2020. Uploaded to Flickr August 6, 2021. Retrieved January 28th, 2024.

Username Andy12-74. "Lawn Jockey". Taken June 3rd, 2006. Uploaded to Flickr November 26th, 2006. Retrieved Janurary 28th, 2024.

Username jeffreyw. "Mmm... meatballs". Taken November 9th, 2010. Uploaded to Flickr November 9th, 2010. Retrieved January 28th, 2024.

Username Anna & Michal. "2009 Au Moulin Dopff Pinot Gris Vieilles Vignes". Taken March 4th, 2012. Uploaded to Flickr March 4th, 2012. Retrieved Feburary 4th, 2024.

Gray, Rex. Username Rex Gray. "1960 Ford Falcon 4d sdn cream fvr". Taken Date Unknown. Uploaded to Flickr September 11th, 2010. Retrieved Feburary 4th, 2024.

Username VasenkaPhotography. "Strand Theater ~ Caro Michigan". Taken July 18th, 2012. Uploaded to Flickr July 19th, 2013. Retrieved Feburary 17, 2024.

Deanrdo, Frank. Username fdenardo1. "Freightliner FLD." Taken May 30th, 2010. Uploaded to Flickr May 30th, 2010. Retreived Feburary 4th, 2024.

McCarthy, Michael. Username MSMcCarthy Photography. "Houmas House-6385". Taken April 9th, 2010. Uploaded to Flickr April 14th, 2010. Retrieved January 28th, 2024.

Username couleewinds. "Dust Devil in our back yard". Taken August 31st, 2008. Uploaded to Flickr September 20th, 2008. Retrieved January 28th, 2024.

Mirkin, Craig. Username cmirkin. " West bound frieght near Peach Springs AZ.Burlington Northern Sante Fe Railroad.". Taken May 21st, 2012. Uploaded to Flickr May 22nd, 2012. Retrieved January 28th, 2024.

Username sobolevnrm. "Monterey Bay Aquarium". Taken June 30th, 2013. Uploaded to Flickr July 5th, 2013. Retrieved Feburary 4th,2024.

Username denisbin. "Blinman in the Flinders Ranges. The old 19th century wood stove in a miner's cottage." Taken October 6, 2020. Uploaded to Flickr November 28, 2020. Retrieved January 28th,2024.

Schulz, Katja. Username Katja Schulz. "Nut Weevil".Taken July 3, 2015. Uploaded to Flickr July 3, 2015. Retrieved Feburary 4th,2024.

McCarthy, Michael. Username MSMcCarthy Photography. "Laurel Valley Plantation -6009". Taken February 16, 2018. Uploaded February 22, 2018. Retrieved January 28th, 2024. Link

Username x1klima. "Angel of Death". Taken January 3, 2018. Uploaded to Flickr January 21, 2018. Retrieved Feburary 4th, 2024. Link https://www.flickr.com/photos/x1klima/28040991569

Doss, Marion. Username Marion Doss. "Chamber pot". Taken November 26, 2003. Uploaded to Flickr August 21, 2008. Retrieved Feburary 4th, 2024.